Carlos A. Casanova

Genealogies of Rights

On the Origins of Two Conflicting Versions of Rights

To Laura, Ávila, Carlos,
Vicente, Isabel and Rafael

Carlos A Casanova

Genealogies of Rights

On the Origins of Two Conflicting Versions of Rights

EDITIONES SCHOLASTICAE

Bibliographic information published by Deutsche Nationalbibliothek
The Deutsche Nationalbibliothek lists this publication in the Deutsche Nationalbibliographie; detailed bibliographic data is available in the Internet at http://dnb.ddb.de

Our books are distributed worldwide

53819 Neunkirchen-Seelscheid – Germany
www.editiones-scholasticae.de

ISBN 978-3-86838-310-2

2026

Printed on acid-free paper

Printed in Germany

TABLE OF CONTENTS

Acknowledgements

The author must express his gratitude to the anonymous reviewers who forced him to polish this work greatly and so to make it better.

He also wants to express his gratitude to Professors Reinhard Hütter and Matthew Levering for their support and for their valuable advice and corrections of the manuscript. To Professor Elliot Polsky, and to Doctoral Student Adam Bishop, for reading the entire manuscript and helping correct my English style. To Mr. John B. Martino for his advice regarding the form of the manuscript.

I am thankful to Professor John Stinneford as well, who trusted that I could help develop philosophical scholarship in the United States and offered me a job at the Hamilton Center in 2022. Without him, the composition of this book would have been unthinkable.

My thanks to Universidad Santo Tomás for having granted the funds with which I was able to write the first three original Spanish papers (chapters 1-3). To the Chilean Agency of Research and Development (ANID) for granting the funds with which I wrote the fourth original Spanish paper (chapter 4).

To Idoya Zorroza for her hospitality during my visit to the library of the Universidad de Navarra and for her valuable discussions and academic materials.

I must acknowledge the journals where my four chapters were published earlier in the form of papers. All these journals allow for the re-publication of the papers in the form of book chapters. The four papers have been translated, heavily corrected and in some case the title has been changed. They appeared thus:

(1) "Is William of Ockham's Ethic Voluntaristic?", *Acta Philosophica* 28, no. 1 (2019): 113–30.
(2) "Guillermo de Ockham y la concepción nominalista de los derechos subjetivos," *Cauriensia*, Vol. XI (2016) 113–40, ISSN: 1886–4945.

(3) "Was Francis Vitoria a nominalist?", *Scripta Medievalia*, 12/2 (2019): 67–99.
(4) "Are Human Rights the Actual Subject Matter of Human Hope and the Measurement of Political Societies? An Appraisal of the Declaration of the Rights of Man and of the Citizen of 1789 in Light of Augustine Barruel's Critique of its Philosophical Sources," *Díkaion*, eISSN 2027–5366, Año 37 (2023) - Vol. 32 Núm. 1, DOI: 10.5294/dika.2023.32.1.8. This chapter was funded by the Fondo Nacional de Desarrollo Científico y Tecnológico (Fondecyt) project no. 1220051.

I must also acknowledge the courage of my wife, Laura, who dared to move the family from an apparently comfortable position in Chile, when we perceived the dangers of totalitarian tyranny, to the unknown odds of the adventure of moving back to the United States.

I thank finally my sister María Isabel and my aunts Marianela and Moravia for taking care of my aged mother. Without this I probably would not have had the time to develop peacefully my academic work.

My thanks above all to God, who has guided my steps at every turn and has been so good as to let me continue my philosophical life after I had to abandon my Fatherland (Venezuela), and even when afterward my Fatherland was in great measure destroyed.

INTRODUCTION

A careful assessment of the contemporary use of the word *right* reveals that it has many meanings: (1) In Continental Law, Right (*Recht, Derecho, droit, diritto*) appears as equivalent to the objective legal order (e.g., the Law [Right] of Chile, or Spain, or Venezuela). (2) In Continental philosophical treatises on morality, law, or politics (and occasionally in Anglo-Saxon ones as well),[1] the word *Right* is also used for "what is just." Here, *Right* translates the Roman *ius* or Aristotelian *tò díkaion*. (3) In many constitutions, laws, and handbooks on civil law, *rights* seem to be moral powers belonging to individuals or groups. But, again, such moral powers can be understood in a variety of ways.

In *The American Republic*, Orestes Brownson responded to the existential challenge that the Civil War had posed to the Constitution of the United States. There he identified, at the root of that crisis and of the adequate or inadequate responses that it provoked, three different and contending ways to understand "democracy." There is a first way, "territorial democracy," that is in accord with the classical and Roman conception of the republic. There is a second way, "personal democracy" (or, as I would put it, "individualist, voluntarist, democracy"), which claims that political society is "a simple association of individuals, in which all are equally free and independent, and no restraint is imposed on any one's action, will, or inclination, without his own consent, express or constructive." And, lastly, there is a third way, "humanitarian democracy, which," he says, "scorns all geographical lines, effaces all individualities, and professes to plant itself on humanity alone [...]." If the humanitarian democrat achieved his aims, he "would found in the name of humanity a complete social despotism, which, proving impracticable from its very generality, would break up in anarchy, in which might makes right [...]."[2]

---

[1] Such seems to be the case in Leo Strauss's *Natural Right and History* (Chicago: The University of Chicago Press, 1953).
[2] See *The American Republic* (New York: P. O'Shea, 1865), 349–50, 352 and 355.

These ways of understanding democracy correspond to three different ways of understanding "rights" that today nourish the constitutional rhetoric. Norberto Bobbio and Gustav Zagrebelsky have identified these three versions of rights.[3] Slightly correcting these authors, I would say that the three versions in question are: classical-Christian (corresponding to Brownson's "territorial democracy"), liberal (corresponding to Brownson's "personal democracy") and neo-Marxist[4] (corresponding to Brownson's "humanitarian democracy"). "All men are born equal, and endowed with such and such inalienable rights," is a phrase that took its immediate origin from the works of John Locke (and Jean Jacques Rousseau). In Locke's works, the "rights" of property and liberty are innate or existing in the state of nature, and the civil state is created to protect them. This is very far from the Roman "rights" (*iura*) *in re* and *ad rem*, and it is also very far from those chapters of the Continental handbooks on civil law, where the "rights on things" (*derechos reales, droit réels, diritti reali*) are distinguished from the "rights against persons" (*derechos personales, droit personnels, diritti personali*) since all of these exist only in the context of a political society and are not,

[3] See Gustav Zagrebelsky, *El derecho dúctil* (Valladolid: Trotta, 1997), 75–92; and Norberto Bobbio, "I diritti del'uomo oggi," 188 ff, in *L'età dei diritti* (Einaudi, 2014), 184-194.

[4] By "Neo-Marxism" I mean the cultural movement that promotes a Marxist revolution not mainly through class struggle but mostly by creating new social divisions or sharpening old ones. Perhaps the most central document that led to the most effective crystallizing of this movement is Herbert Marcuse's *Repressive Tolerance*. He declares there that the proletarians are no longer the bearers of revolution, that new bearers must be found among the intellectuals and students, and that new ways must be devised to coerce the majority into a cultural change that can destroy traditions that he considers as "reactionary." (See Marcuse, Herbert, "Repressive Tolerance," in Robert Paul Wolff, Barrington Moore, Jr. and Herbert Marcuse, *A Critique of Pure Tolerance* [Boston: Beacon Press, 1969], 81-123.) Among these ways of coercion, I count the new "rights" through which Christian professors, students, hospitals, doctors, lawyers, parents are coerced to abandon their moral standards as "reactionary" and "discriminatory." Perhaps the best source to understand the central role that Marcuse had in shaping the Neo-Marxist movement is the PhD dissertation *Herbert Marcuse's Role in Shaping the New Left: The Reception of the Notions of Repressive Tolerance and Alternative Revolutionary Forces in West Germany (1963-1974) and their Contemporary Legacy*, presented by Svetozar A. Dimitrov at the Freien Universität Berlin to obtain the PhD degree at the Department of the Sciences of History and Culture in 2021, 348 pp. Available here:
https://refubium.fu-berlin.de/bitstream/handle/fub188/39829/Dissertation_Svetozar_Dimitrov.pdf?sequence=3
Unfortunately, this dissertation deals only with Marcuse's influence over West Germany. It is important, however, because it performs the work that is needed to establish Marcuse's strong influence in shaping Neo-Marxism by researching the actual personal and epistolary influence of Marcuse over the revolutionary leaders, often not documented in a way traceable to formal publications by Marcuse.

therefore, inherent in the human individual separated from political society. But all the aforementioned Lockean and Roman meanings are together very different from the new "reproductive rights" or the "environmental rights," which, at least in part, have their origin in completely different doctrinal and ideological sources.[5]

Moreover, one and the same phrase can today be understood in strikingly different ways. That human beings have a "right to life" can be understood at least in these two divergent ways: First, it may be understood as signifying that life is a good possessed by the living subject and that the one who takes life may both be charged with and punished for a crime, such as murder, and be forced to indemnify the relatives of the deceased. (This is the "right to life" as Francisco de Vitoria understood it in accordance with the classical tradition,[6] which means that it is a subject's moral power understood in the context of jural relations with other subjects.) Second, the same phrase could be understood very differently, as meaning that a living subject, an individual separated from society and enjoying existence previously to that of society, even while completely isolated, has possession of his own life or a power over his own life. For fear of losing such power, the individual is pushed into agreeing with other individuals to establish a community in whose bosom the violation of the right would be understood as violation of positive laws, and, therefore, would give rise to probable and deterrent punishment.[7]

---

[5] Ralph McInerny forcefully demonstrated a similar diversity of meanings in contemporary Catholic discourse. See "Natural Law and Human Right," *American Journal of Jurisprudence* 36 (1991): 1–14.

[6] In this book, when I use the expression "classical" (conception or understanding) I have in mind very specifically the Aristotelian, Ciceronian, Roman Law and Thomistic conception or understanding. Most times it could be extended to the strand of Platonic and originally Augustinian (of St. Augustine himself) classical thought, but I will be focused on the Aristotelian one. I hold that both these strands are at odds with the nominalist conception of rights, but this cannot be demonstrated in this book.

[7] Villey identifies a category of subjective rights that he thinks must be separated from the other two categories. He calls them "claim rights" such as the "right to healthcare." See John Lamont, "In Defence of Villey on Objective Right," in *Truth and Faith in Ethics* (Charlottesville, Virginia: Imprint Academic, 2011), 177-198 at 185. Francis Oakley understands the expression "claim rights" in a different sense, as rights "that are dependent for their existence on the obligation of others," Francis Oakley, *Natural Law, Laws of Nature, Natural Rights* (London: Continuum, 2005), 88. In Oakley's sense, Francisco de Vitoria's *subjective right* would usually have this meaning.

A similar observation can be formulated concerning many other rights, such as "equality." When a text declares that "all human beings are equal," such statement might be understood in a way compatible with classical Roman jurisprudence. In such sense it means that no arbitrary discrimination is allowed, although those who are unequal in relevant senses can justly be treated unequally. Or it might be understood in the nominalist/individualist way, which, for example, implies that all must equally share in power and no authority over men could exist except that based on the consent of the subject. In this latter case, the meaning is potentially revolutionary, while the meaning in the former is not.

Thus, there is great confusion in our day concerning this central concept or term in jurisprudence, *right*. It is necessary, therefore, to distinguish and clarify its diverse meanings to clarify the contemporary legal debates. In this book, I collect in one place four essays, previously published in Spanish, examining the origin of two different ways of giving subjective meaning to the word *right*—one nominalist and the other in continuity with classical philosophy and Roman jurisprudence. I also illustrate how the nominalist version, as shaped by Locke and his French disciples, burst into prominence in Continental Europe through the 1789 French *Declaration of the Rights of Man and the Citizen*. In the two previous great revolutions—the *Glorious Revolution* in England and the War of Independence in the United States—the careful observer might find an important difference from the French Revolution. Hannah Arendt contrasted the American and French revolutions in this way:

> The [American] Bills of Rights [...] were meant to institute permanent restraining controls upon all political power, and hence presupposed the existence of a body politic and the functioning of political power.[8] The French Declaration of the Rights of Man, as the Revolution came to understand it, was meant to constitute the source of all political power, to establish

[8] This is so much so that the Constitution of the United States was approved before the amendments that contained the bill of rights, and this state of affairs was upheld with insightful arguments by Alexander Hamilton (see, for example, *The Federalist* [Indianapolis, Liberty Fund: 2001], n. 84, 445-446).

> not the control but the foundation-stone of the body politic.[9]

Before commencing this exploration of the origin of the rival versions of subjective rights, a preliminary warning is necessary for an Anglophone context. Since the very beginning of Roman law (or, rather, Roman Right) in England, there was an ambiguity that has remained to this day. Henry de Bracton had already confronted this difficulty and, attached as he was to old traditions, decided to keep using *law* where the Romans used *Right*. As Paul Vinogradoff expresses it, "He [Bracton] finds himself confronted with a peculiarity of English phraseology, namely, with the absence of an equivalent in English to the word *ius*. Though writing in Latin, he does not want to make his teaching dependent on a foreign use of terms, and therefore he introduces, though very shortly, the terms *lex* and *consuetudo*—law and custom—explaining that they correspond to *jus*, which in this case would be rendered by the English word 'law.'"[10] According to Vinogradoff, by "law," Bracton meant "the objective order of things and duties."[11] However, since the prevalent meaning of *ius* in Roman law actually is "what is just" in the concrete case (what the judge should pronounce or determine, and the mean of the virtue of justice found in things and in each concrete juridical relation), in dealing with the distinction between the subjective and the objective meanings of *right*, when I am talking about something that the Romans would express with *ius*, I keep the word *right* and avoid the word *law*. For this reason, I use the capitalized *Right* for the objective meaning of *ius*,[12] but the lowercase *right* for the subjective meaning of *ius*; I reserve the word "law" for what the Romans called *lex*. Keeping this in mind, we can continue.

Another preliminary point that the reader must bear in mind is the Aristotelian framework in which I am going to place my

[9] *On Revolution* (New York: The Viking Press, 1973), 104. See also 148. On July 26, 1793 Robespierre expressed exactly this view concerning France: "the French Revolution is the first that will have been founded on the rights of humanity [...]." See Simon Schama, *Citizens, A Chronicle of the French Revolution* (New York: Alfred A. Knopf, 1989), 841.

[10] See *Roman Law in Medieval Europe* (New York: Harper and Brothers, 1909), 94.

[11] See *Roman Law in Medieval Europe*, 94.

[12] William Blackstone uses the word "Right", at least occasionally, in its objective sense. See, for example, *Commentaries on the Laws of England* (Oxford: Clarendon Press, 1765), Vol. 1, 12. David Schindler, citing Thomas Mautner, equates "objective right" to "law." See *The Politics of the Real* (Steubenville, Ohio: New Polity Press, 2022), 114-115. I reject this equation.

philosophical reflections. In *Nicomachean Ethics* 5, Aristotle distinguished at least seven senses of the word "just" (*tò díkaion*), each of which I translate as *Right*. The main distinctions that will be presupposed here are the distinctions between the *just* understood as whatever is conforming to the laws, on the one hand, and, on the other, the *just* as a sort of equality. The second sense is subdivided into the proportional equality (which must be kept in the rules of distribution established by the legislator) and the arithmetical equality (which must be kept in particular transactions that are in the power of judges and courts to protect). In a cultural landscape in which Locke has a strong influence, the most difficult concept to grasp is the just consisting in that proportional equality that must be kept in distributions. According to Aristotle, political society is a cooperative enterprise. Since man is not an isolated individual, but a political animal, no one can achieve maturity and develop fully as a human being without cooperation with other human beings. Such cooperation aims first at bare living, and this is why it requires the division of work or labor: some will be shoemakers, others will be tailors, others architects, and so on. But cooperation also aims at *living well*, and that is why it requires magistrates, courts, priests, and so on. (*Living well* means living virtuously.) The community both produces a variety of goods (e.g., houses, shoes, safety, knowledge, good habits) and requires or occasions a variety of burdens, privations, or evils (e.g., military drafts, crimes, punishments). All these must be distributed and to this end the legislator enacts a system of acquisition and transmission of property and of taxes and even punishments. Since no work is individual, the deed and title to property cannot be just "work" as Locke proclaimed (and Marx agreed). Actually, any deed and title to private property presupposes the production in common and the rules of distribution. And, since we do not live together just for the purpose of not harming each other, but for the purposes of *living* and *living well*, taxes can fund more than defense and policing (*pace* Robert Nozick),[13] and laws can forbid more than those actions that physically harm other individuals. The judges presuppose the system of acquisition and transmission (the rules of distribution, in other words), and, with that presupposition they adjudicate the cases trying to find what is just, Right, in each case, attending to the laws and to the nature of the exchange brought to their

[13] See *Anarchy, State and Utopia* (Oxford: Blackwell, 1999), especially chapter 3, 26-53.

court for consideration. This is the Aristotelian framework that I will presuppose throughout this book.

I suppose the reader would be grateful if I gave a clear example of the two meanings of the just as "equal." A College of Arts and Sciences might have three kinds of income: private donations, tuition, and public funding. This income is received in a common account. Let's suppose that the Dean of the College designs a table of salaries for the different kinds of people employed at the college: full professors, associate professors, assistant professors, lecturers, administrative assistants, and so on. He also establishes a table of bonuses for a variety of works: for assuming *this* or *that* responsibility, for such and such kind of publication, and so on. This table represents a distribution that might be just or unjust. It is just if people who are different in relevant ways receive different payments and people who are equal in relevant ways receive equal payment. The differences in payment must be proportional to the differences in qualifications or "merits" of the persons. (Aristotle does not use the word "merit," but the word "dignity.") The result is that in this "distributive just" we have at least two persons (with their respective dignities) and two salaries; and the proportion between the salaries must equal the proportion between the "dignities" (or "merits") of the two persons; or, put differently, the proportion of personal "merit" to salary must be the same for the two persons. Now, once the different salaries have been established, every month the college owes, in justice, according to the table of salaries, a concrete quantity to each employee: according to the rules of distribution, a person X must receive Y quantity. If the college pays Y minus 10, then an injustice is committed that could be redressed by a court, if the employee asks the college for redress and, not receiving it, decides to sue the college.

There is something analogous in political society, where the Criminal Code distributes punishments in accordance with merit, judged from the viewpoint of the connection of the crime to public order; and the laws distribute taxes in accordance to some other criterion; and other laws establish the variety of ways in which property can be acquired and the protection to which the proprietors are entitled, and so on. Now, once a particular crime is committed, the balance between criminal and victim, and between criminal and political community has been broken. By imposing the due punishment, the judge restores that balance and "corrects" the injustice. But the due punishment is precisely that which was previously established by the law that has distributed punishments in accordance with the gravity of crimes and other similar considerations. We must keep these distinctions in mind to understand what is peculiar to the nominalist version of *right* in subjective sense and what is peculiar to the version of *right* in subjective sense that keeps continuity with classical jurisprudence.

An interesting presentation of one of the problems posed by the nominalist and individualist version, at least in its modern forms (that conceive that political society exists exclusively to prevent that one member of society harms another or that a foreign power harms the citizens) is that by Patrick Deneen contained in a remarkable passage of his recent book, *Regime Change, Toward a Postliberal Future*. There he demonstrates the way in which the influence of John Stuart Mill's conception of "liberty," which implies that justice may be reduced to the mere prevention of mutual harm,[14] has eroded the transmission of the Western philosophical and theological tradition and has made our society helpless against ideological fashions that tend to destroy basic rules that, in the Codes of Criminal Law, for example, protect the public order. Rules such as the prohibition of consensual incest or of drug dealing or consumption have been deemed as protecting not any good that deserves judicial protection but just an irrational moral custom.[15]

The present work is a philosophical work with historical underpinnings. I am searching for the historical origins of philosophical doctrines that one can find today in the practice of the legal profession. I am not interested in tracing the entire historical line of transmission of the original insights or the original experiences to this day. Thus, for example, as I will establish later, one finds in the work of William of

---

[14] (Sentinel: 2023). See chapter 2, section on "Identity Politics and the Will to Power." Deneen does not take this step, but we can observe that Neo-Marxism is the ideology that has taken advantage of the obvious weakness of the liberal-utilitarian ideology, advancing the third kind of "rights" that I have mentioned in this introduction, which are straightforwardly "subversive." See *supra*, note 4.

[15] Concerning incest, see Enrique Cury, *Derecho Penal. Parte General* (Santiago, Ediciones Universidad Católica de Chile, 2005). Concerning drugs, see Steven Debbaut, "The legitimacy of criminalizing drugs: Applying the 'harm principle' of John Stuart Mill to contemporary decision-making," *International Journal of Law, Crime and Justice*, 68 (2022), 1-12. Article 100508. https://doi.org/10.1016/j.ijlcj.2021.100508.

Ockham the first time that a first-rate thinker stated in all seriousness that the courts may apply only positive laws. That is an extremely important landmark. If you then find the same doctrine, and based on similar reasons, in Hobbes and Locke, then you do not need to trace the line demonstrating how that doctrine was transmitted to Hobbes or Locke. In such a case, you do know that these authors belong to the same school on this very essential point.[16] In any case, in one way or another they defend a nominalist, individualist version of subjective rights. A very similar exercise to the one I undertake in this paragraph has been performed by Francis Oakley. He has argued that the epistemological nominalism, the parallel individualism, the expelling of teleological preoccupations from the realm of morality, and the idea of a moral law imposed extrinsically—all these important philosophical novelties *vis à vis* the teachings of great philosophers of the classical and medieval worlds—certainly are present in Hobbes and Locke (as Leo Strauss pointed out) but had their origin three centuries earlier in the works of William of Ockham. So, it was in the 14th century, holds Oakley, when a fundamental shift was engineered "in the way in which the nature and grounding of natural law was understood."[17] And it seems to me that this is well stated even if Oakley does not trace the concrete way in which those ideas coined or forged in the 14th century were transmitted to the 17th and 18th centuries.[18]

---

[16] I can point out, however, that there is evidence that political theorists, and especially Huguenot theorists read Ockham's philosophical and political works in the 17th century. See Janet Coleman, "Ockham's Right Reason and the Genesis of the Political as 'Absolutist," 35-36, *History of Political Thought*, Vol. XX, No. 1 (Spring 1999), 35-64.

[17] Francis Oakley, *Natural Law, Laws of Nature, Natural Rights*, 94. See also 100. Oakley cites Strauss in the first passage.

[18] In the third volume of his trilogy on "The Emergence of Western Political Thought in the Latin Middle Ages," *The Watershed of Modern Politics: Law, Virtue, Kingship and Consent (1300-1650)* (New Haven: Yale University Press, 2015), Francis Oakley attempts to trace a more concrete history of influence from William of Ockham (but not only Ockham) to John Locke, regarding especially the politics of consent. A sketch of the line of influence is depicted in 285. However, Oakley himself is aware of the difficulty of the task of charting such line (see ibidem, 2), so that he comes to state: "[...] it is long since time for historians to liberate the word 'influence' from the veritable embarrassment of quotation marks that has come to surround it. However sloppily the influence concept may conceivably have been invoked in the past, it always has (and always has had) an important and probably indispensable role to play in the history of ideas" (7). I think that when one identifies the birth of a symbol used by an author with a specific, contingent and conventional meaning in its problematic context, and then finds the symbol appear used by a different author with the same meaning in later times, one may assert that a version of that symbol is common to both authors and that probably the origin of such

Until a few decades ago, Michel Villey and Michel Bastit had established the thesis according to which William of Ockham, having upheld a nominalist theology and metaphysics, had also upheld a voluntarist moral and legal doctrine;[19] and, moreover, had prepared a revolution in legal philosophy and practice by coining the notion of *right* in the subjective sense and elaborating for the first time a systematic conception of the juridical discipline articulated around this notion. Furthermore, Villey held that any use of the subjective meaning of *right* after Ockham was a sign of the nominalist nature of the moral and/or juridical doctrine of the author who made such use. Based on this, Villey accused the Spanish scholastics of the sixteenth century in general, and Francisco de Vitoria in particular, of being nominalist.

Before we start to portray the history of the reception of these doctrines, it seems expedient to briefly explain what the essential mark of a nominalist theology and metaphysics is. As Janet Coleman explains, Ockham's epistemology holds that "universality and commonality are not properties of things." They "are properties only of signs, that is, of linguistic expressions and of acts of thought that may also be expressed in language."[20] For this reason, nominalism asserts that only individuals and their powers are real. These are the essential metaphysical theses of what I have called "nominalism" in this book.

Villey's first two theses have been severely challenged. In the history of law, it has been Brian Tierney who has led their demolition.

---

version (it being a contingent and conventional meaning of the symbol) must probably be in the first author that used it. And this is so even if one cannot find a definite line of transmission.

[19] See Michel Villey, *Philosophie du droit* (Paris: Dalloz, 1978), Vol. 1, 137-146; and Michel Bastit, *Nascimento da lei moderna* (Sao Paulo, WMFMartinsfontes, 2010), chapter 9, 288-337.

[20] "Ockham's Right Reason and the Genesis of the Political as 'Absolutist,'' 40-41. Coleman does not cite the source, but her statements clearly find grounds in *Summa totius logicae* (Oxford: 1675), book 1, chapters 14 and 15, 29-33. (What is most impressive in this passage is the total absence of the Aristotelian notion of form or formal cause.) This is precisely what I call "nominalism," although some call it "conceptualism." For the purpose of this book, the distinction between nominalism and conceptualism is not very relevant. Both doctrines deny the real existence of the intelligible *good* or *Right* and that is the relevant point of contrast with the Aristotelian tradition. We can use here the brief, but incisive definitions given by Edward Feser: nominalism "denies that universals and the like are real"; conceptualism, in turn, "acknowledges that they are real but insists that they exist only in the mind [...]." See *The Last Superstition* (South Bend: Saint Augustine Press, 2010), 41. Michel Bastit shows that Ockham denies that concepts are grounded in universals that are real, in potency or in act. See *Nascimento da lei moderna*, 297.

In the field of moral philosophy there has been a plethora of authors, especially in the Anglo-Saxon world, who have questioned them. Among such authors we must count, for example, Lucan Freppert, David Clark, Marilyn McCord Adams, and Kevin McDonnell.[21]

From this dispute I am interested in studying two very specific points: first, whether it can be said that the moral theology of William of Ockham is voluntarist, and second, whether it can be argued that Ockham's legal philosophy and theology constituted the inauguration of the nominalist version of subjective rights. It seems to me that there can no longer be any doubt that the subjective sense of the word *ius* existed before Ockham. On that point the dispute seems to me settled. The voluntarist character of Ockham's moral philosophy is the subject of the first chapter of this book. We are forced to study this aspect of Ockham's work in our research on the notion of subjective right because this is the only way to really understand what he means when he talks about "natural Right" in his political works, and the profound difference that separates his conception of "natural Right" from the Aristotelian and other classical non-nominalist ones. The second point—whether Ockham's use of the subjective notion of right actually constitute the inauguration of the nominalist version of rights—is the subject of the second chapter.

I add a third chapter in which I consider whether Villey is correct when labeling Francisco de Vitoria as "nominalist." A careful analysis of the work of Vitoria, grounded on the previous studies by Alejandro Guzmán Brito, will reveal that Villey's approach to this subject is too simplistic. It is true that Vitoria was influenced by the nominalist theology prevailing in Paris at his time, but it is also true that he reacted energetically against that influence and for the restoration of a purely Thomistic moral theology. He kept the word *right* in its subjective meaning, but he thoroughly changed the word's content and context—so much so that we can see in him the founder of a second way of understanding *right* in subjective sense, a non-nominalist way and

[21] In due time we will examine their works and arguments.

one that we find in the handbooks of civil law in Italy, France, Spain, and Spanish America.[22]

The contrast between Vitoria's conception of subjective right and the nominalist conception is very notable: In the first place, he holds that the rights in subjective sense are always actually or potentially the active side of a juridical relationship between two persons or subjects of rights and obligations; they are never a power that an isolated individual possesses. In contrast, in the nominalist understanding of reality, there are no real relations and, for this reason, the powers belong to isolated individuals like those existing in the Lockean state of nature.[23] In the second place, Vitoria presupposes that all rights exist in the context of a moral order which is often a political order (although not always). In such order, the courts may equally apply positive or natural law in the protection of subjective rights. In contrast, in the nominalist understanding things and actions are not good due to their nature, but due either to the will of God[24] or to them being pleasant.[25] This is the ground for conceiving that the political order must be based not on the common good, but on consent and an arrangement of rights. It is also the ground to claim that the courts may not apply anything but positive laws in the protection of rights. Moreover, Vitoria sees individual property as a right that might appear in a pre-political moral order but that is transformed once absorbed into a political community. In contrast, the nominalist thesis in some of its 17th century instances sees property as a right that is prior to political order and that remains in it as its foundation. Finally, Vitoria holds that there is a community between all human beings who are children of Adam, and, for this reason, there might be relations of justice between

---

[22] I do not mean that all authors who ever used in recent centuries the word *right* in its subjective sense and in continuity with the Roman and classical tradition and in a systematic way depend directly on Vitoria. I just mean that he was the first highly influential philosopher and theologian to do so.

[23] Javier Hervada holds a similar view of *right* when he states, according to Petar Popovic, that "the focal point of juridicity [is] essentially a relation between a thing – "right" – and at least two persons, one who is the title-holder and to whom the thing is due in a relation of justice, and the other who is the debtor." "The Concept of 'Right' and the Focal Point of Juridicity in Debate between Villey, Tierney, Finnis and Hervada," *Persona y Derecho* 78/1 (2018), 65-103 at 98.

[24] See below our presentation of Ockham in chapters 1 and 2.

[25] See John Locke, *An Essay Concerning Human Understanding*, in *The Works of John Locke in Nine Volumes*, (London: Rivington, 1824 12th ed.), Vol.1, book 2, chapter 20.

men of different political communities so that they do not find themselves in a Lockean "state of nature" (i. e., of war) in their mutual relations.

Therefore, because there are at least two ways of understanding *right* in a subjective sense, we must establish some fundamental criteria besides the notion of *right* in the subjective sense to determine whether an author is a nominalist or not. Villey did not feel the need to do so because he simplified the problem too much by labeling as "nominalist" any author who used *right* in the subjective sense.[26] I must clarify that my departure from Villey's interpretation of the scholastics reflects an important difference between my conception of *ius* and Villey's conception. I will not be able in this book to explore this difference in all its ramifications. The book will only elucidate the difference regarding the compatibility of one version of subjective rights with the classical conception of *ius*.

Two criteria can be formulated in the area of civil law, of *personal rights* (*credita* and other *iura*) and *real rights*[27] (rights over things, *res*), in order to distinguish the two versions of subjective rights. A first criterion, which I established years ago, is whether the author situates the right in the context of distributive justice or conceives of it as a power of the individual prior to the constitution of the political community.[28] It is standard nominalist doctrine that there are no real relations.[29] Therefore, all that is real in political communities and in any kind of collective persons is the individuals and their powers. It is an elementary philosophical insight that this implies that society is a fiction or just an conglomerate of individuals based on an arbitrary will, which could be the consent of its members or just the will of the

---

[26] John Lamont summarizes well this aspect of Villey's central views in "In Defence of Villey on Objective Right," 183-184.

[27] "Real" not as opposed to "unreal" but as opposed to "personal."

[28] See "Nominalismo jurídico, escolástica española y tradición republicana," *Dikaiosyne* VIII/15 (2005): 59-74. Hannah Arendt insightfully perceived that the French revolutionaries proclaimed "the existence of rights independent of and outside of the body politic [...]." This trace of their doctrines allows the scholar to place them squarely in the nominalist version of understanding subjective rights. *On Revolution*, 147.

[29] This is Annabel Brett's doctrine when she cites John Mair. See her *Liberty, Right and Nature* (Cambridge: Cambridge University Press, 1997), 43-44. We will have to return to this point with additional bibliography later in this work. The starting point of the total negation of relations as an accidental reality distinct from the substance and other accidents is William of Ockham, *Summa totius logicae*, book 1, chapters 49-54, 97-112.

stronger.[30] An Aristotelian is non-nominalist and takes political society as a real entity subsisting in the relations between the individuals and lesser societies that compose it. In that network of relations, two important subsets are those that correspond to distributive justice and those that correspond to commutative justice. If an author has a basically Aristotelian conception of society but postulates the notion of subjective rights, he or she conceives them (even the natural ones) in the context of distributive justice. A nominalist author cannot do that.

A second criterion that I established in my recent research is the following: if the author holds that the judge must apply Right in its entirety, with its positive and natural elements, then he is no nominalist; if, on the other hand, the author holds that the court may only apply positive Right, as William of Ockham claimed, he is a nominalist.[31] Indeed, the authors who embrace the nominalist, Ockhamist, version of subjective rights hold that the human, political courts can apply only human laws, and, therefore, protect positive rights. The reason for this distinction is that the nominalist author thinks that "right" and "justice" are nothing in the nature of things if they are not individuals, powers of the individuals or expressions of such powers. For this reason, rights are only powers that derive their "rightness" from conformity to arbitrary laws (which are expressions of individuals' wills), be them divine or human. These are the two primary and most certain criteria.

As should be clear from the previous paragraph, another three criteria can be established in connection with political power. The first two criteria address: (a) whether political society is conceived of as a

[30] See, for example, J. M. Bochenski, *Philosophy: An Introduction* (Springer Science and Business Media, 1964), 96-98.

[31] See "Guillermo de Ockham y la concepción nominalista de los derechos subjetivos," *Cauriensia*, Vol. XI (2016) 113–40, ISSN: 1886–4945. Concerning many of our handbooks of Continental civil law we find an ambiguous situation. Because they clearly understand *right* within a political and a legal order and as the counterpart of actual or potential obligations or duties (so they are within the classical tradition), but at the same time they, because of the strong influence of the positivist tradition, claim in general that all these rights emerge from the [positive] law. However, I know of no handbook of Continental civil law that claims that there are no gaps in the law; and most are aware that very important "sources of obligations [and correlative rights]" were established by the decisions of the courts because justice required so, although the law was silent. Among such sources we can count, for example, "abuse of right" and "objective liability" (neither of which was established in the French Civil Code).

conventional entity or a natural entity; and (b) whether political authority is conceived as an essential integral part of society or as a structure added to the already existing society by the consent of the latter's members. If society is conceived as "natural" in the Aristotelian sense (necessary for the human being to achieve his or her flourishing),[32] then some kind of authority structure is also natural. It is not held that a particular kind of authority structure (democratic, for example) is natural, but that it is natural for society to have any kind of authority structure concretely realized (monarchic, aristocratic, democratic, mixed). In the non-nominalist understanding, political authority is conceived as an essential part of political society. Instead, if only individuals and their powers are conceived as real, then society can only be an conglomerate of individuals that are united by the exercise of their powers (and among the powers of the individuals, their will, their consent, is the most relevant). From this fundamental metaphysical difference, a third political criterion emanates: (c) Since "justice" in the nominalist view does not mean anything real in the nature of [the just] things, except conformity to a law emanating from an arbitrary will, the authority based on such law will be an arbitrary imposition on the subjects, unless such authority can also be based somehow on the will of the subjects.[33] The third criterion is whether the legitimacy of authority and the freedom of the subjects are connected just with the will of the subjects who through their consent create the authority (as in many of the nominalist views), or with the intellect. If the authority and power necessarily existing in some way or another are actually subject (in their formation and in their exercise) to laws, while the laws in turn are an act not of arbitrary will, but of reason, stating (and commanding) what *in truth* and according to the nature of things belongs or is directed to the common good, then such authority and power are considered legitimate and its subjects as free, even if such authority is monarchical and cannot count with the affection of its

[32] See Aristotle, *Politics* (Leipzig: Teubner, 1894), 1.2, 1252b28-1253a38.

[33] However, in Ockham's theistic version there is divine law, known through right reason or through revelation. For this cause, political authority is subject to a higher law, as Ockham stated in his pages on the three modes of natural law in his II-III *Dial.* iii 6, whose revised text was published by H. S. Offler in "The Three Modes of Natural Law in Ockham: A Revision of the Text," 212-218 (*Franciscan Studies* 37 [1977], 207-218). In secularist versions this is not the case.

subjects.[34] These three differences emanate from a direct application of standard nominalist doctrines, contrasted with the Aristotelian view.

My fourth chapter deals with the first attempt to build a political society on the foundation of *rights* understood in a subjective sense and in the nominalist version. This first attempt was the French Revolution and the 1789 *Declaration of the Rights of Man and the Citizen*. This chapter adds an important angle to the book, because it allows us to assess whether *subjective rights* in the *nominalist sense* may or may not be the measure and goal of political society and what the most essential problems are in this area. This final chapter is linked to the previous three due to the nominalist character of the philosophical works that inspire the *Declaration* and to some other important factors.

The reader must be warned that this fourth chapter is not a study of the French Revolution as such. It focuses only on the document of the 1789 *Declaration of Rights* and on its philosophical sources. One of the central tasks performed in this chapter is to apply the criteria developed in the previous chapters to demonstrate that the *Declaration* and its philosophical sources embrace a nominalist version of subjective rights.[35]

As should go without saying, this book cannot solve all the problems arising today from the enormously polysemic character of the word *right*.[36] The book aims rather at laying the groundwork for understanding the provenance of the two primary and original versions of subjective *rights* and the philosophical and theological context in which subjective *rights* were understood. It seems to me that this understanding is an important step toward clarifying the current rhetorical landscape.

---

[34] See Aristotle, *Nicomachean Ethics* 5.1, 1129b14-27; 5.6, 1134a26-b7; 10.9, 1179b34-1180a18. According to Ockham, it should be noted, political authority is above human laws. See Janet Coleman, "Ockham's Right Reason and the Genesis of the Political as 'Absolutist,'" 51.

[35] In the three first chapters all translations from the Latin are mine, unless otherwise indicated or unless I am citing explicitly other author's translation. In the fourth chapter, I use a very early English edition of Abbé Augustine Barruel's originally French work.

[36] For an incomplete but extensive survey of the plurality of meanings of *right* in the present cultural landscape, see Bruce P. Frohmen and Kenneth L. Grasso, "Introduction. Rights in a Multicultural Landscape," in *Rethinking Rights. Historical, Political, and Philosophical Perspectives* (Columbia: University of Missouri Press, 2009), 1–33.

A final observation seems necessary. There is currently a strong debate in Catholic circles between liberals, who adhere to the notion of individual subjective rights,[37] and integralists and others, who often reject this notion or at least attempt to knit it into a communal fabric.[38] I do not wish to enter this debate in this book. It seems to me, however, that both sides of the debate could benefit from (i) gaining a greater awareness of the existence of two different versions of subjective rights—one that accepts Ockhamist, nominalist presuppositions, and a second one that has striven to correct such presuppositions since the time of Francisco de Vitoria—and from (ii) the criteria here devised for distinguishing the nominalist from the non-nominalist use of the subjective notion of "right."[39]

[37] See, for example, John Finnis, *Natural Law and Natural Rights* (Oxford: Clarendon Press, 1980); Dominic Legge, "Do Thomists Have Rights?" *Nova et Vetera*, English Edition, Vol. 17, No. 1 (2019): 127-147; Christopher McCrudden, "Alasdair MacIntyre's Critique of Human Dignity: A Response," *Law and Justice: The Christian Law Review* 189 (2022): 110-125.

[38] See, for example, Alasdair MacIntyre, "Community Law, and the Idiom and Rhetoric of Rights," 103-105, *Listening: Journal of Religion and Culture* 26 (1991): 96-110; Felipe Widow, *Autonomía de la razón práctica y derecho subjetivo en la filosofía jurídica de John Finnis [Estudio crítico y confrontación con Tomás de Aquino]*. Doctoral dissertation submitted to the Faculty of Law of the Pontificia Universidad Católica de Chile, and approved on July 6, 2016, 345-359); Patrick Deneen, *Regime Change* (New York: Sentinel, 2023), 113.

[39] David Schindler in *Freedom from Reality* (Notre Dame: Notre Dame University Press, 2019) and in *The Politics of the Real* (Steubenville, Ohio: New Polity Press, 2022), 115, has the right intuition that there is a notion of subjective rights that can be understood in continuity with the classical philosophical and juridical traditions, and a rival version that, due its nominalism, is a rupture with such traditions. This book, by philosophically reflecting on historical sources, brings experience in aid of his metaphysical intuition.

CHAPTER 1

Is William of Ockham's Ethics Voluntarist?

As was stated in the Introduction, Michel Villey and Michel Bastit have held the theses that, along with his nominalist theology and metaphysics, William of Ockham had also espoused a voluntarist moral and legal doctrine and, moreover, had revolutionized legal philosophy and practice by introducing the notion of right [*ius*] in the subjective sense. These theses have provoked a long controversy. In the present chapter, I will consider only an important aspect of the dispute concerning the first thesis, whether William of Ockham's moral, practical theology can be said to be voluntarist. This preliminary discussion is very relevant for the clarification of the discussion of Villey's second thesis. I expect that by the end of Chapter 2 the reader will understand the connection between the voluntarist understanding of morality by Ockham and his views on legal philosophy.

In service of formulating the problems underlying the dispute, I will use Brian Tierney's defense of William of Ockham.[40] This defense can be summarized, as far as the first point is concerned, as follows:

> [Ockham was not a voluntarist because he] did not, as has been suggested, abandon the idea of a rational natural law by emphasizing arbitrary divine commands and then fill the resulting void with a body of natural rights based on individual wills. Instead, whether he defined natural right (*ius poli*) in a subjective sense or an objective sense, in either case his definition was grounded on right reason: 'the *ius poli* is nothing other than a power in conformity with right reason [...], this is sometimes called natural law' [*Opus nonaginta dierum*, in *Opera politica*, vol. 2, 65, lines 574–9]. For Ockham a natural right was not an assertion of naked will but a power conformed to reason. Similarly, when Ockham gave his more complex, multi-layered definition of natural law in the *Dialogus*, each of the three modes

[40] I see Tierney's interpretation of William Ockham as a "defense" because Tierny seems to think that classifying Ockham's ethics as "voluntarist" involves a negative assessment.

he described was derived from reason as it was exercised in different contingent circumstances.[41]

Immediately following the transcribed passage, Tierney exemplifies Ockham's use of reason in his moral and juridical conceptions:

> Ockham deployed the argument from reason at every level of his discourse. [...] Ockham's teaching on the origin of property in the *OND* seems a precise exemplification of his rational moral theory. A 'dictate of reason' showed that individual properties [ownerships] ought to be established among sinful humans; a series of voluntary acts that implemented reason's directive. On the highest level, the criterion for determining the licitness of a Pope's command was 'necessary reason', along with scripture.[42]

From this Tierney concludes that if one were compelled to classify Ockham as a "voluntarist" or a "rationalist" (although all authors of the late Middle Ages who considered questions related to the foundations of morality and law realized that in the conduct of human affairs the use of both reason and will was necessary), then one would have to state that Ockham, far from being a voluntarist, clearly belongs to the camp of the rationalists.[43]

This conclusion of Tierney's defense of Ockham shows that it is necessary to specify from the outset that a certain type of rationalism is not incompatible with metaphysical-moral voluntarism, as is evident in the moral works, for example, of Immanuel Kant and Thomas Hobbes. Whoever, due to his nominalism (or conceptualism), denies that the intelligible good is both real and knowable, must ban it altogether from the consideration of moral philosophy or theology, or else reduce it somehow either to an arbitrary will or to the passions. But, starting from this metaphysical-moral voluntarist (or "appetitionist") presupposition, it is possible to construct a very "rational" moral doctrine, which even tries to imitate the organization of geometrical science in axioms, theorems, and corollaries. The decisive point,

---

[41] Brian Tierney, *The Idea of Natural Rights* (Grand Rapids: Eerdmans, 2001), 199.
[42] B. Tierney, 199.
[43] See B. Tierney, 199.

therefore, that separates a nominalist moral theory from a rational one must be marked here: whether it is accepted that there is a real intelligible good that can be known and can constitute the final cause of the will, which good, consequently, can be the source of morality. If there is not, then the ultimate source must be some kind of appetite, be it an arbitrary will[44] or a passion, even if the possible connections between these ultimate sources or between them and human acts are studied in a hyper-rational way.

The crux of Tierney's defense lies in the Ockhamist notions of "right reason" and "natural law (or right)." It is therefore necessary to resume the examination of the Ockhamist work at this precise point. The meaning of "natural law" (or *Right* in the objective sense) depends, as we shall see, on the meaning of "right reason." Thus, if, in examining the meaning of "right reason" in an Ockhamist context, we were to find that, as Servais Pinckaers has pointed out, it is merely a mediator between divine law and human will,[45] or little more than that, we would have to conclude that Ockham's morality is indeed voluntarist. This issue, therefore, demands a very careful analysis.

The elucidation of this delicate point requires exploring several subtopics: (1) what does Ockham mean by the "good," both metaphysical and moral? (2) What is the relation he establishes between right reason, law, and moral good? (3) Are all principles of morality contingent? (4) What does he hold to be the object of moral knowledge, and how is that knowledge obtained? (5) What is the relation between the divine will and divine wisdom? After all this, we will be able to answer the question: (6) What is the role played by "natural Right" in the whole work of the *Venerabilis inceptor*?

Of course, throughout our research we must keep in mind a standard of judgment. If that standard of judgment were a philosophical "system" different from the system of the author we are discussing, our judgment would probably be biased, as Lucan Freppert has argued

[44] Thomas Ward understands "voluntarism" in this sense exactly: all normative properties depend on the arbitrary will of God. See "The Incoherence of Ockham's Ethics," 225, in *Grounding in Medieval Philosophy*, eds. Carling Normore and Stephan Schmid (Springer 2024), 225-37.

[45] See *The Sources of Christian Ethics* (Washington, DC: The Catholic University of America Press, 1995), 248–51.

against many of those who hold the traditional interpretation of Ockham.[46] But, if that pattern is the most accurate conception we can establish about the ethical discipline, then it would be a "type concept" that can be used correctly, and without which there can be no judgment at all as Max Weber demonstrated.[47] When I contrast Ockhamist views with remarks of Aristotle or St. Thomas, I will do so at points where it seems to me that Aristotle or Aquinas are not mistaken, and thus in the spirit of understanding Ockhamist conceptions in the context of the discipline of ethics.

1. What is good, according to Ockham

Ockham considers that things are not good in themselves. He claims that the "*passiones*" of being, the transcendentals, such as *unity* and *goodness* are things different from *being*, although being is predicated of them.[48] This means that when he states that "goodness" is "every being *qua* willed" he is not saying the same as Aquinas did when in turn Aquinas stated that *good* is being *qua* desirable.[49] According to Aquinas, indeed, the transcendental notions are not synonyms of *being* because they add meaning to *being*. However, they don't add "some [other] nature";[50] they just unveil one face or aspect of the same *nature* or formality signified by *being*. Ockham cannot use the transcendentals in the same way, because he claims that all universals are only in our minds. Thus, one cannot have two different meanings that denote two faces of the same real formality (which is not just in our minds). If you have a different meaning, then you have a different "nominal essence" as Locke would say. So, "goodness" is something different from being, but "being" can be predicated of goodness. Goodness would be "being *qua* willed" or something of the sort, states Ockham.

Now that we have the context, we can take a second step. Considering the "*passiones*" of being, Ockham adds this definition of

---

[46] See *The Basis of Morality* (Chicago: Franciscan Herald Press, 1988), 171.

[47] "The Meaning of 'Ethical Neutrality' in Sociology and Economics," 40–43, in: *Max Weber on the Methodology of the Social Sciences* (Glencoe, IL: The Free Press of Glencoe, 1949), 1–47.

[48] *Sent.*, I, d. 2, q. 9, *Opera Theologica* (St. Bonaventure: Franciscan Institute ed., 1970), Vol. 2, 321-322.

[49] Thomas Aquinas, *De veritate* q. 1, c.

[50] *De veritate* q. 1, ad 4m.

"goodness": "the good is that which is the object of the will, according to right reason."[51] But the very use of this definition reveals that, according to Ockham, there is, properly speaking, no metaphysical goodness, independent of its rational proportion to our action and of the will. He seems at this point to have started the encirclement of the concept of the good within the confines of ethics.

Going beyond Ockham's statements, however, Jenny Pelletier[52] wants to ground, based on the principles found in Ockham's work, a metaphysical notion of "goodness" as a transcendental. According to the scholastic tradition within which he writes, Ockham speaks of the transcendentals, *being, unity, truth* and *goodness*. Now, as Pelletier herself acknowledges, according to Ockham, *being* as a concept is the subject matter of metaphysics. She adds immediately: "if metaphysics is to be a real science that studies extra-mental or mind independent beings, then there *must be* some sense in which an account of the transcendentals is not merely semantic."[53] So, she has to go beyond what Ockham actually stated and correct him, adjusting him to the Aristotelian conception of metaphysics, which must be different from logic.

Could Ockham, however, really take this step without contradicting himself? If there are no actual or potential universal natures in reality that ground our words and concepts, could Ockham really have searched for "the natures of beings, of substances, qualities, and God," as Pelletier[54] would like him to have done? In any case, even if we concede that he could have, what did he actually hold about the

---

[51] *Scriptum in I librum Sentetiarum Ordinatio* (St. Bonaventure: Franciscan Institute ed., 1970), in *Opera Theologica*, Vol. 2, d. 2, q. 9, 321. D. W. Clark, cites this passage in *William Ockham on Right Reason*, 23, in *Speculum*, vol. 48 (1973), No. 1, 13–36. The difference between this statement and the classical conception is subtle: according to the classical conception, whatever is, is good. The good is a transcendental of being (see St. Thomas Aquinas, *Quaestiones disputatae de veritate*, q. 1, a. 1, c. All the works of St. Thomas have been consulted in the *Corpus Thomisticum*, edited by Enrique Alarcón, and available here: www.corpusthomisticum.org). The good is not what is actually loved, but what deserves to be loved. The will can love or desire what is metaphysically good with an ordered act (conforming to what the good deserves and to the situation) or with a disordered act. In the second case, it does not will "according to right reason" and, therefore, there is no moral good. But there is still metaphysical good (see *Summa theologiae* I-II q. 18, a. 1; a. 2, especially ad 1m).

[52] "Is There an Approach to the Transcendentals in Ockham: The Case of the Good," in *The Language of Thought in Late Medieval Philosophy*, eds. Pelletier & Roques (Springer 2017), 111-24.

[53] Ibidem, 116-117. The italics are mine.

[54] See 117.

"good"? He stated that all that is, is good. But what does that mean, if "universality and commonality are not properties of things," but "only of signs, that is, of linguistic expressions and of acts of thought that may also be expressed in language"?[55] Pelletier acknowledges that the nominal definition that Ockham gives is precisely the one given above: "a being that is willable in accordance with right reason."[56] She notes that in that definition Ockham seems to have in mind the moral good. But then she tries to expand it. She states that "he *must have* in mind a minimal notion of rationality rather than the richer moral notion."[57] In her exploration of the possible candidates, she tries to find the key in God's will. He creates everything, so, his will that presupposes the distinction between what is possible and what is impossible must be what provides with content the "transcendental" *good* because He is Good and the things caused by Him must be good as well.

Now, two things are clear in Ockham's works: according to him, that God creates by an act of his will is not demonstrable;[58] and he criticizes Aquinas, states Pelletier, for arguing that we name God as "good" because he is the cause of the created things that are good. According to Ockham, if it were so, we could give to God the name of "asses" or of "angels" as well.[59] Pelletier overlooks this point, but what this critique means is precisely that Ockham claims that both categorial (ass, angel) universals and transcendental universals are just concepts or words, not real natures. He claims, moreover, that neither of the two kinds of concepts or words may be participated in different degrees, as a real analogical formality could be present in eminent way in the first analogate and in a secondary and more imperfect way in the other analogates.[60] Pelletier wants to bring Ockham to have stated that there

[55] J. Coleman, "Ockham's Right Reason and the Genesis of the Political as 'Absolutist,'" 49.
[56] 123.
[57] 123, my italics.
[58] "Ideo quantum ad istum articulum dico quod non potest ratione naturali demonstrari quod Deus contingenter et libere agit vel causat illa quae causat." *Scriptum in Librum Primum Sententiarum Ordinatio.* Distinctiones XIX-XLVIII (Saint Bonaventure University, Saint Bonaventure [New York State], 1979). *Opera theologica*, Vol. IV, d. 42, q. 1, 617, li. 5-12. In the context, where causing in this way is opposed to causing physically (as to the only alternative left), this passage means what my text claims it to mean.
[59] 122-3.
[60] In fact, Ockham thinks that "being" is "univocally" said of God and of creatures, and of all creatures (*Sent.*, I, d. 2, q. 9, 300, li. 1-13; 301, li. 18-20; 316, li. 17-25; 317, li. 8-14; 318-9 and 331, li. 10-2). But "being" does not mean anything *universally real.* It is just an *intentio* of our minds

is participation, not in the Neo-Platonic way, but through efficient causality;[61] that is to say, in the Aristotelian or Thomistic way that Ockham explicitly rejected. So, it is true that, according to Ockham, all beings are willed by God, although we cannot demonstrate this without revelation. It is also true, therefore, that all beings are actually willed and, in that sense, "good." But that this implies that there is a common nature in things that allows for us to call them "good," beyond the fact that God or a creature wills them, is far from having been established by Pelletier.[62]

We can take now yet another step, with André de Muralt: "Because [according to Ockham] we call good that which is desired or wanted by the will, *bonum est idem quod volitum sive volibile*, the will and its act are connoted by the term *good*. It follows that, having God prescribed moral goodness by the force of a precept, of a law, that is to say, of an *a priori* obligation, this obligation obliges not due to the intrinsic goodness of the end towards which it directs the will [...], but due to the authority of that who prescribes it, to the mere fact that it [such end] has been willed, [...] prescribed by the divine omnipotence."[63] This is the deepest reason for Ockham to define the "good" as that which

(*Summa totius logicae*, book 1, chapters 14-15 and 38). This is why it can be univocally predicated of God and creatures, despite the idea that "there is nothing in creatures, either essential or accidental, that has perfect similarity with anything that is in reality in God" (*Sent.*, I, d. 2, q. 9, 317, li. 3-6; see also 300, li. 1-13). He thinks that "being" is a genus and, therefore, is not in the *ratio* of the differences with which the species of being are formed, as if there could be *nugatio* in such case (ibidem, 320, li. 14-22; this is openly opposed to Aquinas' teaching in *De veritate* q. 1, a. 1, c). However, according to Ockham "being" is said equivocally of the ten categories (see *Commentary on Porphyry*, Chapter 3, § 10, in Kluge, Eike-Henner W. [trans.], 1973–1974, "William of Ockham's Commentary on Porphyry: Introduction and English Translation", *Franciscan Studies*, 33: 171–254 and 34: 306–82). He, moreover, denies that there is analogy (*Sent.*, I, d. 2, q. 9, 294, li. 14-24: this is Scotus' opinion, but Ockham does not reject it), or equates it to "aequivocatio a consilio" (ibidem, 326-9).

[61] 122-3, note 37.

[62] Actually, "in his mature discussions, he [Ockham] attributes final causality to the end of the intelligent agent and not to nature [...] He suggests that if it were not for revelation we might think that there are no final causes in nature, since we would not know that there is someone who orders them to an end." (This means that the thing is not naturally desirable, *i. e.*, "good." Rather "goodness" is an extrinsic connotation of "being." The citation is from Thomas Osborne, "Ockham as a Divine-Command Theorist," 8, *Religious Studies*, 41/1 [Mar. 2005], 1-22.)

[63] See *L'unité de la philosophie politique. De Scot, Occam et Suarez au liberalisme contemporain* (Paris: Librairie Philosophique J. Vrin, 2002), 33.

is willed in accordance with right reason, that is to say, in accordance with God's will.

Therefore, we can reiterate our statement that there is no metaphysical goodness, according to Ockham. Moreover, as we shall explain, moral goodness is a "circumstance" added to the substance of acts. From the point of view of ethics, this "circumstance" is of the essence, but from the physical or metaphysical point of view it is just that, a circumstance.

In his criticism of Duns Scotus, Ockham seems at times to depart from his general nominalism (or conceptualism) and from the natural consequence of nominalism in morals, which is "voluntarism," the claim that what is morally good or bad is determined by an arbitrary will. So it is with the following passage, for example:

> From this it is manifest that goodness or malice adds something to the substance of the act; for in one manner it is to be said according to this way [Ockham's] and in another according to John's [Scotus, *Quodl.* 18, nos. 7–8; Waddings-Vives ed. 237–8]. For John states that the substance of the virtuous or vicious act may be the same, but it is said to be virtuous on account of conformity to the requisite circumstances, of which he does not affirm that they are partial objects of the virtuous or vicious act. Therefore, through him [Scotus], goodness adds something to the substance of the act with respect to conformity to all the circumstances... But according to this way [Ockham's], which states that all the circumstances required for the act are partial immediate causes immediately required for the perfectly virtuous act..., this substance of the act is this goodness of the act, and in a similar way it can be applied to the wicked [*vitioso*] act, this substance of the act is this malice of the act [...].[64]

A superficial reading would suggest that here Ockham is asserting that morality is a quality intrinsic to the substance of the act. To grasp his true meaning, we must examine a couple of other texts in which he

---

[64] *Sent.* III, q. 10, P. David W. Clark cites this text in an attempt to prove that moral value is not extrinsic to the act (o. c., 24), but the text, as we shall see below, proves the contrary.

explicitly holds that the conformity or non-conformity of an act to law or right reason is a "circumstance" from which its goodness or malice flows:

> Virtuous and wicked are connotative names and signify the act itself, not absolutely, but by connoting with this action the activity of the will and prudence. And when something connoted is lacking, such action is not called virtuous.[65]

> I say that although 'hating God,' 'stealing,' 'committing adultery,' and the like actions have bad circumstance annexed to them in relation to the common law, inasmuch as they are performed by one who is bound to the contrary by divine precept; yet, as to their absolute being, those acts can be performed by God without any bad circumstance annexed, and they could also be performed in a meritorious manner by a wayfarer [a man who has not reached heaven], if they fell under the divine precept, as now, *de facto*, their opposites fall under the divine precept [...]. And, if they were committed by a wayfarer meritoriously, then they would not be mentioned or called 'theft,' 'adultery,' 'hatred,' etc., for these names signify such acts not absolutely, but connote or imply that he who performs such acts is bound by divine precept to the contrary.[66]

Then, according to Ockham, the "circumstance" (from the physical or metaphysical point of view) of the relation of the act to the divine law or to "right reason" constitutes the "substance of the act" from the moral point of view (i.e., insofar as "virtuous" or "wicked").

For the moral point of view adds a connotation to the names of actions—namely, their relation to the divine law. This "connotation" is given through prudence or conscience, which is precisely the voice of the law

---

[65] *Sent.* III, q. 13, F. Cited by D. Clark, o. c., 25.

[66] *Sent.* II, q. 19, O. Cited by D. Clark, cit., 24. Lucan Freppert comments on another text (*II Sent.* 15), but that text shows exactly the same thing: acts considered absolutely are neither good nor evil; goodness or evil derives from the "circumstance" that the act is commanded or forbidden (that is why God can perform any act without sinning).

within man. According to A. S. McGrade, since the "dictates of natural law" are "themselves [...] *indirect* or 'tacit' divine commands,"[67] the arbitrary will of God is what defines the moral nature or connotation of our acts. As stated in the pages of the excellent systematic presentation of Ockhamist morality, Lucan Freppert's book, *The Basis of Morality According to William Ockham*,

> What is the norm of morality? We find that in answer to this question two norms are proposed: a subjective and proximate norm consisting in man's right use of his reason and will; an objective and ultimate norm, consisting in the will of God. More accurately, these two norms together form a twofold norm of morality.[68]

In conclusion, the good is ultimately nothing but conformity to the divine will, and such "good" is a circumstance of the action, from the metaphysical point of view. On the other hand, from the moral point of view, since moral concepts connote precisely the relation between action and its norm, "good" or "evil" is the substance of action. Consequently, the interpretative thesis of Servais Pinckaers is confirmed without a shadow of a doubt. But from this follows another thesis of Pinckaers: that Ockham's morality is a "morality of obligation," that is, of conformity to divine precept.[69] This can be seen in the aforementioned book by Freppert.[70]

However, we still have a task ahead of us. Marilyn McCord Adams has argued that we must distinguish natural morality from positive morality in Ockham's work; or, in other words, the "good" or

---

[67] Thus Francis Oakley (*Natural Law, Laws of Nature, Natural Rights*, 79) summarizes McGrade's thesis in "Natural Law and Moral Omnipotence," 276-9, in *The Cambridge Companion to Ockham* (Cambridge: Cambridge University Press, 1999), 273-301. See also Oakley, ibidem, 99. We will return to this point in the next section of this chapter.

[68] *The Basis of Morality*, cit., 13. The article by Kevin McDonnell *Does William of Ockham Have a Theory of Natural Law*, in *Franciscan Studies* 34 (1974): 383–92, points in the same direction on this point.

[69] See *The Sources of Christian Morality*, cit. 305–6. Thomas Osborne comes to this very same conclusion and he also revindicates Pinckaers, although he does it with this qualification: Pinckaers does "not fully take into account the way in which Ockham is a divine command theorist [...]." However, he is "right to emphasize the importance of Ockham's theory for the development of later moral thought" (Th. Osborne, "Ockham as a Divine-Command Theorist," 18). Osborne identifies, moreover, that Ockham's ethics is revolutionary (ibidem, 17).

[70] See L. Frepert, o. c., 161–6.

the "virtuous" that would be natural, on the one hand, from the "meritorious" that would be "positive," on the other. Positive morality and the meritorious would be what derives from political laws (jurisprudence) or from divine-positive laws (moral theology and, in part, canon law). But natural morality and the *right* or virtuous would be what is discovered by right reason, which would not be affected by a change in divine legislation.[71]

Against this interpretation, many more or less clear passages could be opposed. Several of them are quoted by Adams herself. Let us look at them:

"[...] given the existing divine precepts for the opposites [of hatred, theft, adultery, etc.], no one could do such acts meritoriously or [do them] well, because they could be done meritoriously or well only if they fell under the divine precept."[72] "[...] the created will is obliged by God's precept to love God, and therefore given that precept it cannot act well by hating God or causing an act of hatred."[73] "Whatever could be a right act here below, could also be a right act in the Fatherland [=heaven]. But hating God can be a right act here below; therefore likewise in the Fatherland."[74] According to Adams, these passages refer only to "merit." But, in fact, the very words Ockham uses exclude that interpretation. Indeed, he says "meritoriously or well" (not just "meritoriously"), in the first text; "acting well" (not just meritoriously), in the second; and he speaks of what is "just" (not only what is "meritorious"), in the third.[75]

But there are other texts on which she herself comments that are even clearer, if this is possible: "Ockham holds," says Adams, "that

---

[71] See M. M. Adams, *The Structure of Ockham's Moral Theory*, 15–23, in *Franciscan Studies* 46 (1986): 1–35.

[72] *Q. in II Sent.*, q. 15, 353. *Quaestiones in II librum Sententiarum (Reportatio)* (Saint Bonaventure, New York State: Saint Bonaventure University, 1981). *Opera Theologica*, Vol. V. This text is quoted by M. Adams in o. cit., 29.

[73] Ibid. Cited ibid, 29–30.

[74] *Quaest. In IV Sent.*, q. 16. Cited by M. Adams, o. cit., 31.

[75] Thomas Osborne concurs in this opinion: "Adams suggests that, whereas right reason is the basis of good actions, divine commands are the basis of meritorious actions. Ockham himself does not make this distinction." He, like any other Christian theologian, distinguishes between merit and virtue, but "this distinction between merit and virtue does not imply on its own that right reason and divine commands are similarly distinct." "Ockham as a Divine-Command Theorist," 4-5.

God in His freedom could positively command [...] the acts we now call 'theft,' 'adultery'[76] and 'fornication.'[77] (Logician that he is, Ockham notes that if God were to enjoin such acts, they would no longer receive those labels, the nominal definitions of which connote that God has forbidden acts of this type)."[78] But, the fact that Ockham asserts that "moral evil" connotes the violation of a divine precept constitutes sufficient proof that natural reason does not take its rule from itself or from the nature of things, but from the divine commandment. Thus, Adams's identification of the natural-positive distinction with the good-meritorious distinction appears contrary to the spirit of Ockhamist theory.[79]

2. Relationship between right reason and divine law.

We have already noted the core of this relationship succinctly, because it was presupposed in the previous section. But now we will explore it in detail.

We can start with two texts that lay the foundations for what we will say in this section:

As for the first text, its context must be understood. Ockham holds that an act of the will, for example of abstention, cannot be virtuous, without a prescriptive act of reason. It cannot be virtuous, even if the voluntary act is based on the apprehension of objects and of the proposition "one should abstain for God's sake at such a time and place." To explain his point, he adds: "[...] right reason should dictate

[76] *Quaest. In II Sent.* q. 15.

[77] *Quaest. Variae*, q. 7, a. 4.

[78] M. Adams, "The Structure of Ockham's Moral Theory," cit. 22. I suppressed two words of the text to make her mind clearer to the reader who does not have the context. Ockham explicitly upholds the doctrine of connotation in *In II Sent.* q. 15, 352–353.

[79] Other texts could be added. For example, *Quodl.* III, q. 19, answer to the question; and *Quodl.* VI, q. 2, answer to the main argument. Thomas Osborne specifically refutes Marylin McCord Adams' thesis in his "Ockham as a Divine-Command Theorist," especially 2-11. He states his case very carefully, and his conclusion is that, according to Ockham, "moral judgements [of the pagans or Christians] are ultimately made true or false by divine commands" (10).

that abstention is to be willed for God's sake, because it is so dictated by right reason, otherwise it would not be right reason, but erroneous."[80]

Note that, to the apprehension of objects and the order to God as grounds of the good voluntary act, the transcribed text adds just this: "[it must be willed] because it is so dictated by right reason." That is to say, for the act to be good, according to Ockham, one must be aware that one wills what one wills because it is so commanded by right reason, which conforms to the law. It is not enough that the will conforms to real goods ("to objects," as Ockham would say) for God's sake, nor that the agent is aware of this conformity. He must be aware that he is also conforming to a "prescriptive act," to "right reason."

The point is more explicit in this other passage: "But precisely because the divine Will wills this, right reason dictates what is to be willed."[81]

These texts show that the necessity of conforming to divine law cannot be said to be an essential characteristic of meritorious acts only, as Marilyn McCord Adams and, before her, Erik Hochstetter have argued. It is, in fact, an essential characteristic of virtuous acts, especially perfectly virtuous acts. Lucan Freppert responded very well to Hochstetter, in *The Basis of Morality*:[82] the human will, to be upright, must conform to a norm; but that norm can be neither the "autonomous reason" which, according to Freppert, would be the norm postulated by both Kantianism and Stoicism, nor an "impersonal" law of natures or essences.

Freppert's response is interesting, because it reveals the rationality underlying Ockhamism, and it also reveals the misunderstandings present in Freppert's own philosophy, which prevented him from *seeing* the turn that Ockhamism represented in the

[80] *Quodl.* III 16. From this text (and from *Quaestiones variae* 7, a. 4), Freppert argues, following Ockham, that the Gentiles ["pagans"] could not have perfect virtue, because they could not do "for God" the good things they do (see o. cit., 78). But it seems to me that the latter (that they could not do for God the good things they do) is true neither of Socrates, nor of Plato, nor of Aristotle.
[81] *In I Sent.*, 41, un.
[82] Cit., 79–82.

history of Christian morality, turn that Servais Pinckaers described so well.

Let me explain. The realistic morality of St. Thomas and Aristotle is not based on an "impersonal law," but on the notion of practical truth.[83] The proportion between, on the one hand, the nature of the things among which man finds himself as an agent, and, on the other hand, the being of the agent himself *qua* agent, constitutes the rule to which the judgment on which a choice is based must conform. This practical truth is founded on the highest truth, on God (see *Metaphysics* alpha 1), which in this sphere and in a Christian context is called First Truth and Eternal Law. Practical truth, in turn, marks the path by which the agent can achieve his fullness.[84] And God commands us to act according to it because His will is preceded by wisdom.[85] In other words, the divine essence *qua* will is not the supreme rule of the universe; the divine essence *qua* wisdom is.[86]

Freppert does not perceive that within the Decalogue is enclosed a wisdom that scrutinizes the depths of the human heart and the nature of the things among which we men are to act. The second rule of morality is practical truth, but this is an expression of the ultimate cause, which is the Eternal Law. Now, the Eternal Law is primarily the act of a wisdom rather than of a will, although it is also the act of a will. That is why it is called "law."[87]

The not inconsiderable change introduced or consolidated[88] by Ockham at this point is this: he postulates that the ultimate rule of the

---

[83] See *Nicomachean Ethics* VI 2, 1139a23–35; 5, 1140b4–5 and 20–21; and III 4, 1113a21–35, with the comments of St. Thomas.
[84] See Carlos A. Casanova. "La verdad práctica como piedra angular de la ética," section 2, in *Cuadernos Salmantinos de Filosofía*, Vol. XXXIV (2007): 403–34; *Racionalidad y justicia* (Santiago: Globo Editores, 2013), chapter IV, section 3. "¿Ha sido derrotada la teoría clásica del Derecho natural con el argumento de la falacia naturalista?" *Logos, Anales del seminario de metafísica*, Vol. 47 (2014): 37–54.
[85] See Aquinas, *De veritate*, q. 23, a. 6, c.
[86] This is why St. Thomas says in his commentary on Psalm 26, that the *Will of the Lord* is "*the reason willed and disposed by God.*" There is no divine will without divine Reason.
[87] As Aristotle and St. Thomas have shown, *law* is "an ordinance *of reason* to the common good, made by him who has the care of the community, and promulgated." *Summa theologiae* I-II q. 90, a. 4, c. See *Nicomachean Ethics* X 9.
[88] It had already been brewing to some extent in Franciscan theology, which was becoming increasingly voluntarist. Think of Duns Scotus's teaching on the second table. But it should not be assumed that all Franciscan theology was pre-nominalist. In P. J. Olivi's "Quaestio '*Quid ponat*

universe is a will (the divine) detached from all other rules, because it would be the origin of all rules. In this sense Ockhamism can be seen as the deepest source of Kantianism. For Kantianism does not postulate, as Freppert thinks, an "autonomous reason," but an autonomous will. The moral law would have to be a categorical imperative of the human will, without reference to any object.[89] Kantianism is a sort of secularized Ockhamism. Both teachings, by denying that there is a real nature signified by the word "good," must make the meaning of the word depend on an autonomous will. Ockham, being a Christian, postulates as the origin of the good the divine will to which human reason and will must submit. But Kant, who denies that we can *know* the existence of God, holds that the human will is the origin of the categorical imperative. There is a world of difference, then, between Stoicism and Kant. Many Stoics do not, in fact, argue that there is an autonomous (human) reason. I could develop this line further, but the point I want to illustrate now seems to already be sufficiently clear.

In any case, Freppert maintains that the "pagans" could only perform imperfect virtuous acts, because they could not know the decisive rule of human acts, which is the divine will or law. Philosophy, therefore, would be very limited in the knowledge of morality, and only the Christian could attain perfect knowledge, which would be theological knowledge.[90]

---

ius vel dominium' ou encore 'De signis voluntariis'" (321, lines 25–28. Edited by F. Delorme, in *Antonianum*, XX (1945): 309–30), on the difference that introduces "the right" in reality, one can notice a clearly descending perspective, from God to the world. But (a) it is true that God, His wisdom and His will, are the ultimate and most important cause of the moral order and of all rights, and (b) Olivi recognizes that the divine will is preceded by wisdom: "it must be *known that there is a certain order absolutely prefixed and included in the same absolute reason of justice in such a way that God cannot and must not will the opposite of it,* and, therefore, rational nature must be brought to it in a most absolute and completely immobile way. That ought is included partly by indifference in its [rational nature's] essence, partly in the essence of its gratuitous accidents insofar as they are its own. And this order is commonly called the order of natural right." As can be seen, Olivi does not deny the secondary causes, but focuses rather on the First Cause. And his conception of this, the First Cause, is fundamentally correct, as far as I can see.

[89] See I. Kant, *Critique of Practical Reason*, Part 1, Book 1, Chapter 2, 171-172, in *Critique of Practical Reason and Other Writings in Moral Philosophy* (New York: Garland Publishers INC., 1976), 110-111 of original edition.

[90] See *The Basis of Morality* cit., 80. Paradoxically, however, Ockham holds that the act of loving God above all things performed in a natural way may not differ specifically from the supernatural act. See 91–2, citing *In I Sent.* 17, 2.

In Freppert's view, only one obstacle remains in the way of attributing to Ockham the identification of good and precept. While Freppert generally upholds the identity of these in Ockham's thought, he argues for their differentiation on one point. The illustrious interpreter claims that in Ockham's late works, in particular the *Quodlibetales*, a human's love of God appears to be a necessarily virtuous act apart from any command. Let us briefly examine this matter.

The most important passage Freppert quotes reads: "[...] this act [whereby one loves God above all things and for God's sake] is virtuous in such a way that it cannot be vicious [...]: [...] for all are obliged to love God *pro loco et tempore* above all things."[91] It is true, then, that the divine precept is not expressly mentioned as a foundation, but it is obvious that it is mentioned implicitly. Firstly, because "to be obliged," according to Ockham, consists in being under a precept, a norm; secondly, the expression *pro loco et tempore* is technically linked to the interpretation of positive precepts. The first point is easy to prove. In the *Quodlibetales*, Question III, 15 (reply to problem 2), Ockham expressly holds that "the deformity is not an absence of the justice or rectitude that should exist in the *act*, but instead a lack of the rectitude that should exist in the will itself—which is nothing other than to say that the will is obliged by a divine precept to elicit some act that it [in fact] does not elicit."[92] Similarly, in the *Quaestiones variae*, q. 8, he states that a man sins when he departs from the rule to which his will must conform, which is that to which the divine will wants the human will to conform.[93]

But there is a third reason why it is obvious that the passage quoted by Freppert simply means that in the present divine dispensation, under the precepts now in force, to love God above all and for his own sake is a virtuous act that cannot be vicious. An analysis of the context reveals this. In Question 14 of the *Third Quodlibetal*, what Ockham attempts to prove is that there is a necessarily virtuous act of the will. Acts that are not of the will, or even acts of the will other than

[91] *The Basis of Morality*, cit., 121. *Quodlibetales* III 14. William Ockham, *Quodlibetal Questions*, Yale University Press, New Haven 1991. English translation by Freddoso, Alfred; and Kelly, Francis.
[92] The brackets were added by Freddoso.
[93] See *The Basis of Morality*, cit., 118 and 120. See also, *Quaestiones variae* 7, a. 4, lines 155–64. In: *Quaestiones variae* (Saint Bonaventure, New York State: Saint Bonaventure University, 1984). *Opera theologica*, Vol. VIII.

that of loving God above all and for His own sake, are not necessarily virtuous because the intention that animates them can always be twisted. But the act of the will to love God above all and for His own sake cannot have an intention that does not fall within the actual divine precepts. It is therefore a necessarily virtuous act. But it is so, as it says in the text, "provided that the relevant divine precept remains in force." (ibidem, thesis 2)[94]

All in all, Freppert reinforces his interpretation with a powerful reasoning that, nevertheless, can be defeated. Such is, approximately, the reasoning: what it means to love God above all is precisely to be willing to obey him in everything;[95] but the reason for obeying is love. Therefore, a precept that states that one must love God is not a true precept because in obedience to any precept, love is already presupposed. It cannot be that the love of God is sought because of obedience because, in that case, it would not be seen why obedience is obligatory. From here, Freppert argues that the thesis that Ockham defends in the *Commentary on the Fourth Book of Sentences*, 16—namely, that God could command us to hate him, and that, therefore, in heaven we could hate him[96]—simply contradicts the rest of his doctrine.[97] He

---

[94] Freppert returns to this text on pages 145-9 and tries again to argue that the fact that Ockham separates acts that are not of the will from the act of loving God above all and for His own sake could imply that the latter is necessarily virtuous independently of the divine precepts. But this interpretation is untenable and does not really take into consideration the context of the texts. The relevant difference between the two types of acts, that of loving God above all and for His own sake and the other acts, lies not in their relation to the precepts (dependent or independent from the precepts), but in their relation to the intention that animates them (one act is necessarily informed by an intention that is always right as long as the relevant precept remains in place while the other acts could be animated by different intentions, according to precepts or not). Therefore, the clause "as long as the relevant divine precept remains in force" applies to all acts, including that of loving God above all and for His own sake. In the same sense, see T. Osborne, "Ockham as a Divine-Command Theorist," 13. I think Thomas Ward misses this qualification, that to love God is necessarily virtuous *as long as the relevant command is in place*. See "The Incoherence of Ockham's Ethics," 231-3.

[95] Ockham says things similar to this, but always based on divine precepts.

[96] It should not be forgotten that this thesis is held by Ockham in opposition to the thesis of Duns Scotus, who thought that the first table of the Decalogue was necessary.

[97] Benedict Spindler demonstrates that this is precisely the argument with which Vitoria dismisses Ockham's system of ethics. Vitoria argues that if God could command us to hate him, then we would have to love and hate God at the same time, since "obeying a divine command is an expression of love." "Law, Natural Law, and the Foundation of Morality in Francisco de Vitoria and Francisco Suárez," 184, in *The Concept of Law (lex) in the Moral and Political Thought of the "School of Salamanca,"* eds. Kirstin Bunge, Marko J. Fuchs, Danaë Simmermacher and Anselm Spindler (Boston: Brill, 2016), 172-97.

adds that it is a thesis of his youth and that it caused his condemnation in 1326, but that it is a thesis that he later abandoned, as can be seen in the cited passages of the *Quodlibetales*, in which he makes no mention of any precept when he speaks of the love of God as a necessarily virtuous act.[98]

Against this powerful objection, we must reply as follows: First, we have already shown that in the *Quodlibetales* love is indeed linked to the precept. Second, according to the pre-nominalist Christian view, the precept of loving God can make sense precisely because the most fundamental precepts do nothing but make explicit what is implicit in the nature of things. The very fact that Freppert does not see this already indicates that he is far from the pre-nominalist moral conception. Third, to accept that loving God is a precept that cannot change is already to accept that the truth of morality, the ultimate "objective norm," to use Freppert's expression, is not the bare will of God, but the wisdom of God, which guides his will.[99] That is to say: the nature of things and their ordering to the good of the universe and to man's own good, constitute the final *ratio* behind the divine precepts. That is why there can be a "natural law" or a "natural Right."[100] But Ockham does not recognize that final *ratio* as something that precedes the precept. He thinks that the ultimate objective rule is the bare will of God and that this owes nothing to the nature of things. Most particularly, Ockham considers as morally irrelevant the nature of love, perhaps because he neglects to intellectually penetrate in such nature. Human love, which is the basis for understanding divine love, he seems to think is a simple passion that is good or bad not according to a

[98] Carlos Isler, although he rightly and sensibly holds that Ockhamist ethics is voluntarist, makes an exception for the hatred of God: according to him, God could not command us to hate him, and, apart from the exclusion of contradictions, this would be the only limit to Ockham's ethical voluntarism. In this he follows a fairly widespread opinion, but which, for the reasons I explain in the text, seems to me to be mistaken. Something similar occurs on another point: Isler holds that the first principles of morality, as Ockham understands them, are purely formal and necessary. In this he follows David Clark. But, again, although this is a widely held view, it seems to be partly mistaken, as I will show below, in section 3 of this chapter. See "El nominalismo, ¿está asociado necesariamente a una concepción voluntarista de la ley natural? El caso de Ockham y Hobbes," 179, 183, and 184, in *Praxis Filosófica* Nueva Serie, No. 38 (January-July 2014), 175–200.

[99] We will consider again later the connection and distinction between divine wisdom and will.

[100] Ockham speaks very little of natural law, except in his polemical writings, as Freppert acknowledges.

rational order, but according to whether or not it conforms to an arbitrary divine precept:

> If you ask about conversion to God with an act of charity, and aversion with an act with which one loves the creature that God does not will one to love, that is, with the act of fornication, thus they are not repugnant to each other formally and naturally, but are compatible in the same subject, at least regarding the nature of the acts. But they are repugnant only because of an extrinsic cause, that is, because of God who commands that such a creature should in no way be loved by the created will; and, thus, the will that loves such a creature does not love God above all, because, if it loved him thus, it would not love a creature that God hates [...] or that he does not wishes the will to love. And, therefore, it is only because of the ordination of such an extrinsic cause that they seem repugnant to each other. This is evident because, if the established law were repealed, these acts of loving would already become compatible in the same subject; and if that law were to command that creature to be loved, then not only the two acts of love could be simultaneous, but the love of that creature would then be meritorious.[101]

In the light of this text and our previous considerations, it is clear that Ockham could not help but think that the sovereign will of God has the right to command us to hate Him.[102] What would be the basis for this obedience? In the text of the commentary on Peter Lombard on the possibility of God commanding us to hate Him, one can glimpse the foundation: salvation. Whoever wants to go to heaven will have to conform to this precept.[103] And, if in the present dispensation there can

---

[101] *Quaestiones variae* 7, a. 4, lines 353–66; Freppert cites this in *The Basis of Morality* cit. 96.

[102] Eric Hagedorn shares my opinion on this point. See his "On Loving God Contrary to Divine Command: Demystifying Ockham's *Quodlibet* III 14," *Oxford Studies in Medieval Philosophy* 9 (2021): 222-45.

[103] In this light it can be understood why Luther held Ockham to be his true teacher. See *Dr. Martin Luthers Werke* (Weimar: Bölaw, 1883). WA 6, 600, line 11. Thomas Osborne suggests something similar. He states that we could obey the precept of hating God based on the love of concupiscence for those precepts: in order to achieve salvation, we obey. See "Ockham as a

be no salvation without divine love, the omnipotent will of God is not tied to the present dispensation.

The above conclusion is confirmed by Ockham's and Freppert's treatment of another, closely related problem: whether God can wholly and exclusively cause in a created will an act of hating God. In a Christian and non-nominalist metaphysics this is absolutely impossible for several reasons. In the first place, an act of hating God is intrinsically evil and could never be good. But while God sometimes permits evil to obtain greater goods, He does not cause evil. Hatred of God is the sin *par excellence*, and God cannot cause sin insofar as it is sinful. That is to say He causes sins insofar as, *qua* First Cause, He concurs with the creature in the acts of the latter; everything positive in these acts comes ultimately from Him (including the love of the created good that leads to aversion to the Creator), but, insofar as they are disordered, they do not come from Him. Sin is a privation of due order. This aspect, disorder, God tolerates only to protect a higher good: the place of the creature's freedom in the universal order. Secondly, it is impossible for God to cause wholly and alone in the will of the creature an act of hating Him because it would not be an act of the created will. If the Ockhamist principle that God can cause wholly and alone by Himself whatever He can cause concurring with the second cause[104] is true, it is true with one restriction: God cannot cause wholly and alone the very act of created causation without the act of the created cause because that would be contradictory. But the act of the will ("hating God") is the very act of the created cause.[105] Therefore, God cannot cause wholly and alone the act by which the created will hates Him.

Divine-Command Theorist," 15-6. Thomas Ward points out a similar solution to the problem of God commanding creatures to hate Him, but then he abandons it because he thinks that it *cannot be* that Ockham did not think that God deserves to be loved. But this is precisely why he is compelled to find Ockham's ethics incoherent, because he does not want to accept the consequence pointed out by Osborne. See "The Incoherence of Ockham's Ethics," 235-7.

[104] See *II Sent.*, 15; *Quodlibetales* VI 1, 6. Freppert, *The Basis of Morality*, cit.

[105] The way Ockham explains the connection between created and divine causality is erroneous. He maintains that God is a partial cause of the acts of the creature because He does not always act with all his power, but sometimes leaves room for created causality (see *In IV Sent.*, 10–11. Freppert, *The Basis of Morality*, cit., 130). But, according to the truth of things, God is not a partial cause, but total and first. The creature is also a total cause, but second. Just as a brush is the total cause of the painting, the painter is also the total cause. Such are the ordered causes. (I have proved this in the following paper: "A Restatement of the Fifth Thomistic Way to Prove the Existence of God," *Rivista Angelicum*, 96/1, 2019, 29-59, section 1.2. William Carroll

Thus, William of Ockham maintains that God can totally and exclusively cause an act by which the created will hates Him, and Lucan Freppert fails to draw from this fact the due consequences.[106] Let us take a closer look at the reasons Ockham gives to support this far-fetched thesis:

(1) God never sins "*because he is no one's debtor*" (*Quodlibetales* III 4; *Quaestiones variae* q. 7, a. 4, lines 320–31). And, "precisely because God wills something, therefore it is right that it should be done" (*In IV Sent.*, qq. 10–11;[107] *The Basis of Morality*, 134). That is to say: the source of every obligation is the divine will. Since to sin means to violate an obligation, it would be contradictory to say that the will of God can sin.

(2) God can cause this act because He can exclusively cause any act that the creature can cause with his co-causality. But it is obvious that the creature can hate God (cf. *In IV Sent.*, 10–11.[108] It is also obvious that the creature can command that God be hated, by the way: *The Basis of Morality*, 137).[109]

(3) More explicitly, Ockham holds that God can be the exclusive cause of anything positive that the creature causes, especially if what is caused is absolute. Therefore, He can be the exclusive cause of the act of hating God (*In II Sent.*, 15.[110] *The Basis of Morality*, 135).

---

has proven the same point in "Thomas Aquinas on Creation and Science," in *Investigación científica y fe católica*, Carlos Casanova ed. [Santiago, Chile: RIL Editores-Universidad Santo Tomás, 2016], 89-198.) Ockham also holds that God is first and immediate cause of all effects (for he understands by "immediate" that without which the effect cannot be produced: *In II Sent.*, 3–4. Freppert, *The Basis of Morality*, 131; see, also, *Quaestiones variae* 7, a. 4, lines 312–13). But from these two Ockhamist statements a paradox follows: Does the causality of creatures that is the non-divine part of the causality of created effects depend on God? Is not that created causality, too, an effect of God? But, then, should it not be said that God is the total cause of all effects? There is in Ockhamist theology, because of the absence of an adequate notion of participation and order, a constant danger of absorption of created causality in divine causality.

[106] In contrast, Carlos Isler does evaluate the implications that, according to Ockham, God can do evil. See o. c., 186–7.

[107] 198, lines 2–9. *Quaestiones in IV librum Sententiarum (Reportatio)* (Saint Bonaventure, New York State: Saint Bonaventure University, 1984). *Opera Theologica*, Vol. VII.

[108] See 198, lines 13–16.

[109] It follows that God could command us to hate Him, through the act of at least one creature.

[110] See *In II Sententiarum*, q. 15, 342, lines 22–343, line 2; 343, lines 16–22; 352, line 3–353, line 2; 353, lines 11–3.

(4) Moreover, only in the sin of omission can its substance be said to be a simple privation. The sin of commission does not consist in a simple privation and, therefore, because it is a positive action, God must be its cause (cf. *Quaestiones variae* q. 7, a. 4, lines 299 ff.).

From all these reasons it follows that, according to Ockham, the nature of evil consists simply in the lack of conformity to the divine will. Also, moreover, that the divine will (source of general laws or of particular decrees) is absolutely autonomous, dissociated from any wisdom that could precede it. Its only true limit would be the non-contradiction with the being of things (being that Ockham understands as stripped of all intrinsic goodness) or with the previous acts of the same divine will. Finally, we can apprehend the strange blindness of the Ockhamist intellect, unable to perceive the disorder intrinsic to sin or "moral evil" and unable to perceive, therefore, the imperfection and turpitude contained in this disorder, turpitude that is simply repugnant to the divine holiness. God cannot cause sin by His will (which is the only way God causes), but not because His will is the one cause that arbitrarily defines what sin is, as Ockham claims, but because the intrinsic deformity of the sinful act (e.g., hatred of God) is repugnant to the beauty and goodness of the divine being.

3. Contingency of the moral standard

A further objection can still be opposed to the present thesis. Analytic philosophers have taken up the question of whether the traditional interpretation of Ockham's moral theory is accurate. David W. Clark, for example, argues that the principle "act according to natural reason" is a necessary principle of morality, according to Ockham. Therefore, he cannot be a voluntarist.

In considering this objection, we start by asking ourselves whether the principle "act according to natural reason" is a necessary and universal principle of morality according to Ockham, or else if it is just a principle *within the present divine dispensation* (because it happens to be the case that, within this dispensation, right reason is what conforms to the divine law). Clark's thesis could be reformulated, then, as follows: "act according to natural reason" is a principle of morality, necessarily enjoined in any divine dispensation; as a result, under any dispensation, man would have to act according to his right reason since this would always be what conforms to the divine law. Thus, although the concrete precepts which in the present divine dispensation constitute the content of the law are contingent, it could be said that "act according to right reason" would be a necessary and immutable principle of Ockhamist morality. If, however, we examine the Franciscan's work carefully, we see that not even Clarke's thesis is correct—not even the principle of acting according to natural reason is immutable.

To settle the question, let us review the following text, which does not belong, according to Freppert, to the early works of William of Ockham:

> [The act of prudence] is an efficient cause necessarily required for the virtuous act. It is impossible for an act to be virtuous without the act of prudence, *so long as the divine ordination which now exists remains*, because for a virtuous act the activity of the act of prudence and the activity of the will are required in a necessary way, so that the two causes are partial causes together with God with respect to the virtuous act.[111]

[111] *Quaestiones variae* 7, a. 4, lines 440–2, cited by Freppert, *The Basis of Morality*, cit., 64. Emphasis added. Francis Oakley, unlike Clarke, is aware of the implications of passages such as the one cited: "When [...] it comes to determining whether or not Ockham's teaching on moral or juridical natural law is indeed voluntarist and aligned with the template constituted by his views on the order of physical nature (it *is* voluntarist and *is* so aligned), his use of such crucial qualifications as 'in the present order' [...] can be and has been ignored only at the price of severe misunderstanding" (*Natural Law, Laws of Nature, Natural Rights*, 80). A. S. McGrade overlooks this passage, and its implications, in his article "Natural Law and Moral Omnipotence." In: *The Cambridge Companion to Ockham*, ed. Paul Vincent Spade (Cambridge: Cambridge University Press, 1999), 273–301. Of course, a divine ordination in which we should not obey right reason (the act of prudence) would, in reality, be absurd, unless right reason and obedience to divine precepts were separated from each other. But, in that hypothetical case (which does not exist in our world as we know it, according to Ockham) what would happen, perhaps, would be something like the state of things that Luther envisions: reason is the devil's prostitute because it proposes to us a rectitude that is not what God expects of us. So, although it cannot be said that Ockham's doctrine is equal to Luther's on this point, it can be said that Ockham's doctrine may have paved the way for Luther's. For in having so emphasized divine omnipotence, and separated it from wisdom, as we shall see, he made at least conceivable a clash between God's actual will for us and the apparent natural rectitude of reason. Thomas Osborne also overlooks this passage in his paper "Ockham as a Divine-Command Theorist," 16. However, Osborne is right that there are some aspects of the present

It is not only the content of morality but its very structure and deepest foundations that could vary if the omnipotent will of God so disposed. There could be a divine ordination in which the virtuous act did not require the act of prudence. There is only one limit, that of non-contradiction. There is no other limit to what God could will or command. For example, God could command us to hate Him, but He could not command us to will and not to will at the same time and in the same respect. Ockham argues this explicitly in a late work: in the present dispensation in which God is to be loved above all things, *because He is not contradictory*, God can command that for a time someone should not love Him, because He must devote himself to study, e.g.[112] But he cannot command [within the present dispensation] that we hate Him. Since this is the only limit that Ockham conceives, according to him, therefore, there is no intrinsic order rooted in the nature of things.

The possibility that the moral good and the prescription of prudence diverge allows us to enter briefly into a theme connected with the next section: in the present order established by God, right reason is governed by principles that are in harmony with the divine law, but these principles do not proceed from things. They proceed from an internal ordering of the human mind by God. There is a kind of [extrinsic] "law" written in the hearts of all men, to paraphrase Romans 2:15. Freppert correctly interprets Ockham on this point:

> by the natural light of reason, man is capable of acquiring a knowledge of the order established by God in the universe. This includes a knowledge of the moral

---

dispensation of morality that would be necessary in any dispensation. "For example, He [God] could not make digestion virtuous or vitious because digestion is not free" (ibidem).

[112] *Quodlibetales* III 14. As Freppert comments, in such a case, the one who receives the command could not be distracted from study in an act of loving God above all things, because such an act would be disobedience and, therefore, would not be an act of love (in the present dispensation). Such an explicit act of love would be contradictory and impossible. However, it would be possible, through obedience, to perform an implicit act of love. See *The Basis of Morality*, 137–40. Eric W. Hagedorn considers this passage and the problems that it poses at length. His solution is in harmony with Freppert's interpretation. He adds that, since the precept that commands to love God is a positive precept, it must be fulfilled at certain times and places, which Ockham explicitly states in *Quod.* III 14, lines 66-67, and is a general scholastic teaching with which Ockham concurred. So, there is no contradiction in abstaining to elicit an act of loving God above all things for a period of time because God has so commanded, and it would be contradictory and impossible to elicit it. See "On Loving God Contrary to Divine Command: Demystifying Ockham's *Quodlibet* III 14."

> order. In accordance with his knowledge of the moral order man constructs a code of ethics, a philosophy of right action by which he can guide his life with practical certitude. In following the precepts of this code of ethics, man's right reason is the norm which he must follow. The moral goodness or depravity of an act is measured in terms of its conformity to right reason. God's will, however, as manifested in a positive act of revelation, may supersede the demands of the moral order and the commands and prohibitions of a humanly constructed code of ethics [...].

But Freppert gives this thesis a foundation that seems to me to be alien to Ockham. He cites St. Bonaventure, in fact, to state that there is a "natural revelation" because, starting from created things, the human mind begins its journey towards God.[113] In the work of St. Bonaventure, it is presupposed that there are good or bad things in themselves, and that, therefore, the will of God is preceded by His wisdom.[114] In this important aspect Ockham's work departs from the work of the great master, the holy Franciscan doctor, St. Bonaventure. And, insofar as it departs, the *Venerabilis inceptor* makes it possible to conceive of a dissociation between natural reason and the moral law, as I have pointed out: only in this dispensation the object of rational moral knowledge is not the intrinsic order of created nature, but the arbitrary law of God and its application to the acts of the human will.

4. The object of moral knowledge

In this section we will focus our attention on natural morality and leave aside Ockham's notion of "positive morality." From what has been said so far it is clear that, according to Ockham, the object of moral knowledge is constituted, in the first place, by the divine law itself

[113] *The Basis of Morality*, 177 and 178. He cites the *Itinerarium mentis in Deum*.

[114] In the *Itinerary of the mind to God*, 1, 14, it is presupposed that the divine Power is always exercised according to wisdom and, therefore, from the order of created being we can have a glimpse into the Creator's Mind. That is to say, this writing presupposes the precedence of the reason of wisdom over the reason of Power in God's acts. It is for this cause that Bonaventure can intelligibly hold that created things are a ladder of ascension to the Creator.

(insofar as it is impressed on the hearts of men or revealed to them) and, in the second place, by the conformity or non-conformity of human acts to that law through "right reason." The second aspect of moral knowledge is by no means simple, since it requires a profound knowledge of the "circumstances of the act," including its relation to the law. As for the first aspect, we must bear in mind that, although divine law is the first directive rule, right reason can be considered the rule of the human will because reason manifests the divine law to the person who is the subject of the act of will.[115] (It actually happens in the present dispensation that natural reason and divine law are in agreement.)

One of the interesting facets of the second aspect is that, according to Ockham, natural reason constitutes both part of the object and partial efficient cause of free (moral) acts. The second point I will deal with a little further down. As for the first, it is said to be part of the object because the rectitude of the act, according to Ockham, cannot be known by considering the nature of the things involved in it, like a kind of food and the agent, for example, together with all the essential or accidental circumstances:

> If right reason were not the object of the act of temperance, and food were the object, then it would follow that in apprehending food without right reason (and even with an erroneous reason), the will could elicit a perfectly virtuous act. For to cause an act of the will nothing else is required but God, the will, and the apprehension of the object. These suffice as partial causes in the production of an act of willing.[116]

Note that in the classical view "the food" would not be the object of the virtuous act,[117] but rather the due proportion that exists between that food and the subject's action in the concrete circumstances—a proportion that can be grasped in a judgment of prudence that arrives

---

[115] *Quaestiones variae* 8, at the beginning. Cited by Freppert, *The Basis of Morality*, 51. We will return to this text in the section dedicated to the divine will.

[116] Freppert, *The Basis of Morality* cit., 64, which paraphrases *Quaestiones variae* 7, 4, lines 419–28 and 451 ff. The passage vividly recalls Kant: the rightness of an act cannot come from objects, but from the law of pure practical reason itself.

[117] I am referring here to the "object" of the moral act in technical sense, as opposed to the end and the circumstances.

at practical truth, which is susceptible of being formulated in a general way in a law.[118] But the law would not be the cause of the rectitude of reason, nor of practical truth, but rather a general formulation of that truth.

According to the Ockhamist view, however, right reason is part of the object of the virtuous act both because it (reason) indicates its conformity to the law ("this act is good"), and because it prescribes it (the virtuous act) in a normative formulation ("this act should be done"), in an act of assent.[119] This is how the Ockhamist Freppert interprets the passage in *Nicomachean Ethics* II 4, 1105a: "The agent must be in a certain condition when he does them (the acts of the virtues); in the first place, he must have knowledge; secondly, he must choose the acts, and choose them for their own sakes."[120] It is obvious, however, that what Aristotle means is something quite different: it is not a matter of willing the conformity of the act to the law (equated to right reason), but of willing the action and the good it serves deliberately and for their own sake, and not for a benefit extraneous to them; and of finding in this willing and in the act itself a certain delight, which is not the end of the action, but is concomitant upon it for the virtuous man.

Here we can see the difficulty Ockham has in integrating the reality of the free act in a unitary way. In the Thomistic and Aristotelian understanding of morality, reason, straight or crooked, is the final cause of the free act, while the efficient cause is the will. But reason can be a final cause precisely because it (rightly or wrongly) presents a good that is considered proportionate to the agent (the end is "the good of each one"). And conformity or non-conformity to the law is not part of the object of the free act because the law is a rule extrinsic to the goodness or badness intrinsic to the free act. The disappearance (or at least transformation) in Ockhamist conceptualism of the final cause proper, a disappearance that manifests itself in considering prudence and reason as "partial efficient cause" (and "object") of the voluntary act,[121] ends up producing a disintegration of the moral act. In the first place, it

---

[118] See Casanova, Carlos, *Rationality and Justice*, chapter IV, section 3; and *La verdad práctica como piedra angular de la ética*, cit.

[119] Here I again follow Freppert, *The Basis of Morality*, 52–3, which paraphrase or comments on *In III Sent.* 12; *Quaestiones variae* 7, 4, lines 219–24, 419–20, 443–69.

[120] *The Basis of Morality*, 52. Freppert follows *Quaestiones variae* 8, a. 1.

[121] See *Quaestiones variae* 8, 1, lines 145–47, 216–31, 240–41. Freppert, *The Basis of Morality*, 62.

produces a sort of dualism: (intrinsic) morality would reside exclusively in the acts of the will and would consist in a person willing those things which are willed by the divine will to be the objects of different acts precisely because they are so willed by the divine will. But the judgments of prudence would be mere "natural entities," without any moral entity, except as objects of the will's act of willing: they would be "extrinsically" moral.[122] Secondly, there is an occlusion of the distinction and mutual connection between object, end, and circumstances as elements of the structure of the moral act. For the "object" is the species of the act, which results from the information of the matter of the act (the essential circumstances)[123] by intention and rational judgment.[124] Moral dualism excludes this in-formation. The

---

[122] *Quaestiones variae* 7, 4, lines 108–15 (see also a. 1, lines 100–112). Freppert cites this same passage in: *The Basis of Morality* cit., 58 n. 11. See in the same vein, *Quodl.* 1, 20. It is true that the root of morality lies in the intention of the free agent's acts; but that does not mean that the rest is extrinsically moral. It is intrinsically moral precisely insofar as, *qua* final cause, it can inform the act of the will. But Ockham cannot understand this because, having fallen into a strange blindness about the intrinsic goodness of things and actions, he cannot see them as ends, but as objects conforming to or contradicting the law. Ockham's moral dualism becomes very manifest in this passage:

> [The goodness of the exterior act can be conceived as something different from the exterior act and, in this case, as a relation of conformity to the interior act]. But this sort of relation [also] belongs to the acts of those natural causes that are brought into proximity to the passive principles by the interior act. For example, if (i) the will commands a fire to light a candle in a church in order to honor God, and (ii) the fire is brought into proximity to the candle, then the fire's act straightaway conforms to the will's interior act. Similarly, if (i) the will commands a donkey to defecate in a church and (ii) the donkey is brought to the church and (iii) there is no impediment, then the donkey's act immediately conforms to the will's interior act—and yet the donkey's exterior act does not have its own proper goodness or evilness. Therefore, neither does the exterior act have its own proper moral goodness or evilness in the case under discussion. Hence, an exterior act belonging to the same subject [that has the interior act] has a conformity to the interior act only if an act belonging to an ox or a donkey or fire can have an exactly similar conformity. (*Quodl.* I, q. 20, a. 2, second proof. I quote from the English translation of Alfred Freddoso and Francis Kelly cit.)

This passage allows us to emphasize Ockham's equating any natural cause used instrumentally, on the one hand, with the operations of our own being, on the other.

[123] This conception of the matter of the act can be seen in Thomas Aquinas, *Summa theologiae* I-II, qq. 7, a. 3; 18, a. 2, ad 3m and a. 6, c.

[124] For a detailed study of the notions of object, end and circumstances, see Carlos A. Casanova, *Verdad escatológica y acción intramundana. La teoría política de Eric Voegelin* (Pamplona: EUNSA, 1997), 391–415.

structure of the moral act is reduced to an intention that takes into account all the elements ("objects") of the act of volition and that is caused by all the concurrent "efficient causes."[125]

5. Divine will and wisdom

From what we have said, it is already clear that William of Ockham conceives the divine will as the ultimate rule of all goodness in the universe and, therefore, as a power detached from any rule of goodness. But it will not be superfluous to show some explicit texts or to bring to light the misunderstandings they contain. Here is a text from a work that is not one of the earliest: "The divine Will does not need something to direct it, because it is a directive rule in the first place, and cannot act evilly. But our will is such that it can act rightly or wrongly. Therefore, it needs some reason to direct it."[126] This means, in the proper metaphysical terms, that Ockham does not see (1) that the good is a transcendental, present in all being; (2) that what "can be loved" by the will (the intelligible good, the transcendental proper) presupposes what "can be known" by the intellect. It follows (3) that he perceives neither that the will (including the divine will, insofar as our language can rightly express the life of God) takes its rule from the understanding (which is its final cause), nor that the understanding takes its rule from being. There is no being that is not valuable as *good* (which is the object of the will), but the value of goodness follows being (which is the object of the intellect). For this reason, what is meant by (divine) "wisdom" precedes what is meant by (divine) "will," and we cannot speak correctly about God except according to the intrinsic order of significations. If we did not say that the will is preceded by wisdom we would be, in fact, denying that the will of God is necessarily wise in its acting.[127]

---

[125] On the fusion of the notions of "end," "object," and "circumstances" in the notion of the "object" of the act of the will, see e.g., *Quodl.* 3, 16; and *Quaestiones variae* 7, 4. On the hegemony of the intention, see *Quodl.* 1, q. 20, a. 2, proof 5.

[126] *Quaestiones variae* 8. Freppert transcribes this text in *The Basis of Morality*, 51. As we have seen, P. J. Olivi is in total disagreement with this thesis of William of Ockham. The latter is truly revolutionary on this point.

[127] Ockham cannot see this point in relation to the divine will because he denies that there can be distinct formal aspects of the same real thing (as happens in transcendentals: the referent

A presupposition of not perceiving that the divine will is preceded by wisdom is that Ockham does not perceive that beings possess an intrinsic goodness and, therefore, that the appetite of persons possesses an intrinsic order, endowed with conditional necessity, about which God's will cannot be arbitrary. This is why the above text can be connected with those we have already commented on, concerning the possibility that God directly and exclusively causes an act of hatred toward Himself in the creature.

According to the nature of things, if there are rational creatures, an act of hatred of God would constitute the greatest evil in the universe,[128] and that action, insofar as it is disordered, cannot be caused by God. The disorder of that action does not proceed from an arbitrary disposition of the divine will, but from the nature of the things involved in it. Thus, it is a grave error to claim that God can cause directly and exclusively, without the participation of the free will of the creature, an act of the creature to hate God. It is also wrong to say that God can establish that theft, fornication, or adultery are right. The Fathers of the Church have reflected deeply on the biblical cases that raise doubts in this sense. When the Israelites, for example, are commanded to dispossess the Egyptians, it is not theft, but a punishment imposed by God; when they are commanded to exterminate a people, they are executing divine punishment as instruments of divine judgment; and so on. In such cases they may sin, if their heart does not desire the divine punishment, but is carried away by the thirst for revenge or by avarice. Now, if God were to cause directly and exclusively in the Israelites that act of desiring vengeance or riches, God would sin. To claim, therefore, that He could cause it would be a grave error. As St. Thomas would say, it would be blasphemy.[129]

---

and the formality signified are the same in two transcendentals, but not the "aspect" signified); he wants to deny all formal distinction, if there is identity in the thing; and, if there is difference in an aspect of signification, to deny all identity in real formality; and he seems unaware that our true language about God, because it starts from the multiplicity of the created, must distinguish in Him formal reasons which according to the subject and according to all His reality are identified in Him. See ADAMS, Marilyn McCord, *William Ockham* (Notre Dame: University of Notre Dame Press, 2015), 20–2, 49–50.

[128] That according to the nature of things to hate God would be at least gravely evil (if not the greatest evil) is asserted by Thomas Ward in "The Incoherence of Ockham's Ethics," 232.

[129] See, for example, *Super Sent.* lib. 1 d. 42 q. 2 a. 1 ad 4.

On this point, Ockham is innovative. Although, among the other Franciscans, divine omnipotence[130] and obedience to the will of God[131] were heavily emphasized, it was always taught that wisdom guided the divine will.[132] Paolo Grossi's thesis is plausible—namely, that the nominalist revolution in the conception of subjective rights (which we will discuss in the next chapter) may have been, to some extent, prepared by the conceptual apparatus of Franciscan scholasticism prior to Ockham.[133] However, because other Franciscans subjected God's will to His wisdom, we must be very careful not to attribute a revolutionary character to aspects of Franciscan teaching that simply reflect a new emphasis on perfectly traditional doctrines. I think that Paolo Grossi is not careful enough and, as a result, attributes a revolutionary character to aspects of Franciscan teaching that are not revolutionary.[134]

6. Did Ockham sincerely subscribe to the Aristotelian doctrine of Natural Right (in the objective sense)?

From what has been said so far, it seems to me that a reasonable answer to this question can be given. "Natural Right" can be understood in two ways: (a) as a "law" inscribed in the heart of man, which constitutes the set of principles with which "right reason" deliberates; and (b) as the demands that the natures of things can make on the reason of the agent (and, above all, on the reason of the judge). If "natural Right" is understood in the first way, Ockham held there is such a thing as natural

---

[130] See, for example, P. Duhem, in his *History of Physics*, chapter 8, in *Catholic Encyclopedia* (New York: The Encyclopaedia Press, 1913) Vol. 12, 47–67. Available here: http://www.newadvent.org/cathen/12047a.htm. Accessed on March 17, 2016.

[131] See Olivi, *Quid ponit ius*, cit. for example, where it is held that "law" adds, above all, the will of God and what is willed by it.

[132] This is very clear in the aforementioned work by Olivi, as we have seen.

[133] Probably the Olivian conception of relation ("elsewhere it has been proved that relative reason alone taken by itself without any other quiddity is not something real nor does it add an essence diverse from that on which it is immediately founded," see *Quid ponit ius*, cit.) has prepared the Ockhamist denial of the reality of relation, for example.

[134] In fact, and for example, Grossi ("Usus facti," 135–6, 152, 156, in: *Il dominio e le cose. Percezioni medievali e moderne dei diritti reali*, Giufffrè Editore, Milan 1992, 123–89), in his reading of Olivi, argues that he reduces Law to the will of God, but fails to notice that this Franciscan, focused above all on the ultimate cause, does not reduce Law to that ultimate cause, as we have seen. I could give another example concerning property, but I will deal with it in footnote in the next chapter.

Right. But, if it is understood in the second way, Ockham did not think there is natural Right. Lucan Freppert himself, who has thoroughly examined Ockham's moral writings, tells us that only in the polemical (legal and political) writings does Ockham make use of the scholastic "system" of "natural Right" in his argumentation, as a tribute to the popular conception of law and morals. "In his philosophical writings, [...] Ockham carefully avoids any mention or use of the ethical system of natural law ethics."[135]

It is within this context where one must situate the famous passage of the *Dialogue* concerning "The Three Modes of Natural Law."[136] The first mode or layer is composed of indubitable principles of right, natural reason that were valid before the fall. Again, those principles are not the wise order of things according to their nature, but a presence of God's arbitrary law in human conscience. One principle that is taken here as immutable and belonging to the first layer, "you shall not commit adultery,"[137] for example, is held by Ockham to be a principle just because God so willed it, as we have established above. The second layer is a modification of the first that obtains after the fall. Unlike the first layer, it is mutable because human beings can establish rules that are contrary to what otherwise would belong to natural law.

Thus, we must clarify that Ockham holds that, because the fall moved God to introduce new principles, the first layer does not have universal applicability.[138] For example, according to Ockham, by natural Right of the first kind things should be used by all; but by natural Right of the second kind, things should be possessed in common and there should be no slave. However, the second set of rules may be changed by some human acts and that is why *ius gentium* allows to have private property, on the one hand, and slavery, on the other. The third layer is

---

[135] *The Basis of Morality* cit. 11–2. Kevin McDonnell (op. cit.) agrees with Freppert in this interpretation. Freppert seems to ignore the difference between natural law and natural Right.
[136] See Janet Coleman, "Ockham's Right Reason and the Genesis of the Political as 'Absolutist,'" 51-6; and William of Ockham, "The Three Modes of Natural Law in Ockham: A Revision of the Text," 212-8. As a matter of fact, Ockham uses the word "Right," not "law." However, it is not wrong to translate it as "law" because in English the word is ambiguous and because in Ockham that is the real meaning.
[137] See William of Ockham, "The Three Modes of Natural Law," 212.
[138] That we witness in this second set of principles a further legislative act by God, according to Ockham, can easily be gathered from *Breviloquium* III, chapters 7 and 8. *Opera politica*, Volume IV (Oxford: The British Academy-Oxford University Press, 1997), 97–260.

a "natural Right *ex suppositione.*" It is a set of rules rationally derived from *ius gentium* or from a divine or human act. The said set of rules is valid, unless those who have interest in the issue agree not to abide by it. He gives as an example of this third layer the need to repel violence even by force. This belongs to natural Right *if* there are human beings who unjustly attack others. This kind of rule would not be necessary if men lived in accordance with the second layer of natural law after the fall.[139] This doctrine on the layers of natural law, with all its complications, does not affect the nuclear point that I have made in this chapter, since the ultimate origin of the different layers of rules is always either the laws established by God's arbitrary will or human reasoning that takes as its principles such divine laws and human positive laws as well.[140]

And with this we are coming to the end of the first part of this investigation. There is no doubt that in his polemical writings William of Ockham speaks of "natural right," both in an objective and in a subjective sense. But, in light of what we have just shown one can reinterpret a central aspect of Tierney's defense of Ockham by considering the meaning of "right reason" in Ockham's work. Let us here bring back a central passage:

> Whether he defined natural right (*ius poli*) in a subjective sense or an objective sense, in either case his definition was grounded on right reason: 'the *ius poli* is nothing other than a power in conformity with right reason [...], this is sometimes called natural law' [*Opus.* cit., *Opera politica*, vol. 2, 65, 574–579]. For Ockham a natural right was not an assertion of naked will but a power conformed to reason.[141]

[139] See William of Ockham, "The Three Modes of Natural Law," 212-3, 215. In these distinctions, what Ockham is doing is to subsume Isidore of Seville's teachings on natural right within his own (Ockhamist) worldview. Among the rules of natural Right in the third sense, Ockham includes that a community must elect those who rule over it, unless the community itself yields its right to others (see ibidem, 216).

[140] See ibidem, 218. That God is the author of all natural Right is Ockhamist doctrine (see "The Three Modes of Natural Law", 216), but it is also Aquinas' doctrine that God is the ultimate cause of all natural Right. It is the context of each worldview where such statements acquire their final meaning.

[141] Tierney, Brian cit. 199.

But, as we have shown, according to Ockham, "right reason" does not discover practical truth, the demands of the nature of things. What is its proper work, then? In the moral order, it unveils the divine precepts. This implies that Ockham's morality depends on his theoretical works and is voluntarist.[142] And what is the proper work of right reason in the political-legal order? We will have to try to clarify this in the next chapter.

[142] See Francis Oakley, *Natural Law, Laws of Nature, Natural Rights*, 80.

CHAPTER 2

William of Ockham and the origin of the nominalist conception of subjective rights

As noted above, Michel Villey (and later Michel Bastit as well) held the disputed theses that William of Ockham, espousing a nominalist theology and metaphysics, also (1) espoused a voluntarist moral doctrine and (2) revolutionized legal philosophy and practice through coining the subjective meaning of *right* and developing a systematic philosophy of law around this new notion. In this chapter we are going to study the second disputed thesis, whether Ockham's legal philosophy and theology constituted the inauguration of the nominalist version of subjective rights. To formulate the problems connected with this question, I will use two points of the three found in Brian Tierney's defense of William of Ockham. In Chapter 1 the first of the three points was dealt with: whether Ockham is or is not a moral voluntarist. The other two points are the following:

1) First, according to Tierney, Ockham's work did not involve a semantic revolution that coined the subjective meaning of the word *right* (as Villey argues[143]), nor a "Copernican revolution" (as Bastit argues).

Ockham sought out the texts he needed to serve his own purposes and deployed them creatively. Having reappropriated or reinvented some earlier canonistic understandings of *ius naturale* he went on to apply them to the problems of his own day; in the process they took on some new meanings and revealed new implications. The old texts also acquired a new significance from the fact that Ockham was addressing an audience different from that of the Decretists, not just a narrow circle of professional canonists but the whole intellectual world of the Christian West. The language of rights continued to be used in the

[143] See Brian Tierney, *The Idea of Natural Rights* (Grand Rapids, MI: William B. Eerdmans Publishing Company, 2001), 28–30.

works of late medieval jurists but, after Ockham, it increasingly inhabited the realms of philosophy and political theory.[144]

So, according to Tierney, Ockham did not introduce a semantic revolution, but he did bring about a significant development of thought and language. Among the examples he gives, we have: "he built a coherent theory of property, rather reminiscent of Pufendorf's, around some scattered texts of the *Decretum*"; he unites the natural rights of subjects to the ideal of evangelical liberty; he highlights "an obscure doctrine of canonistic corporation law and turn[s] it into an important principle of political thought."[145]

2) Second, according to Tierney, Ockham's metaphysical and theological nominalism and voluntarism had no influence on his political and juridical doctrine. Against Villey, he argues especially that Ockham's theses on rights are independent of his theological theses; that the subtle speculations of philosophers and theologians on the relations between intellect and will are rarely transferred to the earthlier reflections of law and politics.[146]

The importance of Brian Tierney's contribution to the research on the origin of the notion of subjective right is undeniable. Even before Tierney's work, Villey had conceded that there was a marginal use of *ius* in subjective sense (or in a sense close to it) in Roman Law or Right, in expressions such as "*personae sui iuris,*" "*personae alieni iuris,*" the "*ius*" of "*usufructus,*" or "*iura*" as incorporeal things.[147] But today it is quite clear

---

[144] 202.

[145] In other words, moral persons are a fiction. 203.

[146] See 28–30, 31–32, 52–53, 200.

[147] See M. Villey, *Estudios en torno a la noción de derecho subjetivo* (Valparaíso: Ediciones Universitarias de Valparaíso, 1976), 93. See also Cristóbal Orrego, "La gramática de los derechos y el concepto de derecho humanos en John Finnis," 156, *Persona y Derecho*, 59 (2008), 135–57. Father Dominic Legge, O.P. has argued in the same line that there are at least 23 instances in which Aquinas uses *ius* in the subjective sense and that some of those instances equate to arguing that there are "natural rights" "belonging to persons in virtue of their nature as free and rational creatures" (136). He adds that this kind of right was invoked by the Dominicans in the 16th century against the enslavement of the indigenous peoples of the New World (ibidem). Finally, he states that these rights according to Aquinas belong to human persons, but always considered within a wider teleological order (137, see Dominic Legge, "Do Thomists Have Rights?" *Nova et Vetera*, English Edition, Vol. 17, No. 1 [2019]: 127-147). This last remark contains the key to his view and for this reason I think that I find myself in fundamental agreement with him. However, I must observe three things: (1) in Legge's list, many of the instances of *ius* used in the subjective sense are not really such or at least they have been

that canonists and theologians before Ockham made frequent use of it, since the twelfth century.[148] However, in his reaction against Villey's thesis, Tierney seems to have gone too far. So far, in fact, that his theses led to the formulation of a historiographical and theoretical problem worthy of careful consideration. Indeed, is it possibly true that the main novelty introduced by Ockham consists simply in setting a number of traditional concepts and assertions (including the preexisting notion of subjective rights) "in a framework of discourse about natural rights, the rights granted to human kind 'by God and nature,'" in the *Breviloquium*, as Tierney claims?[149] Or is it rather true that in Ockham's work we discover a conception of Right profoundly different from the classical or Roman one (which is not the case in the work of the previous

strongly disputed. Felipe Widow (see Felipe Widow, *Autonomía de la razón práctica y derecho subjetivo en la filosofía jurídica de John Finnis [Estudio crítico y confrontación con Tomás de Aquino].* Doctoral dissertation submitted to the Faculty of Law of the Pontificia Universidad Católica de Chile, and approved on July 6, 2016, 345-359) has demonstrated this point when he responded to similar lists produced by Fr. Hiacinthus Hering ("De iure subjective sumpto apud S. Thomam", in *Angelicum* 16 [1939]), Héctor Hernández (*Derecho subjetivo. Derechos humanos. Doctrina solidarista* [Buenos Aires: Abeledo-Perrot, 2000], 268-269), and John Finnis (*Aquinas. Moral, Political, and Legal Theory* [Oxford: Oxford University Press, 1998] 132-138); (2) Legge goes too far when he states that the reason why nominalist views of rights differ from the Thomistic one *is not* because "they shift from objective to subjective rights." In the classical and Thomistic view, all subjective rights are actually or potentially the active side of a juridical (objective) relationship because the objective meaning is the fundamental meaning of *ius*, from which all others are derived. The nominalist view, instead, shifts the fundamental meaning of right from objective to subjective. And (3) the Dominicans that argued for the Indians did not properly argue so that the Indians would not be enslaved—because Isabella had already solved this issue much earlier (authorizing the enslavement only of the Indians who were cannibals) and Sepúlveda never argued for their enslavement but for considering them unable to deliberate perfectly and, therefore, in need of legal guardianship. Concerning Sepúlveda, see David Brading, *The First America* (Cambridge: Cambridge University Press, 1991), Part 1, chapter 4, 79-101. On whether the Indians were enslaved or not, see Carlos A. Casanova, *El republicanismo español en América: una evaluación* (Mexico: UNAM, 2015), 34-36. David Lantigua in his book *Infidels and Empires* (Cambridge: Cambridge University Press, 2020), 51-186, portrays very interestingly many debates concerning the Amerindians in which the Dominicans were involved. A defect in Lantigua's book is that the pragmatic history of the Spanish conquest is never told based on the pragmatic historians' account, but always through the Dominican friars' lenses or the lenses of other participants in the European debate, so that a distorted image of the pragmatic events emerges from his narrative. Besides, he often overstates his critique of the jurists, as when in 109 he accuses Sepúlveda of having proposed to enslave the Indians, by identifying them with the *ferae bestiae* of Roman law, although in 165 he clearly states that no Spaniard gave arguments to subject the Indians to chattel slavery.

[148] See Tierney, Brian *The Idea of Natural Rights*, chapter 2, 57 ff. See also Francis Oakley, *Natural Law, Laws of Nature, Natural Rights*, 102-103.

[149] *The Idea of Natural Rights*, 193.

canonists nor in that of St. Thomas), and that such conception is connected to the nominalist notion of the good?

In order to successfully undertake the task of answering both the above questions, it is necessary to keep in mind that rights in the subjective sense can be understood either in a way that is compatible with classical philosophy or in one that is not.[150] If they are seen, for example, as powers that exist in the context of distributive justice,[151] and if they are seen as the actual or potential active side of a juridical relation that also presupposes distributive justice,[152] and if they are seen as what the law allows,[153] in all these cases the use of the word *right* does not imply the adoption of a nominalist philosophy.

We can now use the method employed by Francis Oakley[154] and state that it is an undisputed fact that since the 17th century a non-classical view of political and legal order emerged, and in that view (a) the political community exists just as an conglomerate of individuals, and (b) not with the end that its members cooperate through the division of labor and through the cultivation of virtue to achieve a common good. In this new view, the "civil society" exists, rather, so that its members do not harm each other's rights and so that they protect each other's rights from foreign aggression.[155] This new approach to political and legal philosophy is nominalist and, for reasons that were pointed out in the introduction and on which we will come back later, denies that in political society all rights must be understood in the context of distributive justice. Besides, this new approach holds (c) that the judicial courts must refrain from applying any law that is not

[150] Although Alejandro Guzmán Brito grasped this point in his book *El derecho como facultad en la neoescolástica espanola del siglo XVI* (Madrid: Iustel, 2009), 87–89, he did not elaborate on it.
[151] Such is the case with the expressions *persona sui iuris* and *persona alieni iuris* in Roman Law.
[152] As is the case in many examples of canonists cited by Tierney, and as is also the case in the work of Francisco de Vitoria.
[153] "I am within my right to do such a thing, since the law does not forbid it." This statement, for example, as understood in the work of many canonists and also of Vitoria, is compatible with the classical conception of Right. Only the context will allow us to decide whether the term *right* is used in a nominalist sense or not. For *right* as that which the law allows can be understood in a nominalist way or in a way compatible with the classical conception of Right.
[154] In his *Natural Law, the Laws of Nature and Natural Rights*, 94, he concedes to Leo Strauss that there is a deep difference between the Hobbesian and the Lockean political philosophies, on the one hand, and the classical and medieval; but he then adds that the fundamental shift had taken place three centuries earlier, in the works of William Ockham.
[155] John Lamont, "In Defense of Villey on Objective Right," 184-185.

positive law.[156] Looking back from this vantage point, one can assert that, if (a) Ockham holds the thesis that society is a mere conglomerate of individuals and not a reality above and beyond the individuals and if, in consequence, he further holds the individualist thesis that *right* in the subjective sense is a power existing prior to the existence of the community and, therefore, independent from the network of relations that demand distributive justice; or if (b) Ockham holds the thesis that the judge can protect no other (subjective) right than that which derives from positive norms, from objective "human law," then we are probably faced with a nominalist use of the notion of subjective "right."

We must examine the last of these theses in a very special and relevant case, connected to the controversy on poverty. We should scrutinize all the evidence carefully in order to perceive the difference between (a) those who hold, on the one hand, that because of the original universal destination of goods (previous to the formation of political communities) there is a certain title or deed that grants human beings a *right*, a moral power over material things in case of extreme necessity and that this *right must* be protected by the courts of law,[157] and (b) those, on the other hand, who hold a similar proposition, except that they clearly state that either this title does not grant a *right* that the judge must protect but constitute just a *license* to act against the positive right that the court should ordinarily protect. We need much care because, although the difference is enormous, it is at the same time hard to perceive, so that its perception requires an intellectual power able to grasp very subtle distinctions. This is perhaps the central point that I seek to clarify in this chapter.

Of the two theses mentioned above, the one that would most clearly place us in the presence of a revolutionary doctrine, in the presence of the new juridical nominalism, would be the doctrine according to which the judge can decide the cases brought before him only by using human, positive law. In other words, the doctrine

---

[156] See John Locke, *Second Treatise of Government*, § 136.

[157] According to this view, the person who steals a morsel of food to prevent starvation is not only exempt from liability but is acting legitimately and must be protected by the court that has jurisdiction. In essence what is being done, from the point of view of the Aristotelian theory of distributive justice, is to declare that every man, because of his essential dignity, has the right to receive the minimum of goods necessary to subsist, provided that such goods are available.

according to which the only rights that can be vindicated in the *forum* are the rights derived from human law, and not from natural or divine law.

Of course, if our investigation concluded that there is a considerable difference between Ockham's juridical philosophy and the classical one, it would remain to be shown that he was the person who coined the nominalist understanding of the notion of subjective rights. There are many authors between St. Thomas and Ockham. But I have not been able to find the specific points that we are going to investigate here in any other author, despite there being some thorough publications that have attempted to find precedents to Ockham. One of these is Paolo Grossi's. He sees the nominalist theory in other Franciscans, such as Peter Olivi. However, it seems to me that Grossi is mistaken on this point.[158] Thus, I think that no author before Ockham

---

[158] Indeed, in the previous chapter in footnote we saw how Grossi, in reading Olivi, seems not to notice that this Franciscan is dealing above all with the ultimate cause. But now we can consider another subject more relevant in the present context. Grossi does not pay close enough attention to the fact that the scholastics who reflect on property, and do so not on a strictly juridical but theological level, incorporate in their reflections the teaching of Jesus Christ: "Blessed are the poor in spirit, for theirs is the kingdom of heaven"; or "it is more difficult for a rich man to enter the kingdom of heaven than for a camel to pass through the eye of a needle," et cetera. This is why we find in the work of the scholastics concerning property at least two planes that cannot be confused, and which Grossi does not distinguish: the juridical plane and the theological plane, where spiritual detachment is considered. The fact that it does not highlight sufficiently this distinction, turns this interesting study by Grossi, "*Usus facti*" (in: *Il dominio e le cose. Percezioni medievali e moderne dei diritti reali* [Milan: Giufffrè Editore, 1992], 123–89) into a work in which the interpreter cannot confidently rest. There are passages in Grossi's work in which he turns the doctrine of the Franciscans on its head. Thus, where they speak of the freedom that poverty gives, Grossi speaks of (juridical) property as freedom (see, for example, 157–60). The same lack of distinction leads Grossi to label as "revolutionary" and far removed from the unitarian Thomistic conception of the cosmos that the Franciscan emphasize so much the role of the will in the possession of wealth. Grossi overlooks that, of course, also in the work of St. Thomas the Christian is asked to renounce property in his spirit: he is called to be poor, although sometimes through an attitude of detachment, by an act of his will, not always by renouncing juridical property. Aquinas teaches that he is "rich" in the way contrary to Christian doctrine, not the person who juridically has possessions, but the one who, with his will, attaches himself to them. See, for example, what St. Thomas teaches about habitual poverty in *Contra impugnantes*, Part II, chapter 5: "Item. Marc. X, 23, super illud, *quam difficile qui pecunias habent* etc., Glossa: *aliud est pecuniam habere, aliud amare. Multi habent et non amant, multi non habent et amant, item alii habent et amant, alii vero nec habere nec amare se gaudent: qui tutiores sunt, qui cum apostolo dicere possunt: mihi mundus crucifixus est, et ego mundo.* Ergo actualis paupertas et habitualis simul praeferenda est habituali paupertati. Item. Luc. XIV, 33: *nisi quis renuntiaverit omnibus quae possidet*, Glossa: *hoc distat inter renuntiare omnibus et relinquere omnia: quia renuntiare convenit omnibus, qui ita licite*

was the originator of the nominalist version of rights, although some aspects of Franciscan theology might have prepared the ground.

To elucidate whether Ockham's juridical philosophy breaks with the classical one, we will take the following steps. First, we will review Villey's exposition of the Ockhamist conception of the emergence of positive law and of the *potestates appropriandi, instituendi rectores et condendi leges*. We will then establish the salient features of Ockham's doctrines in relation to the disputed points, through a direct review of the primary sources, in counterpoint with Brian Tierney's interpretations, in order to demonstrate the revolution introduced by Ockham in the use of the subjective meaning of *right*. We hope that a more or less clear judgment on the disputed points will emerge from this. We will conclude with a brief reflection on the continuity between William of Ockham's theoretical work and his political work.

1. Villey's presentation of William of Ockham's doctrines

Michel Villey[159] had attributed to William of Ockham, and in particular to the *Opus nonaginta dierum* and Book III of the *Breviloquium*, the following doctrines:

God is at the top of a hierarchy of power. He has the "*potestas absoluta*" and is the source of all juridical order. He is an individual and has a power that is real, a "subjective right." The juridical order is a divine positive order and is found in Scripture, not in nature. Sometimes, however, Ockham calls this divine Right "natural Right."

---

utuntur mundanis quae possident, ut tamen mente tendant ad aeterna: relinquere est tantummodo perfectorum, qui omnia temporalia postponunt, et solis aeternis inhiant. Ergo relinquere, quod pertinet ad actualem paupertatem, est evangelicae perfectionis; sed renuntiare, quod pertinet ad habitualem, secundum Glossam praedictam, est de necessitate salutis.") So, in all this scholastic literature, also in the Thomistic one, poverty is regarded as a source of freedom that the rich man lacks. I am not sure, but I have the impression that the confusion of these planes, which leads to think that judges should only apply positive law because the natural rectitude is equated to evangelical poverty, alien to the courts, occurs only in the work of William of Ockham, and not before him, *pace Grossi*. I will discuss this Ockhamist confusion at length in the text.

[159] I follow especially, "Droit Subjectif I," in: *Seize Essais* (Paris: Dalloz, 1969), 140–78, at 174–6.

Men receive from God certain *potestates*, which we can discover in Scripture. The first of these, the *potestas appropriandi*, is a consequence of sin (in the beginning everything was common) and of the commandment to cultivate Eden (Gn 2:15), and therefore a certain form of "natural right." But private appropriation needed a complement, and, for this reason, God also gave man the power to establish rulers (*potestas instituendi rectores*) by means of election, a social contract, or pact. The elected rulers would determine the limits of the properties so that they could exist together.

One result of the pact is that the temporal sovereign receives, by delegation of the people, the legislative power: *potestas condendi leges et iura humana*. To establish the limits of property, that is, to legislate. And to this power is added the power of jurisdiction, which must ensure respect for the legally established limits. Here human positivism is born, *as a consequence of the denial that there is a natural order*. The laws established by the sovereign also grant powers to individuals. Ownership, usufruct, *ius utendi* and all other "subjective rights in the strict sense," as long as they are powers granted by human law, imply *potestas vindicandi*.

This theoretical framework was created by Ockham to prove that Pope John XXII was wrong when he held that the Franciscans necessarily owned property since they ate, and goods that are destroyed by their use cannot be legitimately used without property. Based on this framework, Ockham is able to proclaim that Pope John XXII is mistaken when he holds that the law of men cannot *entirely* deprive Franciscans of property or of other subjective rights (especially over goods that are destroyed by consumption): all the rights that can be vindicated before a judge have their origin in human legislation and can be suppressed by it just as they can be granted.[160]

It is not difficult to discover in this scheme a prefiguration of the *theories* of authors belonging to the later Anglo-Saxon empiricist tradition. But it is doubtful whether such a scheme really corresponds to Ockham's thought. There are many inaccuracies in Villey's presentation of Ockhamist doctrines. First, for example, Ockham teaches that God has a *potestas absoluta*, but he also states that he has a

---

[160] See *Seize Essais*, 168–69 and 175–76.

potestas ordinata. Second, Ockham holds that all men, in the present order of the universe,[161] must follow the dictates of their reason. The principles of morality can therefore be known without knowing Scripture.[162] Third, Villey does not sufficiently distinguish between particular appropriation and ownership in the strict sense.

However, it is true that, according to Ockham, moral principles are the result of a sovereign decision of the will of God and that they could change radically if so disposed by that same will, according to its absolute *potestas*.[163] Moreover, it is also true that, according to Ockham, the original domain of divine Right is known to us from Scripture, as we shall see.

In the light of the last two points, it can be concluded that the substance of Villey's exposition is not too far off the mark, even if the presentation is full of inaccuracies that almost invalidate it. For this reason, his disciples, and most notably Michel Bastit, have been able to refine the original intuitions and to formulate them in a much more precise and accurate manner. Thus, for example, in "Ockham as a Precursor of Modern Philosophy of Law," a lecture given at the Universidad Bernardo O'Higgins, in Santiago, Chile (on August 25, 2016), Bastit stated,

> To be sure, the Roman jurists spoke, for example, of the 'sui juris,' and the medieval communities claim their 'jura.' However, these jura are never primitive, they are the result of repartitions. They are rights because they have been justly

[161] This is not necessary; it could change: See *Quaestiones variae* 7, a. 3 (Saint Bonaventure, New York State: Saint Bonaventure University, 1984). *Opera theologica*, Vol. IV). Freppert, *The Basis of Morality*, 64. The doctrine is repeated in *Quaestiones variae* 7, a. 4, lines 440–2.
[162] See, for example, David Clark, "William Ockham on Right Reason," in *Speculum*, vol. 48 (1973), No. 1, 13–36. Also, Carlos Isler, "Is Nominalism necessarily associated with a voluntarist conception of natural law? The case of Ockham and Hobbes," 179–83, in *Praxis Filosófica* Nueva Serie, No. 38 (January July 2014), 175–200.
[163] See, for example, *Quaestiones variae* 7, a. 4, lines 353–66 and 440–42; and *Quaestiones variae* 7, a. 3, which Freppert cites at *The Basis of Morality*, 64.

attributed, and they are not primitive powers.[164] As St. Thomas states 'jus est id quod justum est.'[165]

Bastit has thus gone a long way toward isolating the point of novelty in Ockham's doctrine—namely, his conception of right as a primitive power, abstracted from the political context and from distributive justice. Nevertheless, it seems to me that a detailed exposition of the Ockhamist texts is still necessary to expound as precisely as possible the boundary between a nominalist conception of subjective rights and a non-nominalist one.

To establish precisely where the revolutionary character of Ockham's teachings lies, from the primary sources, let us make an exposition, independent from Villey's, of the way in which, according to the Franciscan, political power and law arise.

2. From the state of innocence to the emergence of civil law proper. The itinerary described by William of Ockham

Adam and Eve were created in a state of innocence. According to William of Ockham, in such a state, they had nothing of their own, everything was common. Our first parents and all their descendants originally received the power to dispose and use temporal things for their utility, but without the power for any person or any special college (or group) to appropriate any temporal thing.[166] This common dominion (which was a right to use) was imposed by divine right, "by special grant of God, to whom all things belonged and still belong, both by right of

[164] I must add one point to Bastit's observations. I had entertained the suspicion that the *fueros* of Spain probably used the word *right* or *iura* in subjective sense. But my reading of *El fuero Viejo de Castilla* has persuaded me that there *fueros* is used as a synonym of *derecho* and that both are taken in the objective sense. Any petition or demand of a party might be conforming or not to *right*, but this means, to what is just. See *El fuero viejo de Castilla* (Madrid: Ignacio Jordán de Asso y Miguel de Manuel and Rodríguez (eds.), 1847), III, 38, 48, 59, 68, for example. In 32–4, *derechos* means *taxes*. A careful reading of the *Magna Carta* of 1215 yields a similar result: it seems to me that *ius* and *iura* are used there in an objective sense, while *liberties* mean what later will be expressed with the word *iura* in subjective sense. See the *Carta* in Charles B. Mont, *Chartes des libertés anglaises (1100–1305)* (Paris: Alphonse Picard, 1892), 24–40.

[165] The author had the kindness to send the umpublished text to me.

[166] *Breviloquium de principatu tyrannico*, book III, chapter 7, lines 7–13.

creation and by right of preservation." We know this through the divine Scriptures.[167]

Immediately after the fall, the universal right to use the created goods became a common dominion, different from the original one.[168] Later, the common dominion that God had given to the human race came to include the power to appropriate temporal things in particular. This particular dominion was imposed with a positive precept (one that binds *semper, non pro semper*)[169] and must be exercised because, due to the fall, there is danger that greedy or evil persons will prevent others from accessing and using necessities, and also because there is danger that, without the particular appropriation, some could fall into indolence and omit the due care that material goods require.[170] This power is recorded, at least implicitly, in Ecclesiasticus 17. On the second type of dominion, Ockham says expressly:

> the power of appropriating temporal things—both rational things, such as wives and children, as well as others—is among the things that must be counted as necessary and useful to the human race to live well after sin, because of the multitude of those same negligent and foolish people whose number cannot be counted, as it is said in Ecclesiastes 1. Aristotle, as we read in II of the *Politics*, reproved the constitution or ordination of Plato, who asserted that a city would be better ordered in which all things were common than one in which things were privately owned. For he [Aristotle] considered that the multitude is evil and inclined to evil, and therefore the common things of the many are less loved and therefore less cared for than the things owned privately. Wherefore, among such [fools, negligent, evil, inclined to evil], the appropriation of things is better than the community of things. But, in the multitude of the perfect or of those who tend with all their might to

[167] *Breviloquium* III, 7, lines 34–39. It refers to Genesis 1. In a similar sense, *Breviloquium* III, 10.
[168] According to the *Opus nonaginta dierum*, the power that Adam and Eve had over the whole material creation was different from the common dominion that they had after the fall. See 14, lines 61-156; 26, lines 50-65; 28, lines 86-89, in *Opera politica*, Volume II [chapters 7-124], edited by J. G. Sikes and H. S. Offler [Manchester: University Press, 1973], 375-858).
[169] See *Breviloquium* III, 8, lines 9–10.
[170] *Breviloquium*, book III, chapter 7, lines 7–13 and 19–33.

> perfection, it is different, because the perfect ones love and care more for common things than for their own [...].[171]

The passage is surprising and fascinating.[172] But, for the purpose of our investigation, we must concentrate on the fact that, according to Ockham, after sin, God gave the power to appropriate temporal things in particular. God also gave to men, and for a similar reason,

> without ministry or human cooperation [i.e., in the context, without the mediation of the pope or the Church], the power to establish rulers having temporal jurisdiction, because temporal jurisdiction is counted among those things which are necessary and useful for living well and politically, and Solomon is my witness [...].[173]

These two powers were given by God both to the faithful and to the infidels. Thus, they fall under the universal precept of God—that is, under a precept belonging to natural Right.[174] But, since it is a positive precept (as opposed to negative), faithful and infidels are subject to it only in case of necessity, can renounce the power given by the precept (except in case of necessity), and can be deprived of this power by legitimate judicial authority (again, except in case of necessity, since "necessity cannot fall under human law or precept").[175] In this way Ockham intends to defeat the pope's arguments in two different

---

[171] *Breviloquium* III, 7, lines 57–69.

[172] It is true, it seems to me, that Plato's desire to have a part of the members of the political community occupied only with the public good and detached from all private property (see *Republic* V, 457c–465e), was as perfectly as humanly possible realized in monasticism, dedicated to the common good of the Church. Precisely because the monks vowed to remain celibate and chaste, they avoided all the disadvantages pointed out by Aristotle in the Platonic proposal (see *Politics* II, 1–5), concerning the disorder of the passions and family love. But Ockham confuses everything when he embraces the possible common possession of women and children. Aristotle could address to him the same critique he directed against *Republic* V. One wonders about the similarity between the doctrines of this Franciscan, on the one hand, and the Albigenses and Cathars, on the other.

[173] *Breviloquium* III 7, lines 72–76.

[174] *Breviloquium* III 8, lines 1–8.

[175] Note well that he refers only to human law. Divine law does govern necessity, according to this text. Note, as well, that both, private property and government came to be due to the wickedness that followed the fall. See William of Ockham, "The Three Modes of Natural Law," 212. See also Janet Coleman, "Ockham's Right Reason and the Genesis of the Political as 'Absolutist,'" 53.

polemics, first between the pontiff and the Franciscans (the latter may forsake private ownership), and second with the emperor, Louis of Bavaria (the authority of the emperor cannot be restricted by the pope).

The first mention of the power of acquisition in particular, Ockham says, appears in the division of property between Cain and Abel, a division which Abel was surely compelled to introduce because of Cain's wickedness and avarice.[176] Scripture shows, moreover, that God gave such power directly in many cases, but he did so only after the division of property had first been introduced by Abel or by other men. Thus, for example, God gave the land of Canaan to Abraham.[177]

Something similar happens with the power to establish rulers: although it is of divine Right, the effective establishment of the concrete authorities, with the exception of Moses, the biblical Judges, and some other rare cases, is of positive (human) right. As Ockham states it, "[...] other authorities obtained jurisdiction over human beings either by election or by the constitution of men or in some other way."[178]

The two powers (particular appropriation and establishment of rulers) appear in Ockham's work as closely connected. In this the Franciscan departs considerably from the Greek and Roman classics and from St. Thomas, while resembling the 17th century political theorists, and particularly John Locke. But there is another similarity with Locke that is found in this same line: the friar states that legitimate power "of positive right" is held by the ruler who has become such either by the

[176] See *Breviloquium* III 9, lines 1–17. A similar argument is used in *Opus nonaginta dierum* (*Opera politica*, Volume I, edited by J. G. Sikes and H. S. Offler [Manchester: University Press, 1974], 292–368) 4, lines 317–25, to prove that the early Christians in Jerusalem should have had legal ownership of their property, even if it was common; Christians should be able to protect themselves, even judicially, from the depredations of the greedy.
On the authorship of the *Opus nonaginta dierum*, see Annabel Brett, *Liberty, Right and Nature*, 56-57. She concludes that although Ockham drew from many previous sources in his response to the pope, the strategy of the response belongs to him and he is "the author of the language of rights contained therein."
[177] In the *Opus nonaginta dierum*, Okcham points out several divisions that took place before the constitution of the political communities and after, by human action or by divine intervention. See, for example, 88, lines 94-108, and 135-79; 92, lines 33-6.
[178] *Breviloquium* III 11, lines 14.27.

consent of his subjects[179] or by just war.[180] On the other hand, the power that has its origin in violence is not legitimate. The rationale adduced by Ockham vividly recalls Locke, once again: "all mortals, who are born free and in no way subject to anyone by positive (human) right, have from God and nature the power to spontaneously establish for themselves a ruler, as any people and any city can constitute Right for itself."[181] Then, the power to appropriate temporal things and to establish laws and positive (human) rights, given by God, was initially in the hands of the individuals composing the people or peoples. These, giving their consent, were able to establish both laws and rulers of various kinds, such as emperors, kings, and so on. In this way, the particular dominions arose, in accordance with positive (human) Right.[182] In the case of the Roman Empire (which Ockham identifies with the Germanic Roman Empire), the people constituted the senate and the emperor; and, therefore, the pope has no authority to depose the emperor, but, if anyone has such authority, it is only the Senate, that is, the body of electors of the Germanic Roman Emperor, and that body has such right only by delegation of the people. Moreover, when the senate makes use of this power, the empire reverts to the people.[183] The concrete dominions, therefore, arise by human, popular will, but, once established, they are no longer under any human authority, but directly under the authority of God.[184] They arise in this way because, according

[179] Janet Coleman concurs on this: public authority emerges from the voluntary consent of the people. She cites, besides the *Breviloquium*, the I *Dialogus*, 6, 8. See "Ockham's Right Reason and the Genesis of the Political as 'Absolutist'," 38.

[180] See *Second Treatise of Government*, §§ 171, 175 and 180, for example.

[181] *Breviloquium* IV 10, lines 55–64 and 75–76. In the same sense, III 13, lines 43–46. Brian Tierney also notes the similarity between certain Ockhamist doctrines and those of Locke and Pufendorf, in *The Idea of Natural Rights*, 167–68. Compare with *Second Treatise of Government*, § 61.

[182] *Breviloquium* III, 14, lines 4–11 and 15–22. See also, IV, 3, lines 9–17.

[183] See *Breviloquium* VI, 2, 25–45. Ockham has difficulty in explaining the enthronement of Pepin the Short, father of Charlemagne, because he wants to exclude any intervention of the pope in the origin of the Roman-Germanic Empire and, therefore, Franco-Roman (*Breviloquium* VI 2, lines 104–20; Ockham does not even mention the beginning of the Ottonian dynasty nor their alliance with the papacy). At one point he makes a reasonable observation: if the pope had the power to pronounce the emperor a heretic, as he seems to have because it concerns spiritual matters, the effect of such a declaration should be to hand the emperor over to the secular authority (as with other heretics) for the secular authority to pass final sentence. Such authority would be, in this case, the "Senate" (VI, 2, lines 69–82).

[184] See *Breviloquium* IV, 6, lines 6–15; see also IV, 13, lines 1–8; and VI, 2, lines 90–2. This is a political indictment, nothing more and nothing less, against the Latin Christian system of the two powers. In the same sense, IV, 8. On this point, Ockham ignores the scriptural authorities

to Ockham, communities do not have existence over and above the individuals (including God) and their powers (the power to consent, in particular).[185] Here, Ockham leaves in the air a problem that his spiritual successor, John Locke, will consider explicitly: if the subjects, by their will, are those who constitute the empire, and this because all mortals are born free, et cetera, why would the children of those who have constituted the empire be subject to it?[186]

It is in this context of particular political power where ownership properly so called arose. The jurists call this right "property," the main power by which a person or certain persons or a special college have temporal things at their disposition. This ownership properly so called is different from the particular appropriation that existed, at least since the time of Abel, before human laws were given.[187] Property, in the strict sense, therefore, was created by positive Right; it was not established by natural or divine Right but by political authority, whether royal, imperial, or otherwise.[188] This

---

on which, for example, St. Thomas based the two-power system, such as I Corinthians 6, 1ff (see *De regno* I, chapters 15–16, and *Summa theologica* II-II, qq. 10, a. 10; 11, a. 3; and 12, a. 2). Brian Tierney too hastily argues that there is nothing revolutionary in Ockham's teaching on the relations between temporal and spiritual power (*The Idea of Natural Rights*, 192). Faced with such a categorical statement, one wonders: why, then, was Ockham an enemy of the pope and a friend of the revolutionaries, Louis of Bavaria and Marsilius of Padua? On this subject I make the following observations: (a) Without the structure of government no unified (political or pre-political) people can exist. Political articulation of scattered human beings or families or tribes is a providential event. Thus, political authority, political power, cannot come from "the people" but from above. Now, political power, although coming from nature or God, can be structured in different ways. It is clear, therefore, that the form of government, in scholastic terminology, is not of "divine right." The power of the pope and the institution of the papacy, on the other hand, are of divine right, although not in all its aspects. (b) Now, a ruler who comes to power by legitimate means can become a tyrant, lose his legitimacy, and justify tyrannicide. This was the common teaching in political thought of Latin Christendom. It appears even in the *Siete Partidas* of Alphonse X, the Wise of Castille (see Partida Segunda, Título I, Ley X). A Christian ruler can also cease to be a Christian. In that case, according to 1 Corinthians, he should not judge over the saints, and, based on this text, St. Thomas holds that he could be removed by the pope. Both scholastic statements (concerning the tyrant and concerning the heretic) are intended to preserve the freedom of the Christian people. It is surprising that neither Ockham nor Tierney addressed this point.

[185] See *Opus* 6, lines 413–55; 62, lines 206-24, 271-3, and 279-85. We will return to this issue.

[186] Locke holds that the children of those who have agreed to a constitutional compact are subject to it if they accept the inheritance of their parents. See *Second Treatise on Government*, § 73 in *Two Treatises of Government* by John Locke, with a Supplement *Patriarcha* by Robert Filmer. Thomas I. Cook (Editor) (Hofner Publishing Company. New York, 1947–reprint of 1964).

[187] *Breviloquium* III, 7, lines 14–18.

[188] See *Breviloquium* III, 15, lines 1–9 and 20–2.

implies that judges, when they hear matters relating to ownership of things, must decide exclusively in accordance to positive law. On this basis, Ockham claims that the *de facto* use of material things differs from the *de jure* use, even with regard to consumable goods.[189] The Franciscans, therefore, could renounce any moral power over material things susceptible of being enforced by the courts and could simply enjoy a license to make a *de facto* use, in conformity with the original divine ordination, but not as an exercise of a faculty of ownership "properly" speaking. Again, by means of this argument, Ockham does two things: he defends Michael of Cesena and the Franciscans in their polemic with John XXII[190] and he lays the groundwork for the imperial allegations against the pope.[191]

Thus, even if Michel Villey has misinterpreted the *Breviloquium* on many points, Villey's interpretation of William of Ockham is

[189] See *Breviloquium* V, 4, lines 78–81. Pope John XXII, following the teachings of Roman Law, held that in the case of consumable goods, use equated to property, since using food implies disposing of it by destroying it.

[190] See *Breviloquium* III, 15, lines 1–9.

[191] On this point Ockham's position fits perfectly with that of Marsilius of Padua, who is one of the first precedents of what will later be known as "the amortizations": the confiscation of the goods of the Church and of the monasteries. For example, note that, according to Ockham, in the origins of Christianity those who sowed the spiritual goods did not own anything but had to be supported directly by the Roman Empire (which Ockham identifies with the Empire of Louis of Bavaria—that is, the Germanic Roman Empire). See, for example, *Breviloquium* IV, 1, lines 51–5. On the one hand, Ockham claims to defend the freedom of Christians ("non peioris conditionis debant esse fideles quam infideles") by clamoring against the diminution of the emperor's powers through the enlargement of the pope's powers (see *Breviloquium* IV 1, lines 163–9; V, 1, lines 9–14). -As if the secular power of the emperor, without the tutelage of the spiritual authority of the pope, were a surer guarantee of the freedom of the faithful than the differentiation of secular and spiritual power. On the other hand, Ockham ignores the progress that the papacy and monasticism meant for the life of Italy and for its countryside (II, 19, lines 77–83), progress that has been recognized, instead, by Arnold Toynbee—by no means a supporter of Catholicism, but a historian respectful of historical evidence. See *A Study of History*, Abridgment by D. C. Somervell (New York: Oxford University Press, 1962), 225–26 and 673. It is therefore curious, not to say amusing, that Ockham cites in support of his rebellion against the pope the text of Psalm 2:3: "sometimes it is lawful to bear the yoke [imposed by the pope] and lawful [equally] not to bear it; and sometimes it is by no means to be borne, but to be cast off entirely according to the counsel or precept of the Psalmist who says: *let us cast off their yoke from us!*" (see *Breviloquium* II 21, lines 68–71). Ockham goes to the extreme of denying the kingship of Christ, the Man, in *Breviloquium* V, 8. According to him, moreover, it cannot be held, as some canonists did, that "there is no empire or ordained power outside the Church" (see *Breviloquium* III, 1, lines 17–28). Of course, if the canonists applied this to the gentile powers existing in the world, the thesis would obviously be wrong. If they applied it, however, to Christendom, that was the standing system when Ockham wrote.

curiously confirmed in that work: the courts may only protect those rights that emanate from human laws based on the right of establishing laws; the authority of the judges is based on a compact; such compact is based on the right of establishing rulers, and so on.

Traces of the same conception of ownership in the proper sense and of particular appropriation can also be found in the *Opus nonaginta dierum*. The resulting schema of Ockham's conception of rights and dominion in the latter work is the following: there are *ius poli* or *ius naturale*, on the one hand, and *ius positivum* or *ius fori*, on the other. The courts can apply only and exclusively positive laws. By *ius poli* we can all use the material goods for our survival. But for that use to be licit, it must not violate any *right*, especially positive right. So, the use can be licit because either one has the positive right to use the thing (in this case one can be the owner or hold a different kind of right, like *commodatum*) or because one has a *license*. A license can be given by a person who has the positive right over the thing, or by *ius poli*, if one is in a state of extreme necessity. In case of extreme necessity, one is not obliged by right nor by previous commitment. So, in the case of extreme necessity the right to use does not belong to the *ius fori* but it does belong to the *ius poli*, and the license to act against the right of *ius fori* is given by nature itself.[192]

In our perspective, the main theses that William of Ockham holds in this other work are the following: (a) that things may be *de facto* used licitly without a strict right of use that is enforceable in court; and, especially, (b) that there can be a licit use of consumable goods separate from any right enforceable in court and, particularly, from property.[193] Of these two theses, the first one has massive support in canonist sources that Ockham interprets correctly. To defend these theses, he makes use of traditional notions, such as that somebody may have legitimate power to use things, although that power does not give the right to set a court in motion if it is denied by certain kinds of people.

---

[192] This schema is especially clear in *Opus* 65, lines 34-89, 119-47, 157-9 and 184-217. Rondo Keele in *Ockham Explained. From Razor to Rebellion* (Chicago and Lasalle, Illinois: Open Court, 2010), 169 explains the distinction between the two kinds of rights and the license to use licitly a thing that is under the ownership of other person. He does not mention, however, the novelty of Ockham's doctrine according to which the courts can apply only rights based on positive laws.

[193] See, for example, *Opus* 6, lines 340–56.

For example, if a landowner in particular gives me license to pluck ears of corn in his estate (as in general did the Old Testament Law), I can pluck them legitimately, without that meaning that I have a right that I could oppose in court to the landowner.[194] But William of Ockham does more than make use of traditional notions in this context.

Indeed, in defending both theses in both works (*Breviloquium* and *Opus nonaginta dierum*), Ockham also introduces new concepts or gives them new meanings. Most notably:

1) Ockham denied the distinction between what we now call the moral person and the aggregate group of human individuals that compose it. The canonists had used a hesitant and inadequate terminology to speak of collective persons. They had called them "imaginary" or "represented" persons. John XXII considered them incapable of carrying out a *de facto* use, such as eating or drinking.[195] Ockham finds John XXII's statement, which is certainly erroneous, laughable. But, in correcting it, the Franciscan introduces no small confusion: he considers the moral person—as Hans Kelsen also much later did in his *Pure Theory of Law*[196]—just a conglomerate of individuals.[197] The underlying reason is the standard nominalist doctrine that relations are beings of reason.[198] This is the metaphysical explanation of Ockham's refusal to accept the existence above the

[194] See, for example, *Opus nonaginta dierum* 2, lines 335–7; 4, lines 398–404.
[195] See the text of the Bull in *Opus* 6, lines 24–6.
[196] Chapter 8, n. 4, of the French edition (which has many original additions and corrections compared to the 1934 German edition), *Theorie pure du droit* (Neuchâtel: Éditions de la Baconnière, 1953): "la personne dite morale ou juridique désigne seulement l'unité d'un ensemble de normes, á savoir un ordre juridique réglant la conduite d'une pluralité d'individus" (106).
[197] See *Opus* 6, lines 413–55; 62, lines 206-24, 271-3, 279-85. The same doctrine is held in *Tractatus contra Benedictum* chapter 8, lines 189-92, in *Opera politica*, Vol. 3 (Manchester: University of Manchester Press, 1956) 165-322. It is explicitly added that collective persons can neither be subjects of rights nor use them.
[198] Marilyn McCord Adams has shown that Ockham denied that the reality of relations could be known by natural reason. This is a typical nominalist doctrine. See *William Ockham* (Notre Dame: University of Notre Dame Press, 1987), Vol. I, 215–76. Janet Coleman underlines that "the focus on the individual is a consequence of what is often called Ockham's nominalism." She also states that, according to Ockham, "the whole is *nothing more than* the decisions of its individual parts regarding the common good." See "Ockham's Right Reason and the Genesis of the Political as 'Absolutist,'" 40 and 49.

individuals of these wholes that are moral persons. This, of course, he extends to the State and to the Church as to the Franciscan Order.

2) This is the foundation to postulate that there are natural rights that are prior to the existence of the political community. Actually, only the individuals have real ontological existence. These natural rights come from the original divine ordination and subsist side by side with positive Right, although they cannot be vindicated in court:

> In the same manner as the common ownership is not less effective to turn licit the *de facto* use of a thing than the special ownership[199] is, because anybody may use licitly the common thing in the same way that he uses his own thing if there is no other special obstacle; in the same way, the most common licit power to use [and not to own] is not less effective than the common ownership to turn licit the *de facto* use. Therefore, for this reason, in order to make the *de facto* use licit, the most common licit power to use is sufficient, so that [common] ownership is not required, although something else is often required. But the most common licit power to use is the power to use that God gave through our first parents to the whole human race before and after sin. Then, if all ownership is removed, and if there is no other [moral] obstacle and a most common licit power to use subsists, the *de facto* use can be licit. Therefore, if there is any good consumable by use that is not under anybody's ownership, the said most common power to use suffices for someone to be able to licitly use that good, if there is no other [moral] obstacle. Then, the *de facto* use of such a thing can be licit without any ownership, and therefore the *de facto* licit use can be separated from any special or common ownership.[200]

---

[199] That is to say, the property acquired according to positive Right.

[200] *Opus* 4, lines 192–207. The argument seems repetitive, but each consecutive proposition adds something so as to come, step by step, to the desired conclusion. The same doctrine is found here:

> [although Michael of Cesena denies that the Friars Minor have ownership or property over consumable things,] he does not thereby wish to exclude the Friars from having that ownership which belongs to the whole human race, if there is any such, nor does he wish to exclude the Friars from that ownership which belongs to the whole community of the faithful, if indeed the whole community of the faithful

Tierney adds an interesting point: it is Ockhamist doctrine that those natural rights that cannot be enforced by the courts (that are not *iura fori*) can, however, be opposed against the encroachments of an absolutist ruler.[201] Here, again, one can see a connection between the political theorists of the 17th century and their 14th century predecessor.[202] Indeed, regarding the jurisdiction of the judiciary courts, Locke is an extreme positivist; but he nevertheless defends the claim that, if the government does not protect property, then the natural right to property can justify rebellion, because the subjects have given their consent to the government precisely to protect property (understood in the broadest sense, which also includes life, since there is a kind of power over one's own being). In such a case, Right disappears, and we return to the "state of nature."[203] In this way, Lockean natural property, although it disappears with positive law, continues to be latent and vigilant. There is a slight difference in the Ockhamist doctrine: the ownership and the right to use, which are natural rights according to Ockham, can be exercised in the political community, so that they are not entirely latent, they are active to some extent, even if they are residues of the pre-political state of the human

has a common ownership over anything temporal, but he wished to exclude the friars from any dominion which they might claim by a court trial, whether initiated by a friar or by the order of the Friars Minor as a whole (*Opus* 4, lines 131–7).

This same point is explained a little more, with the answer to some objections, here: *Opus* 4, 225–54. In this other passage the polemical character of Ockham's ius-philosophical theses is manifest: he is interested mostly in defending the thesis that licit use can be separated from the special ownership of a person or of a college, for that was the point in the debate with John XXII. The same doctrine is repeated many times along the *Opus nonaginta dierum*.

201 See Tierney, *The Idea of Natural Rights*, 165.

202 David Schindler grasps this connection. See *The Politics of the Real* (Steubenville, Ohio: New Polity Press, 2022), 118-119.

203 Despite all the similarities noted between Locke's and Ockham's respective doctrines, we should not lose sight of the crucial differences between them: (1) According to Ockham, unlike Locke (see *An Essay Concerning Human Understanding*, in *The Works of John Locke in Nine Volumes*, [London: Rivington, 1824 12th ed.], Vol. 1, Book 1, chapter 3, §§ 5–13. I deal at length with this issue in a footnote in chapter 4), there is a divine law prior to any covenant. (2) Therefore, the state of man prior to the covenant and after sin is not a state of war of all against all—although there are elements of such a state of war inasmuch as, due to Cain's greed, Abel was forced to use the power of acquisition. (3) Ockham speaks of rights as faculties, but they are faculties that are grounded either in divine laws or in human laws. In Locke's work the "faculties" are probably, rather, physical powers that are exercised in one way or another to preserve self-interest, and interest is judged in a hedonistic way (see *An Essay Concerning Human Understanding* book 2, chapters 20–21); (4) Ockham's work does not hold that the government's *raison d'être* is to protect property.

being. These rights allow the exclusion of the Friars Minor from the realm of positive rights and from the courts. Curiously, these rights, according to Ockham, could lay the groundwork for excluding not only the Franciscans but also the whole visible dimension of the Church from the realm of positive (human) Right by eliminating all property and all effective power in the world.[204]

3) But even clearer and more revolutionary than the other two points is the fact that Ockham understands that the property right in the strict sense is a moral power which can be defended in a court of law, that is to say, *it is a power different from that which belongs to a man merely by natural Right or by primary divine Right* and also different from a simple license to use a thing.[205]

In the Christian tradition there is an explicit recognition of the "universal destination of goods," of God's giving of all things for the

---

[204] According to Ockham, the Church could be turned into an institution with a presence in the world reduced to the sphere of "morality" or "natural Right," in the terms we are about to explain in the text. See, for example, *Opus* 5, lines 35–41, 61–7, 87–96, 152–63, and 252–6. Note that Ockham postulates that evangelical purity would demand that the Church be stripped of all its real estate. There is nothing strange, then, that, as we have already noted, he was a friend of Louis of Bavaria and Marsilius of Padua, nor that he can be considered a precursor of the great despoilments carried out in the time of Henry VIII, followed by the "amortizations" throughout Christendom.

[205] See *Opus nonaginta dierum* 2, lines 333–5. There is a passage that does not seem to fit well with the interpretation given in the text, since he calls "right of property in the strictest sense" that which can be demanded in court and which is not prohibited by natural Right (see *Opus* 2, lines 390–3). The phrase "is not prohibited by natural Right" does not fit well because it seems to give judicial effect to a principle of natural Right. What is Ockham thinking about? He is thinking that the clerics, when they administer the goods of the Church, do not have a right of property in the strictest sense, because, although they have the faculty to protect those goods in a court trial, natural Right prohibits them to do numerous acts that lay owners may do. And he adds the problematic phrase that, if the clerics were to do these acts, "they [the acts] could be revoked by a judge" (*Opus*, 2, 428–30). But this judicial power should mean that by positive Right, and not only natural Right, the clerics do not have the same powers as an owner in the strictest sense. What, then, led Ockham to qualify the limits of this ownership right of the clerics as limits "of natural Right"? I think Ockham used that qualification because the ownership right of clerics is affected by positive law limits and also by serious meta-legal moral limits. For clerics who use faculties over ecclesiastical goods that have not been conferred on them *sin mortally* (see lines 426–27). The limit that is crossed when one sins mortally Ockham labels here as "natural Right." But in this case this limit is established also in positive laws and therefore is at the same time a limit of positive Right, which is why the courts can enforce it.

benefit of all men. In the *Summa theologiae*, this is translated into terminology that can create confusion:

> Community of goods is ascribed to natural Right, not because natural Right dictates that all things should be possessed in common and that nothing should be possessed as one's own: but because the division of possessions is not according to natural Right, but rather arose from human institution which belongs to positive Right, as stated above (II-II q. 57, aa. 2 and 3). Hence the ownership of possessions is not contrary to natural Right, but an addition thereto devised by human reason (II-II q. 66, a. 2 ad 1m).[206]

This passage takes up the doctrine of the universal destination of the goods, but places it in the context of the purest Aristotelian and Romanist tradition. Private property is of natural Right, required by reason in other words, as Aristotle has shown in *Politics* II and Aquinas confirms in the *corpus* of this same article (q. 66, a. 2).[207] But it is up to human reason, through the virtues of justice and prudence, to make the most reasonable distribution, according to the circumstances: in other words, it is up to reason to concretize in the best possible way what natural justice demands. And the judges, of course, when they pass judgment in these matters, must abide by the demands of natural Right, as it is developed or concretized by human reason. The spheres of natural Right and of positive Right cannot be separated, as if the one were the province of judges and the other were not.

---

[206] I have used the translation of the Fathers of the English Dominican Province, available in *documentacatholicaomnia.eu*. I have modified the text in the light of the original Latin, edited by Enrique Alarcón, in *Corpus Thomisticum*, available online (Pamplona: Universidad de Navarra, 2000).

[207] Here is the reasoning: "First because every man is more careful to procure what is for himself alone than that which is common to many or to all: since each one would shirk the labor and leave to another that which concerns the community, as happens where there is a great number of servants. Secondly, because human affairs are conducted in more orderly fashion if each man is charged with taking care of some particular thing himself, whereas there would be confusion if everyone had to look after any one thing indeterminately. Thirdly, because a more peaceful state is ensured to man if each one is contented with his own. Hence it is to be observed that quarrels arise more frequently where there is no division of the things possessed."

St. Thomas's interpretation becomes a bit more complicated because, again following Aristotle, he says that although property is better if it is private, its use is better if it is common, as was the case with the fields in Sparta. And this he connects with St. Paul's first Epistle to Timothy 6:17–19,[208] in the *corpus* of the same article. It is in this context that the Ockhamist confusion arises: according to Aquinas and the tradition, the rich man is morally obliged to communicate his goods, but this does not mean that the poor man has a right to take them away from him if the rich does not communicate them (except in case of extreme necessity).

Ockham, who was not a jurist, and who found himself involved in a juridical polemic, made use of preexisting terminology and words, but perhaps without knowing it, he gave them a new meaning completely foreign to the juridical tradition. Through him, the meta-juridical moral dimension in which the rich man is obliged to communicate his goods came to be equated both with the natural Right of the scholastics,[209] influenced by Aristotle and Roman Right, and with what in Nicholas III's Bull, *Exiit qui seminat*, was called *ius poli*.[210] The same happened with some expressions of the canonists, taken from Isidore of Seville, such as *fas* or *aequum iure divino*.[211] As a result and

[208] "Tell the rich in the present age not to be proud and not to rely on so uncertain a thing as wealth but rather on God, who richly provides us with all things for our enjoyment. Tell them to do good, to be rich in good works, to be generous, ready to share, thus accumulating as treasure a good foundation for the future, so as to win the life that is true life." I follow the translation of the US Conference of Catholic Bishops, available here: https://bible.usccb.org/bible/1timothy/6.
[209] See, especially, *Opus* 65, lines 119-47.
[210] *Opus* 6, lines 154–64; 60, lines 13-6, and 84-118; 61, lines 20-53, 158-65, and 181-4; 62, lines 48-57, 70-74, and 83-87; 65, lines 34-89, 119-147, and 184-217. Certainly, the Bull of Nicholas III declares that the ownership of all things used by Franciscans belongs to the Roman See, and that the Franciscans retain only *de facto* use. But it seems to me that the said Bull: (a) did not have in mind that the *ius poli* gave rise to a subjective right not declarable by a judge (rather it gives rise to a right to which all human laws yield: see 8); and (b) did not consider the juridical-theological problems that were later discussed. In particular, the problem of property over consumable things was not raised. Certainly, in order to save the Constitution *Quia vir reprobus* of John XXII from error, it must be interpreted as holding that consumable goods were held in common property by the early Christians, but only up to the moment when they were used, since the consumption of these things implies a dissolution of the community with regard to them (see *Opus* 6, lines 1–38; and 9, lines 43-65).
[211] See *Opus* 6, lines 174–6. He quotes di. i., c. 1, and its ordinary Gloss.

correspondingly, the properly juridical dimension that can be claimed in court (the *ius fori*) gets reduced to the application of positive laws.

There is a group of important passages in which William of Ockham explicitly argues that judges should make their decisions according only to what is positive (human) Right, and not natural Right or *aequum iure divino*. They are also interesting for the way in which Brian Tierney presents them. He, on the one hand, (a) tries to argue that in them Ockham simply follows the doctrines of the *Decretum Gratiani* and, on the other hand, (b) highlights only that aspect which can be assimilated to the previous doctrines of the canonists.

Let us consider, first of all, a passage from *Opus nonaginta dierum* (6, lines 174–6),[212] which cites di. I, c. 1, and its ordinary gloss, and purports to be based on them. Ockham states there, as we have said, that the judge can only apply positive Right. According to Tierney, what Ockham says does indeed coincide with what the canonists teach.[213] This obliges us to enter briefly into a discussion about the meaning of the text on which Ockham relies. The *Decretum* teaches that, according to Isidore of Seville, "to pass through another's field is divine law [*fas*], not human law [*ius*]." And the glossator comments: "although it is *aequum* by divine Right, nevertheless it is not right [*ius*], that is, it does not give rise to civil action." The truth is that the text of this passage of the *Decretum* is ambiguous. It is necessary to review the context.

In the context, it is said that divine laws are known by nature, and human laws by custom. Gratian equates divine law with natural law, and comments that by the name "human law" is meant the customs written in Right and transmitted. It could be understood that "divine law" is broader than the law applied by the courts, and then, the sense of the Gloss to Isidore's text would be similar to what we have said that appears in St. Thomas: there is a meta-juridical morality, so that every *ius* gives judicial action, but not every *aequum*.

This interpretation seems to be confirmed by two things that follow in the text of the *Decretum Gratiani*: (a) it is said that "ius," which

[212] This doctrine appears again numerous times in the *Opus*.
[213] "Again Ockham took over the juristic definition and expanded on it [...]" (*The Idea of Natural Rights*, 128 and 123). See also 166–7.

means what is just, is broader than "lex."[214] But these notions are understood in the sense of the jurists, not in the Aristotelian or properly Augustinian sense: "law" [*lex*] is always something written; and "ius" embraces what is known by law and by custom. But the *Decretum* clarifies that "customs" are what is known by reason without being written (without this unwritten form making them any less "ius" because reason itself is what leads us to subject ourselves to the law). Then the *Decretum* points out another division of "ius," taken immediately from Isidore, but mediately from the *Corpus iuris civilis*: natural Right, Right of peoples, and civil Right [*ius naturale, ius gentium* and *ius civile*]. Regarding this division, St. Thomas took the trouble to seek an equivalent in *Nicomachean Ethics* 5.7, concluding that the Aristotelian "natural Right" encompasses both the Roman "natural Right" and the Roman "Right of peoples," and that the judge must take care of Right in these three senses, not merely the civil Right.[215] *That is to say, it was never said in the Latin tradition before Ockham that the judge is only competent to apply positive (human) Right.* And (b) the *Decretum* explicitly considers among the things that are of natural Right (and therefore of divine Right) in di. I c. 7, both what belongs to the aforementioned meta-legal morality, as well as institutions whose protection can clearly be brought successfully to court, such as the return of overdue deposits. Again, it was never the intention of the canonists, before Ockham, to declare that the judge can only apply human law, and not natural or divine law.

But let us consider, in addition, and secondly, this other pair of Ockhamist passages: *Opus nonaginta dierum*, 2, lines 320–37; and 3, lines 77–80, pages 306 and 313, respectively. I will transcribe the first one only since the other just applies the first one's teaching to the interpretation of *Exiit*, the Bull of Pope Nicholas III:

> 'Dominion [*dominium*][216] is a principal human power of laying claim and defending some temporal thing in a human court.' 'Human power' separates this dominion from the divine

[214] St. Thomas takes occasion from this way of defining *ius* to connect the *Decretum Gratiani* with the Aristotelian doctrine of *Nicomachean Ethics* 5: see *S. Th.* II-II, q. 57, a. 1, sc, c, ad 2m.

[215] See *Sententia libri Ethicorum*, book 5, lecture 12 and *S. Th.* II-II, q. 57, aa. 2 and 3. In other passages he gives a slightly different equivalence.

[216] In the original, *dominium* means ownership, rulership or mastery. When it means ownership, we will translate it indifferently either as *dominion* or *ownership*.

dominion [*dominium*]; 'principal' separates dominion from bare use and usufruct and from every other right held from the principal owner, and also from the power of an agent, who has power to lay claim to something in another's name. Thus, although one who has bare use and usufruct has power to lay claim to the thing and also to defend it, yet he had that power from another who granted him the use or usufruct, keeping the first right to himself without acquiring a new right. [...] This particle, 'in human court' separates this dominion from that which belongs to a man by natural Right or by primary divine Right; it also separates this dominion from every grace and license to use a thing, though graces and licenses, strictly speaking, are also excluded by 'laying claim to.'[217]

Brian Tierney refers to this and similar passages but only mentions the last clause (dominion is separated from every grace or license), and not the immediately preceding one,[218] which basically supports Villey's interpretation, since it holds that the dominion that can be vindicated in court is only that which is granted by positive (human) Right.[219]

And, thus, Ockham cloaks a novel doctrine in apparently traditional language. Indeed, the Franciscan makes use of the firmly established teaching of the universal destination of goods, which, in Thomistic development of the work of St. John Chrysostom, on the one hand, that a rich man sins if he does not care for the poor and does not place his goods at the service of the indigent. But, on the other hand, the same teaching leads to hold that if a poor person who is not in danger of starvation takes away the goods of the rich, he also sins. For,

---

217 I have followed John Kilcullen's translation, although I have made corrections, mostly to keep the wording coherent with the rest of the book. See *A Letter to the Friars Minor and Other Writings*, eds. McGrade and Kilcullen (Cambridge: Cambridge University Press, 1995), 29.

218 On 66–9 the same idea is contained, but stated in a general way, not referring only to Ockham, but to the context in which he wrote: the continuity between Ockham and the canonists is shown on this point (the distinction between ownership and license), but nothing is said about the other point (that only the ownership of positive Right can be vindicated in a court trial).

219 Annabel Brett seems to miss this important aspect of the *Opus nonaginta dierum* since she presents both the positive *ius utendi* and the natural one as enjoying the same "strict juridicality." See *Liberty, Right and Nature*, 64. In note 44 she cites W. Kölmel ("Das Naturrecht bei Wilhelm Ockham," *Franziskanische Studien* 35 [1953] 39-85) who seems to perceive the point I am making in the text, i. e., only the right or *potestas* that can be vindicated in court is juridical *stricto sensu*.

from the juridical point of view, the poor man has no right over those goods, although from the moral point of view he has a certain title to them. Note, then, that, since Right is only a part of morality, and although "Right" encompasses natural and positive Right, there is a moral dimension that is meta-juridical and is, therefore, not encompassed by "Right." Ockham's novelty lies in a shift: this meta-juridical moral dimension takes the place of natural or divine Right; and within this new understanding of natural Right is included the use or dominion that men had over all created things, either at the beginning of creation or after sin, but before the constitution of ownership *stricto sensu*. Thus, this dominion is considered a "natural right," entirely separate from positive (human) Right, which is the only one protected and applied by the courts.

Thus, in order to defend the position of the Franciscans against John XXII,[220] Ockham lays one of the foundations of the Lockean system. In effect, the competence of the court is restricted to declaring positive law.[221] This is the most important revolutionary change that Ockham introduced into jurisprudence, and it effectively flourished in the political theories of 17th century and in their theoretical and pragmatic sequels.

This modification of traditional concepts alone is sufficient to rightly state that Ockham's work is revolutionary regarding the theory of law. And it is confirmed in a late theological text, the *Quaestiones quodlibetales* (*quodlb.* II, q. 14 a. 3). According to them, jurists deal exclusively with positive laws and positive morals:

> [...] I claim that positive moral science, e.g., the science of jurists, is not a demonstrative science, even though it is regulated by a demonstrative science in many ways. For the

[220] They would have a "natural" right of use over the consumable and non-consumable things they used, so that such factual use was lawful. But, even so, they did not have a human, positive right, enforceable in the forum (at the courts), nor property *stricto sensu*. This is a response, as I say, to John XXII, because he held both that to use a thing without having a right to it was tantamount to using it unjustly, and that one may not use a consumable thing without having *stricto sensu* ownership of it. To "refute" the pope, Ockham had to change the meaning of "right."

[221] See *Second Treatise of Government*, § 136.

> arguments of jurists are based on positive human laws, which do not include evidently known propositions.[222]

Some of Ockham's defenders overlook the implications of this text. Lucan Freppert, for example, is familiar with the passage, but places it in the wrong context. Indeed, because Ockham states there that the science of jurists is not a demonstrative science (because their reasoning is based on positive laws, which do not include self-evident or rational propositions), Freppert argues that Mortimer Adler, a well-known Chicago Thomist, defends exactly the same thesis when he teaches that positive law is not science, but opinion. Freppert does not notice (a) that Adler is not claiming that judges should apply only positive law, and (b) that the science of the jurists is not the same as "positive law."[223]

4) Ockham separates the ownership of consumable things from their use because he wants to assert that the mendicants own nothing although they use consumable things. As a consequence, (a) he slightly obscures the traditional explanation of why usury is illicit;[224] and (b) he has difficulties accounting for the phenomenon of stealing because of extreme necessity, which is not theft, according to Christian Law (canonical or secular).[225]

Here two dimensions are being confused. The two dimensions are the following: (i) a spiritual dimension, the attitude of the mendicants' will to be absolutely detached from all things they use and, therefore, not to sue in court anybody who subtracts from them the things they use in their various activities; and (ii) the absence of any

---

[222] William of Ockham. *Quodlibetal Questions* (New Haven: Yale University Press, 1991). See, also, Marilyn McCord Adams, "The Structure of Ockham's Moral Theory," 15, in *Franciscan Studies* 46 (1986): 1–35.

[223] See *The Basis of Morality*, 16. Adler's quote is taken from a lecture he gave at the University of Notre Dame, "The Doctrine of Natural Law in Philosophy," in *Natural Law Institute Proceedings*, Vol. 1, Notre Dame, 1949, 65–84 (available here: http://scholarship.law.nd.edu/cgi/viewcontent.cgi?article=1001&context=naturallaw_proceedings). Adler simply distinguishes "natural law" (which is enacted by teaching) from "positive law" (which is enacted by the will of a legislative body), but he does not deny that the judge must apply or determine both natural Right and positive Right.

[224] *Opus* 3, lines 215–40, 291–302, 342–43, 625–30, and 660–71; 109, lines 249-77.

[225] See Aquinas, *S. th.* II-II, q. 66, a. 7.

right that potentially could be protected by a court, even if the Franciscans were willing to bring the case to court.

The problem of usury (a) is that it is understood that to charge interest beyond the capital is illicit. The reason is that, in the case of borrowed money, using it is disposing of it, so that one cannot distinguish property from use, and, therefore, capital from interest. This problem, however, can be solved without rejecting Ockham's thesis of the separation of use and property regarding money. Francisco de Vitoria holds the distinction between use and property and, pressed by the problem of usury, devises an ingenious solution: what matters in usury is not whether the *usus* can be separated from *dominion* but rather, that *regarding the exchange value, usus* cannot be separated from *dominion*. This is why usury is unjust.[226]

As for the remaining problem, (b) traditionally it was held that in such extreme need the necessary consumable things (food or drink) become the property of the person in need since such things return to the original common dominion. Ockham denies this and, as we have seen, he even denies that the persons in need have *ius fori* to the things they need. According to Ockham, such persons have only a license that derives from *ius poli*. In order to prove that they have no property, he adduces a clever argument: if the starving person overcomes his hunger and has not consumed the thing (?), he has to return it, so that he does not acquire the property.[227] However, this is a sophistical argument, for when someone is starving he can consume food and the act of consuming it is an act of appropriation. But, if he is not starving, then he cannot consume that food over which he does not have ownership. In this case, then, property cannot be separated from the use of consumable goods.

---

[226] See Idoya Zorroza, "Francisco de Vitoria y Domingo de Soto: respuestas a una problemática común,"125, in: *Francisco de Vitoria en la Escuela de Salamanca y su proyección en Nueva España* (Pamplona: EUNSA, 2014), 113–29.

[227] *Opus* 3, lines 417–24. In one passage Ockham concedes that in things consumable with a single use property cannot be separated from use: *Opus* 3, lines 432–435. But in another he gives an argument that confuses several things: he who uses an estate, he claims, has the lawful use of its fruits, over which he has no ownership (*Opus* 4, lines 266–8. This example is repeated several times). In reality, he who has the right to use an estate and to exploit it has ownership of its fruits; and he who may pluck the fruits of an estate to eat them has a certain right to use the estate but has ownership only of those fruits that he consumes.

Curiously, Domingo de Soto develops a similar argument in defense of the mendicants' renunciation of all property and the separation of property and use of consumable things.[228] Soto distinguishes two types of dominion: a broad one, any licit power over the thing; and a restricted one, which is the juridical property and implies the power to dispose of the thing, to apply it to any use. He then proposes an example. If a friend invites you to a banquet, you do not thereby become the owner of the delicacies, for you cannot grab them and take them home, but can only eat them; licitly, you can only use them in that restricted way.[229]

To de Soto I would answer that in cases like this it seems that it is the owner who invites me who is using the meal through me; he is using it to treat me. One could say that I, who at the invitation of my friend eat his food, have an *usus facti*. I concede this. However, the mendicants can do much more than the friend invited to a banquet with the consumable things they use. They can store such things, they can give them to the poor or they can consume them. But this does not affect the Franciscan vow of poverty, which can be understood in the spiritual way already indicated.

However, one can take another step and concede that the mendicants use things *qua* things belonging to a different person, as the servant or an employee does with the things given to him by his master or employer.[230] In this way, this second point, the separation of use and property, would be revolutionary only if it led (and in the measure it led) (a) to blur the arguments against usury; or (b) to restrict the courts' decisions to the application of positive laws (as shown *supra*), and, as a consequence, to blur the way of understanding the case of extreme necessity as a *right* (not just a *license*) that can be protected by a court (for example, in judging that no theft was committed and no liability was incurred). This is the case in Ockham's works. And this is the subtle distinction that we had anticipated. From the court's view point, in case

[228] See *De iustitia et iure*, IV, q. 1, a. 1, vol. II, 281–83 (Madrid: Instituto de Estudios Políticos, 1968). Cited by Idoya Zorroza, "Francisco de Vitoria y Domingo de Soto: relación y comparación de sus respuestas a una problemática común," 126–27.

[229] This argument antedates de Soto. It is stated with different examples from Scripture. See *Opus nonaginta dierum* 20, lines 93-143.

[230] See *Opus nonaginta dierum* 30, lines 21-83. In the case of consumable goods, however, Pope John XXII would be certainly right.

of extreme necessity, eating food over which other people have *iura fori* would not be a *right*, according to Ockham, but it would be just permitted because necessity does not acknowledge limits.

3. The continuity between Ockham's theoretical and ethical philosophy and his political and legal philosophy

In his theoretical works, the *Venerabilis inceptor* makes use above all of the term "natural reason," and makes very little use of the expression "natural Right." In his political works, however, he mainly uses the expression "Right" and "rights," natural or positive (human), although he also uses "natural reason." A careful consideration of both types of works leads one to think that there is no opposition or even heterogeneity of doctrines on this point between them. Indeed, many of the natural subjective rights of which Ockham speaks are powers which, according to the Franciscan, arise from principles of natural reason (the universal destination of goods), which happen to have also been revealed by God. Moreover, positive (human) right (in objective and subjective senses alike) also arises as a requirement of natural reason: for protection against the greedy and the foolish.[231]

But we must keep in mind that Ockham's use of "natural reason" does not oppose either his voluntarism or his nominalism (or conceptualism), since the principles of practical reason coincide with the laws established by the will of God.[232] This conclusion, which I have reached in chapter 1 ("Is William of Ockham's ethics voluntarist?"), can be applied to discover that "natural Right" is identified with God's precepts as much as the principles of natural reason are. Let us consider a quite clear passage, such as the following:

> The aforesaid double power (of particular appropriation and of establishing rulers with temporal jurisdiction) [...] has been

[231] Brian Tierney also points out the same thing, that rights as conceived by Ockham are discovered by natural reason. See *The Idea of Natural Rights* cit., 199.

[232] The will of God establishes these laws arbitrarily and can command us what is now forbidden and make it so that the newly commanded action (such as hating God) will be in conformity with natural reason. But the arbitrary will of God could, according to his absolute *potestas*, dispose even that the principles of natural reason should not be respected (see chapter 1).

> given by God immediately both to the faithful and to the infidels, so that it falls under precept, and is counted among the purely moral things: for which reason it binds all, faithful and infidels. And, therefore, in the same way as the infidels are required by God's precept and by natural Right to honor father and mother and to do other things that are necessary to their neighbors, in the same way are they also required by God's precept and by natural Right, according to the circumstances, to have special ownership and to establish others over them as secular powers.[233]

As can be seen, "natural Right," and the universal precepts of God are here identified, while in Chapter 1 we have seen that the principles of right reason and the universal precepts have also been identified.[234]

For this reason, "rights" must be powers emanating either from the arbitrary provisions of God's will (and these are "natural rights") or from the provisions of human authority (and these are "positive [human] rights," such as property in the strict sense). It is to this that Kevin McDonnell points, with an observation intended as praise for William of Ockham:

> There is no genuine conflict between Ockham's earlier and later writings because the principles of right reason perform in the former the same function as the principles of natural law in the latter. Ockham probably avoided, where possible, natural law terminology both because he was sensitive to the confusions of naturalism and because he wished to reject any limitation of God's power.[235]

McDonnell is absolutely right: (a) "the confusions of naturalism" would consist in stating that there is a good that does not depend on a law given by God or by man; and (b) to state that there is a moral truth that God cannot modify would be, according to Ockham, to pretend to limit

[233] *Breviloquium* III, 8, lines 1–8.
[234] This is so at least in the present divine dispensation.
[235] "Does William of Ockham have a Theory of Natural Law?" *Franciscan Studies*, Vol. 34 (1974): 383–92. In a more general statement, Jane Coleman also thinks that Ockham's political writings rely on his epistemology and logic. See "Ockham's Right Reason and the Genesis of the Political as 'Absolutist'," 37-38.

the omnipotence of God's will, which has no other limits than contradiction and those that it imposes on itself.

Ockhamist natural Right is profoundly different from classical natural Right. This difference manifests itself above all in the fact that the authority charged with the task of ensuring corrective justice, whom Aristotle called "the animate just," i.e., the judge, has to limit himself to the application of positive Right, according to Ockham. This "symptom" alone constitutes a revolutionary change that would be impossible to hold if metaphysical nominalism, and, consequently, moral voluntarism had not been embraced in relation to the notion of the good and the just.[236] When metaphysical nominalism is not held, then ethics and politics are understood as the subalternating disciplines of all practical rationality, including judicial prudence, and, therefore, natural Right cannot be excluded from the deliberations of the courts.[237]

John Lamont points out another clear connection between Ockham's theological and philosophical nominalism, on the one hand, and his notion of subjective rights, on the other, thereby refuting Brian Tierney and Charles Zuckerman[238] who held that there was no connection. Here is Lamont's argument:

> [...] Villey, in referring to nominalism, is [...] talking about a school of medieval philosophy of which Ockham was one of the most significant figures. This school is characterized not only by its rejection of universals, but also by its rejection of the reality of relations. It is this rejection of relations that is important for subjective rights, because objective right is a relation. If relations are banished explicitly from one's ontology, it is impossible to consistently postulate the existence of objective right, and a replacement for it is needed, which subjective rights provide. There is undoubtedly a logical connection

[236] Michel Bastit comes to the same conclusion in *Nascimento da lei moderna* (Sao Paulo: WMFMartinsfontes, 2010), 293-310.
[237] See Aristotle, *Nicomachean Ethics* book 1, chapter 2, 1094a18-b7; book 3, chapters 3-4; book 5, chapters 7 and 10; book 6, chapter 11; Thomas Aquinas, *Summa theologiae* I-II, qq. 57, aa. 2.3, 60, a. 5, ad 2m ; H. L. A. Hart, *The Concept of the Law* (Oxford: Oxford University Press, 2012), 210 and 230; Cristóbal Orrego, *H. L. A. Hart, abogado del positivism jurídico* (Pamplona: EUNSA, 1997), 239.
[238] See Charles Zuckerman, "The Relationship of Theories of Universals to Theories of Church Government: A Critique of Previous Views," *Journal of the History of Ideas* 35 (1973): 579–90.

> between Ockham's development of a philosophical conception of subjective right and his nominalist ontology.[239]

Lamont is totally correct in this passage. We must make clear, however, that, as we will see in the next chapter, holding the existence of subjective rights as a moral power of subjects presupposes nominalism only when such thesis is tied to the denial that there are relations and, therefore, objective right, *ius*.[240]

The preceding pages have established beyond doubt the claim that Ockham introduced a revolutionary change when stating that the courts can only pronounce on positive rights. And this point alone justifies stating that William of Ockham is the starting point of a juridical style that uses terminology borrowed from the canonists, but that profoundly modifies the meaning of the words. There is not, therefore, just one version of the notion of *right* in the subjective sense. There are at least two: the nominalist one, which begins in the 14th century, precisely with William of Ockham; and the non-nominalist one, which we find in the canonists and which, as we hope to demonstrate in the following chapter, is strongly represented by Spanish scholasticism from Francisco de Vitoria onwards.

In conclusion, only two of Villey's theses ended up being disproved. First, that *right* in the subjective sense was used for the first time by William of Ockham; and, second, that any use of *right* in the subjective sense is a manifestation of an underlying nominalist metaphysics and voluntarist moral theory. All his other theses turned out to be correct, although often inaccurately formulated.

---

[239] Lamont, "In Defence of Villey on Objective Right," 194-5.

[240] As Francis Oakley has pointed out, to postulate the existence of subjective rights does not entail to deny the existence of objective right. (See *Natural Law, Laws of Nature and Natural Rights*, 99). David Schindler agrees on this point. See *The Politics of the Real* (Steubenville, Ohio: New Polity Press, 2022), 115. However, if one postulates subjective rights *and* denies that there are relations, then the set of subjective rights must replace the notion of objective right, which presupposes the existence of relations.

CHAPTER 3

Was Francisco de Vitoria a nominalist?

This chapter is divided into two parts plus the conclusion. The first part examines the notion of subjective right or dominion used by Vitoria in his commentary on Thomas Aquinas, *Summa theologiae* II-II, q. 62. We apply a set of criteria for establishing whether Vitoria's notion of right is a nominalist notion or not. In the second part, this chapter examines specifically the notion of political *dominium* with the same goal in mind. The conclusion is that Vitoria's notion of *dominium* is not nominalist.

As we have seen in chapter 2, during the twentieth century and so far in the twenty-first, there has been considerable debate about the relationship between juridical nominalism and the notion of subjective right. This discussion was initiated by Michel Villey, who originally argued that William of Ockham had coined this notion[241] in the context of his controversy with John XXII over Franciscan poverty, and that the notion was therefore inextricably linked to the nominalist conception of Right and politics, which had been passed on in its entirety to Thomas Hobbes and John Locke. He also argued that an author's use of the notion of subjective right was a clear indication of that author's ascription to the nominalist tradition. This latter claim is what we will submit to criticism in this third chapter of our investigation. A careful scrutiny of Francisco de Vitoria's work, in particular questions 62 *et seq.* of his commentary to the II-II of the *Summa theologiae*, leads to the conclusion that Vitoria made a systematic use of the said notion and that he received it from none other than John Gerson,[242] former

[241] See, in this sense, Alejandro Guzmán Brito, "Historia de la denominación del derecho-facultad como 'subjetivo'," *Revista de Estudios Histórico-Jurídicos* 25 (2003), 407-443, at section II. Guzmán Brito clarifies that Villey thought that this notion had to have appeared previously in common, non-technical language in Latin Christendom before Ockham used it technically. One can find a less precise presentation of this particular aspect of Villey's work in Petar Popovic, "The Concept of 'Right' and the Focal Point of Juridicity in Debate between Villey, Tierney, Finnis and Hervada," 73.

[242] Michel Bastit adduces as evidence of his thesis this dependence of Vitoria on Gerson. He defends Villey's theses on the nominalist character of the Spanish scholasticism in his book *Nascimento da lei moderna* (Sao Paulo: WMFMartinsfontes, 2010), chapter 11, 375-410. However,

Chancellor of the University of Paris (+1429), and an important author in the nominalist tradition.[243] It would seem, therefore, that Vitoria was a nominalist. But was he really?

Brian Tierney has established beyond any reasonable doubt that the use of the word *right* in the sense of a faculty can be found a long time before William of Ockham composed his works. Apart from discussions about its appearance in Roman Right (in texts referring to "real rights" as faculties or powers of persons over things [*res*], or in texts referring to the powers of some persons over others, for example), canonists made use of the word "ius" in this sense as early as the twelfth century.[244] Among the uses documented by Tierney, there is, for example, the right of the monks to choose the Abbot; or the use of "right to administer" as equivalent to "power to administer"; or the right to do what is not forbidden either by the Lord or by human law.[245] Francis Oakley adduces another, very convincing example: "Huguccio de Pisa (d. 1210) [...] not only distinguished between the objective and the subjective usages, but also asserted as primary the subjective use of *ius naturale* to denote 'a [natural] force of the [individual] soul.'"[246]

However, Tierney went too far when he argued that William of Ockham's legal theory was not nominalist. In chapter 2 I established

---

he directs his attention to Suárez rather than to Vitoria, although Vitoria is explicitly mentioned (see 379).

[243] "In the neo-Thomist tradition stemming from the sixteenth century authors of the Dominican School of Salamanca, Gerson and Summenhart are invariably treated together as moderni or neoterici (authors of suspect nominalist philosophical tendencies) [...]" (Annabel Brett 2003, 35). Conrad Summenhart lived in the second half of the 15th century and until 1502 and developed his work in the German Empire. He followed the teachings of Gerson but took one step further when he identified every right with a kind of *dominium* (Annabel Brett 2003, 36).

[244] See Tierney, Brian *The Idea of Natural Rights* (William B. Eerdmans Publishing Company, Grand Rapids, 2001), chapter 2, 56 ff.

[245] On the last example, see ibid, 67, note 81. William of Ockham in the *Opus nonaginta dierum* cites Isidore, who is cited in turn by the *Decretum Gratiani* in di. I, c. 1 *Omnes*. Isidore states: "to pass through another's field is *fas*, it is not *ius*"; and his gloss adds: "even if it is *aequum* by divine right, it is not *ius*, that is, it does not give civil action" (*Opus nonaginta dierum*, chapter 6, lines 174–76). Vitoria held that all licit use is right, but there can be a licit use that is not *ius* in the sense in which the *Decretum Gratiani* use *ius*. On this point Ockham is right: not every licit use would be *ius*, but only that which gives civil action. In any case, it seems clear (although not certain) that in the second part of the gloss *ius* is used in a subjective sense. Something analogous seems to me to occur in the Bull of Nicholas III, *Exiit*.

[246] *Natural Law, the Laws of Nature and Natural Rights*, 103.

that, on this point, Villey was right: Ockham is the person who coined the nominalist version of subjective rights. However, Tierney has a point when he argues that although Aquinas gave no prominent place to the subjective meaning of *right*, his works are not incompatible with certain ways of using such meaning, which is part of what we are going to prove in this chapter.[247]

Tierney's discoveries oblige us to carefully re-examine Villey's theses and the sources he cited, because the said discoveries show that authors who certainly did not belong to the juridical nominalist camp used the notion of *right* as a faculty or moral power. The case of Francisco de Vitoria also requires special caution because this author studied in Paris and received a strong nominalist influence but reacted against it[248] and strove to recover the authentic sense of the moral (and juridical) doctrine of St. Thomas Aquinas, without ceasing to argue in the language of his contemporaries.

To discern in general whether an author is nominalist or not, therefore, some fundamental criteria must be employed other than the use by the author in question of the notion of *right* in the subjective sense. In the introduction and in the previous chapter we have already refined some such criteria. The first one is the following: if the author holds that the judge must apply Right in its entirety, with its positive and natural elements, and protect both positive and natural rights-as-faculties, he is not a nominalist author; whereas if the author claims that the courts may only apply positive Right or protect positive rights, as William of Ockham claimed, then he is a nominalist author. The second criterion is whether the rights are conceived individualistically, as if

[247] This means that Finnis was wrong in his controversy with Tierney when he claimed that in Aquinas there is an actual theory of *subjective* rights. Finnis does not seem to grasp that *ius* is the only object of virtue that is found in things (in other virtues it is found in the agent subject) and that, for this reason, it can be coerced or even performed by a third party. Moreover, it is not always something that benefits the person receiving "his *ius*" (for example, when "his *ius*" is punishment). See Brian Tierney, "Natural Law and Natural Rights Old Problems and Recent Approaches," *The Review of Politics*, Vol. 64, No. 3 (Summer, 2002): 389–406; John Finnis, "Aquinas on ius and Hart on Rights: A Response to Tierney," ibidem, 407–10; Brian Tierney, "Author's Rejoinder," ibidem, 416–20.

[248] See María del Carmen Rovira Gaspar, "La influencia del nominalismo en el pensamiento de Francisco de Vitoria," 63–4, in: *Francisco de Vitoria en la Escuela de Salamanca y su proyección en Nueva España*, EUNSA, Pamplona, 2014, 61–70. Annabel Brett's book *Liberty, Right and Nature* is helpful to identify a sort of "etymology" of the words *right* (in subjective sense), *dominion*, *power*, and other similar terms, as they are used by Vitoria.

they were powers that belong to the individual even if he is entirely isolated; or the rights appear as necessarily immersed in a network of juridical relations. The third criterion is whether the author situates the rights in the context of distributive justice or, alternatively, conceives of right as a power of the individual prior to the constitution of the political community.[249]

Two further clarifications should be made: (a) "subjective right" is a type of moral power belonging to the individual.[250] Powers of all kinds can be included in the notion, those corresponding to *real rights* (rights over things [*res*]), to *personal rights* (*credita* and other *iura* such as the *potestas* of the *pater familias* over the slaves) or to political authority. And on each of these levels the distinction between the nominalist and the classical versions of the understanding of subjective rights may require the use of different criteria. The criteria mentioned in the previous paragraph refer to the powers known as real and personal rights. As far as political powers are concerned, the crucial points lie in determining whether political society is conceived as a conventional entity or a natural entity; and whether political authority is conceived as an essential integral part of society or as a structure added to the already existing society by the consent of the latter's members.

The underlying metaphysics behind these two criteria is this: society may be understood to be a mere aggregate of individuals which has unity only because the individuals will to belong to such an aggregate. This is the nominalist view, which denies the reality of relations. Society may be understood as a substance, of which the individuals are mere cells or parts, which is the collectivist view that I am not considering now. Or society may be seen as a real entity but not substantial but accidental, subsisting in the individuals but existing in their real relations.[251] This is the Aristotelian view, which adds one more

---

[249] In the second case, it is immaterial if the power is conceived as subsisting with the political community or not.
Alasdair MacIntyre identifies the causes why the individualist conceptions of rights have turned a rational debate on just relations into a near impossibility. The four causes identified by him are similar to the three criteria that I am enumerating here as marks of a nominalist conception of subjective rights. See "Community Law, and the Idiom and Rhetoric of Rights," 103-105, *Listening: Journal of Religion and Culture* 26 (1991), 96-110.
[250] There could be rights-as-faculties whose subjects are moral (collective) persons as well.
[251] It must be remembered that the inexistence or unknowability of relations is standard nominalist doctrine.

point: the being of society is not only real, but "natural" in the sense that human beings cannot achieve the fulness of their being without political society. Thus, although the will of the adult members of political society plays, without a doubt, a causal role in the existence of political society, it is preceded by an order that requires certain acts of the wills as due in justice. Besides, since society is an organism and not a mere aggregate of individuals, its hierarchical structure is an integral part of its nature. Not a particular hierarchical structure but some structure. For this reason, social authority cannot be the result of mere social conventions.

And the second clarification: (b) the moral or natural law can appear equally in the nominalist and in the classical versions, but in the former it depends entirely and ultimately on the arbitrary will of God, while in the latter it depends on divine wisdom. This crucial difference manifests itself in the fact that in one version, it is held that the law is given because the good of the creature or the nature of things demands it, while in the other it is said either that the good of the creature, by God's arbitrary decision, depends on subjection to the law for its own sake (Ockham);[252] or that the law is independent of the good of the creature (Luther).[253]

With all these criteria in mind, let us begin the exploration of Francisco de Vitoria's work.

---

[252] This can be concluded from a combined consideration of several of Ockham's texts which contain: (a) that in the present dispensation, the most important precept, which serves as a basis for all the others, because it is the ground of obedience, is the precept of the love of God; (b) but God could change this dispensation and command us to hate him. Then, why would we obey the law? (c) We would obey God, only to assure our salvation. See *In IV Sent.* qq. 10–11 (*Quaestiones in IV librum Sententiarum (Reportatio)* [Saint Bonaventure, New York State: Saint Bonaventure University, 1984]. *Opera theologica*, Vol. VII, 198, 2–9, 13–6), q. 16; *Quaestiones variae* 7, a. 4, lines 353–66.

[253] See *The Bondage of the Will* (Grand Rapids, Michigan: Fleming H. Revell, 1957), 287-9. To try to live by the law and be saved by it would lead to damnation. The only use of the law would, then, be to reveal sin, and thereby prompt exclusive trust in grace and the abandonment of self to faith, which alone justifies.

1. The notion of right-as-faculty[254] in Vitoria: nominalist origin but later absorption into a rather classical theoretical structure

Before I start the discussion on whether Vitoria's use of *right* in subjective sense was or was not nominalist, it will not be idle to briefly situate the author in context. Francisco de Vitoria was born in 1480 and died in 1546. He was a Dominican who studied in Paris, where he found that the *via moderna* (nominalism) was prevalent. He reacted against it and strove to recover the original spirit of Thomism. In 1526 he became the principal Chair of Theology in Salamanca, and he kept that position until 1546. He inaugurated "a movement for the restoration of scholastic philosophy and to give to theological science a purer diction and an improved literary form. With foresight and ability he devoted all his energies to this undertaking and his success is attested by the many excellent theological works that were produced in Spain during the sixteenth century. [...] He is justly styled the father of the Salmanticensis School [...]."[255] Vitoria

> trained an entire generation of theologians who would define the Spanish Second Scholastic. Among his most accomplished pupils and colleagues were Melchor Cano and Domingo de Soto. Both succeeded him as *Prima* Chair. Both participated in the Council of Trent and intervened in important theological disputes concerning the doctrine of grace and the sacraments. During Vitoria's Parisian sojourn in theological studies, he [...] dabbled in the theological *via moderna* of John Mair and others, though his commitment to the teaching of Aquinas developed under the tutelage of Peter of Crockaert. The Flemish Dominican Crockaert imparted a novel method of theological formation that principally adhered to the *Summa theologiae* rather than Lombard's *Sentences*. [...] When Vitoria came to Salamanca [...] he brought the new theological method of teaching clerics with Aquinas' *Summa*.[256]

With the aid of the new Spanish Thomistic school, Vitoria indirectly marked the course of the Council of Trent and laid the

---

[254] This is another way of saying *right* in subjective sense. It is frequently used in Spanish.
[255] Joseph Schroeder, "Francis of Vittoria," in *Catholic Encyclopedia* (New York: The Encyclopaedia Press, 1909), 232.
[256] David Lantigua, *Infidels and Empires* (Cambridge: Cambridge University Press, 2020), 95.

theological foundations for the administration of justice in the Spanish empire, particularly in the Americas.

In his efforts to draw intellectual sap from St. Thomas Aquinas in order to breathe new life into scholastic philosophy and theology, Vitoria adopted the study of the notion of *right* in its classical, objective, meaning (in his commentary to *Summa theologiae* II-II q. 57). However, he also strove to assimilate whatever was true in the new Parisian teaching and to place it in classical context (in his commentary to *Summa theologiae* II-II q. 62).

Alejandro Guzmán Brito, an important Chilean historian of Law, argues that Vitoria is the initiator of the private-Law systematics[257] centered on the notion of right as faculty.[258] The reason is that, according to him, in the commentary to question 62 of the *secunda secundae partis* of the *Summa theologiae*, a systematic presentation of the notion of *right* as faculty appears for the first time in history. Vitoria's presentation encompasses the origin of the whole juridical order (which is placed in God), the emergence of the political order and of the moral powers of men over things or over other persons (real or personal rights with a determined object), and the transmission of those moral powers by means of the will of their holder or by means of the law of the prince.[259] Guzmán Brito's observations are interesting because they underline the central value that Vitoria's juridical theology gives to the notion of rights-as-faculties.

---

[257] In Spanish, *dogmática jurídica de Derecho privado.*

[258] *El derecho como facultad en la neoescolástica española del siglo XVI* (Madrid: Iustel, 2009), 60–1, 79–82.

[259] It is, however, doubtful whether Vitoria really has priority in this matter, because in Ockham's *Breviloquium* there is already a similar presentation of the origin of the "rights" or powers of men over things or over other human beings, although he does not go into the question of how property is transmitted. It is true, however, that, after Ockham, the discussion of this subject by Vitoria's immediate predecessors, Gerson and Summenhart, had arisen from purely theological interests and had led to a remarkable confusion of the subject, which, without Vitoria's clarifying and ordering intervention, would probably have prevented it from being translated into a private law systematic like that of Donellus. The consideration of the circulation of goods in a systematic way also constituted an important contribution of Vitoria to juridical systematics, as Guzmán Brito points out. But it should not be forgotten that Vitoria's treatment of the subject also has a theological intention, often opposed to the intentions of the jurists.

The point I wish to elucidate is not that of priority in the inspiration of juridical systematics, but simply whether Francisco de Vitoria, by the fact of having used the word *right* in the sense of moral faculty over things or persons, can be considered a nominalist author. Let us briefly examine his exposition of the rights-as-faculties in the commentaries to questions 62 ff. of the *secunda secundae partis* of the *Summa theologiae*, and apply to them the criteria already enumerated for this purpose.

(a) The unfolding of the notion of right, power, or dominion in the broadest sense of the term (encompassing ownership, rulership, and mastery).

As Guzmán Brito points out, in Vitoria's work, the notion of right-as-faculty has a central place, while it does not appear in the work of St. Thomas or, if it has at all a place in it, it is a very secondary one. Moreover, in interpreting Aquinas, Vitoria attributes to some passages the use of the notion, although, in reality, it does not appear there.[260] The commentary to question 57 remains considerably faithful to Aquinas's terminology, contrary to the opinion of Guzmán Brito,[261] but in questions 62 and following, Vitoria adopts the terminology current in Paris—and, apparently, in Spain—because it seems adequate to the study of the moral problem of restitution and other similar problems.

---

[260] Notably, he interprets the ad 2m of article 1 of q. 57 as if *right* were understood there in a subjective sense, as if the law was the prudential reason with which the individual finds his moral power or *right*, which is not the case in Aquinas' text. What is really held there by Aquinas is that the law is the prudential rule through which we find what is just (the Right in objective sense). See *Commentary* on *Summa theologiae* II-II, q. 62, a. 1, n. 5.

[261] Vitoria, for example, does not hold there that one of the senses of *ius* is law. Buridan, instead, erroneously, claims that the primary sense of "ius" is "law." See Vitoria, op. cit., q. 57, a. 1, n. 7; and Guzmán Brito, *El derecho como facultad en la neoescolástica española del siglo XVI* cit. n. 9, 37. When Vitoria focuses on natural Right, he does refer indistinctly to natural law or natural Right, but I think that this happened at times in Aquinas's own work, and it is more or less unavoidable, because the law is a prudential reason for finding the Right. This conflation, along with the nominalist influence, is what explains, I think, the text that Annabel Brett cites in *Liberty, Right and Nature*, 126: "[...] it is natural right that fire ascend and burn; but this is not common to all animals, because not to a stone." She is citing Vitoria's commentary to *Summa theologiae* II-II, q. 57, a. 3, 2.

He distinguishes there, in q. 62, three senses of "dominion" (*dominium*),[262] and adopts the broadest one, which he identifies with *ius*. This sense embraces all human power over things or even over persons. For this reason, in q. 62, a. 1, n. 10 he says that all dominion comes from God, and cites Proverbs 8:15: "By me kings reign"; and Romans 8:15: "there is no power that does not come from God." But after this brief mention, Vitoria leaves aside the power over persons in the context of q. 62, a question that deals with restitution: he speaks almost exclusively of the power over things and goods and over one's own body. The reason he gives for adopting the very broad sense of "dominion" is debatable, but it is clear from the outset that his perspective is neither individualistic nor nominalist. Indeed, Vitoria argues that when someone suffers an injustice (*iniuria*) he becomes entitled to restitution, precisely because "what is his," what belongs to him, what is in his possession or dominion, his right (*ius*), has been violated. The injury can affect property in the strict sense, another right over things, a right over persons, a bodily good,[263] the honor or fame, and/or even a spiritual good (as it happens in the sin of scandal). All these goods and things, then, can be subject to a juridical or legal power, which is why, if the goods and things are damaged, a right to restitution arises whose subject is the victim.

Now one can reasonably ask, what exactly does Vitoria understand by *right* (as faculty) or dominion? Dominion in the broadest sense "is a certain faculty to use a thing according to the Rights ["*iura*"] or according to the laws reasonably established."[264] Let us briefly examine the elements of this definition:

---

[262] In Latin, the word *dominium* is wider than in English the word *dominion*. It is not easy to translate *dominium* for this very reason. But Brian Tierney has suggested the use of this translation, dominion, encompassing ownership, rulership, and mastery. See *The Idea of Natural Rights*, 56.

[263] The right that suffers injury by homicide would be inalienable, according to the *Fragmento sobre si es lícito guerrear a los pueblos que comen carnes humanas*, 127, in: Francisco de Vitoria, *Relección sobre la templanza o del uso de las comidas y Fragmento sobre si es lícito guerrear a los pueblos que comen carnes humanas o que utilizan víctimas humanas en los sacrificios* (Felipe Castañeda, compiler) [Bogotá: Universidad de Los Andes, 2007], 115–34: a Christian prince may make war on peoples who make human sacrifices, so as to protect the innocent, even if they do not ask for protection and even if they refuse such protection.

[264] Q. 62, a. 1, n. 8. The italics are mine. Here "according to the rights" probably means according to the system of justice applicable to a determinate person or community. Thus the expression probably has objective meaning.

(a) As we have seen, the object of this faculty can be any good—external, bodily, or even spiritual.[265] (b) This "using" can be carried out by means of any power of the rational soul. In this case, the faculty in question is a natural faculty. But this does not detract from the fact that this "faculty" is also juridical. (c) In the very broad conception of dominion, Vitoria explicitly states that the use of such natural faculty, if allowed by a reasonable law, is a right (*ius*).[266] But, since it is a right, it can be vindicated in court, in case it is damaged.[267] Vitoria then expressly states that the dominion in the broadest sense implies the duty of others to respect it; and that it gives standing to the holder so as to be able to go to a court of justice if someone tries to damage it or in fact damages it in some way: the victim can request restitution in a legal battle or a court trial.

Having established that he is going to deal with dominion in the broadest sense, Vitoria investigates the types of dominion, much as Ockham had done in the *Breviloquium*, but with an entirely different purpose. (He is not in a polemic with the pope but is simply trying to aid confessors in assigning restitution to penitents before absolution.) Having determined the meaning of "dominion" to be discussed, which encompasses everything that, if damaged, requires restitution, he hypothesizes about the origin of the faculty of dominion.

In the beginning, God is Lord of all. He granted men common property over all things, common property which, therefore, is of natural Right, according to Vitoria, who follows the *Decretum Gratiani*. Gerson, from whom Vitoria probably takes the notion of right-as-faculty, claimed that God had given "ius," "dominion" (*dominium*), or

---

[265] Consider that if someone, against my will and against the law, prevents me from using something, he causes a damage and is liable for it; if someone causes my brain to be damaged, so that I lose my faculty of reasoning, that person is subject to liability; if someone deprives me of my faculty of using a hand (e.g., by cutting it off), he causes a damage and again is liable for it, and so on. The good for which the victim can seek redress can be of his or somebody else's property in the strict sense. Vitoria says so in a phrase that recalls Pope John XXII: "then, if it is licit for him to use another's thing, he has a right over that thing [*ius ad illam rem*]" (q. 62, a. 1, n. 7).

[266] One could ask, is the right a natural power that receives legal recognition? Is this recognition only that of positive law? Guzmán Brito, *El derecho como facultad en la neoescolástica española del siglo XVI* cit., 50.

[267] Q. 62, a. 1, n. 6. If something is a *ius*, it can be protected by the courts. Vitoria gives one example: because the son has *ius* over the father who must provide food, "the son could sue his father and bring him to court, if [the father] denies him food."

"power" not only to humans, but also to all natural things—such as animals, plants, and the sun. But Vitoria rejects this extension of the term with two arguments: The first is taken from both Aristotle and St. Thomas. Because only intellectual beings have mastery (*dominium*) over their acts (i.e., free will), it can hardly be said that irrational beings have dominion (*dominium*)—when they have mastery (*dominium*) neither over their operations nor over the "use" of anything. If they have no mastery (*dominium*) over their acts, moreover, they can neither be responsible nor subject to obligations or duties; therefore, neither can they have rights.[268] The second argument is a *reductio ad absurdum*: if irrational things had "ius," they could suffer "iniuria," which is ridiculous.[269]

So, human beings, and only human beings, have dominion and "ius," but it was a common dominion in the original state. After sin, that community had to be dissolved. The dissolution did not occur according to natural Right because the community was of natural Right and natural Right is immutable, as taught in the *Decretum Gratiani*.[270] But, although the division of goods was not accomplished according to natural Right, neither was it accomplished against the primordial natural Right, because this dominion in common was not commanded, but only granted.[271] Nor was the division accomplished in accordance

---

[268] This coincides with what he says briefly in the *Relectio de indiis*, I, 6: dominion is founded on the image of God, which exists in us due to our rational powers. *Sobre el poder civil, sobre los indios, sobre el derecho de guerra* (Madrid: Tecnos, 1998), 55–150.

[269] Alejandro Guzmán Brito overlooks the first argument, and claims that the second incurs in *petitio principii*: see *El derecho como facultad en la neoescolástica española del siglo XVI* cit., 46–50. As can be seen in the text, I do not think it incurs in *petitio principii*. I hold that it is a correct *reductio ad absurdum*, although nowadays people are less able to see the absurd implied. In any case, even today I do not think many people would claim that a horse is liable for the damages that one of his kicks could cause to a person.

[270] See Vitoria, op. cit., q. 62, a. 1, n. 20, citing d. 6, § *His ita respondetur* [ca. *Non est peccatum*].

[271] Vitoria, op. cit., q. 62, a. 1, n. 20. St. Thomas's solution to the same problem in one passage of the *secunda secundae* (already commented in the previous chapter) is much better, since it receives the doctrine of the universal destination of goods but frames it within the context of the purest Aristotelian and Romanist tradition. (See *S. th.* II-II q. 66, a. 2 ad 1m). In another passage Aquinas clarifies even more the traditional doctrine originated in Isidore, that the common possession of the goods of Earth was originally of natural Right: "A thing is said to belong to the natural Right in two ways. First, because nature inclines thereto: e.g. that one should not do harm to another. Secondly, because nature did not bring in the contrary: thus we might say that for man to be naked is of the natural Right, because nature did not give him clothes, but art invented them. In this sense, "the possession of all things in common and universal freedom" are said to be of the natural Right, because, to wit, the distinction of possessions and slavery were not brought in by nature, but devised by human reason for the

with positive Right, although it was not accomplished against positive (human) Right.[272] It was accomplished by a sort of tacit agreement between men, like many other realities of the law of nations.[273] It came about in this way: when one man occupied one land, the others went to another. The first division occurred at the beginning, just after the sons of Adam acquired the use of reason, and again with the sons of Noah. This division took place "because, after sin, as men were more inclined to [care] for their own things than for common things, it seems that their life together could be neither comfortable nor peaceful, unless the division of things took place."[274]

Certainly, in this context a crucial difference appears between Vitoria and one of the most conspicuous representatives of the

---

benefit of human life. Accordingly, the law of nature was not changed in this respect, except by addition." *Summa theologiae* I-II, q. 94, a. 5, ad 3m. Jacques Maritain clarified a bit more in his early book *Three Reformers* (London: Sheed and Ward, 1928), 127: "[...] the word nature can be taken in the metaphysical sense of *essence* involving a certain finality. Then what is natural is that which answers the requirements and propensities of the essence, that to which things are ordered, by reason of their specific type and finality, by the Author of Being. And it can be taken in the material sense of an actual primitive state. Then what is natural is that which actually existed before all developments due to the intelligence." Private property is of natural Right in the first sense, as Aristotle has shown in *Politics* II (see *corpus* of the same article 2 of q. 66). Vitoria gives a similar solution with regard to political power: although the authority is of natural law and the regime, on the other hand, results from human determination, this does not detract from the fact that the authority of the ruler comes from God. We will consider this doctrine below. As far as the division of property is concerned, Vitoria's final appeal to the Right of Peoples as the basis for private property, is very close to the Thomistic solution, because, according to Vitoria, the Right of Peoples is quasi-natural.

[272] In the sense of St. Thomas, human law can be a simple development of natural law, as mentioned in the preceding note. Vitoria mentions dist. 8, canon *Quo iure*, which says that the division was made by right of the emperor. But Ockham already criticized this thesis ably in his *Breviloquium*. Vitoria simply leaves it aside, as will be seen in the text.

[273] It is difficult to get a clear idea of the relationship between natural, civil, and positive Right. For the first two are terms which change their meaning and extension. In I-II q. 95, a. 4, St. Thomas states that the Right of peoples is positive, but that it is some kind of conclusion that follows from the principles (of natural Right), unlike the positive Right *stricto sensu*, which would be a particular determination of natural Right. However, in the commentary on Book 5 of the *Nicomachean Ethics*, St. Thomas includes the Right of peoples, together with the "natural Right" of the *Corpus iuris civilis*, within the Aristotelian "natural just." Vitoria says that jurists take the Right of peoples in a sense in which it would be natural, but he takes it in a sense in which it is positive, but quasi-natural, because it is a Right without which the natural cannot be preserved and which almost necessarily follows from the natural. See II-II q. 62, a. 3, 4, Ex. Cod. Ottob. Lat. 1.015.

[274] The transcription is from q. 62, a 1, n. 24. The rest is taken from nn. 23–24.

nominalist version of rights in subjective sense, John Locke.[275] Indeed, according to Vitoria, the American Indians, whether or not they had agriculture, because they had occupied part of the territory of the new continent, were the owners of it and had separated it from the common property of humankind. And, since they were not under the authority of the (Spanish or Christian) republic, neither the king nor the pope could dispose of their goods.[276] Locke, on the other hand, advisor to Carolina and author of its Fundamental Constitutions, established that ownership of land is not acquired by occupation, but exclusively by cultivation.[277] Since the Indians did not cultivate the land, they had no right to it. Therefore, the Fundamental Constitutions of Carolina established that any settler who held as title or deed of property the sale or donation by a "native" was to suffer confiscation of all his property and perpetual banishment from the colony.[278] In the light of this provision, one wonders if the Lockean thesis that the title to land is its cultivation is a purely theoretical thesis.

Be that as it may, once private property is constituted, Vitoria continues, it is transmitted either by the will of the owner or by law. Regarding the transmission of property by the will of the owner, Vitoria tells us: "he who has priority of dominion can do so [transmit the property by an act of the will], according to natural Right, unless the authority of somebody else precludes it."[279] This statement allows us to infer that, although Vitoria uses the terminology of the *Decretum Gratiani* in some contexts (according to which natural Right is immutable), in other contexts he follows Aristotle in conceiving that natural Right can change, although there are immutable principles. In the origin the community of goods was of natural Right; but later it is of natural Right that the private owner can transmit the property by his individual will, in principle. Of course, this power to transfer would be

[275] In this chapter, the next, and in the conclusive reflections we will identify all the traces of Lockean doctrine that place him without a doubt within the nominalist version of subjective rights.
[276] See q. 62, a. 1, n. 28.
[277] *Second Treatise of Government*, §§ 27, 34, 40, 42, 45. *Two Treatises of Government* by John Locke, with a Supplement *Patriarcha* by Robert Filmer. Edited with an introduction by Thomas I. Cook. Hofner Publishing Company. New York, 1947; reprint 1964.
[278] See art. 112 of the Fundamental Constitutions of Carolina. At: http://avalon.law.yale.edu/17th_century/nc05.asp, Accessed November 26, 2023.
[279] Q. 62, a. 1, n. 29. In nn. 29–31 he speaks of voluntary transmission according to natural law.

an instance of a more general principle: the owners in general (whether one or many) can transfer the property. Moreover, in the beginning, the co-owners had the power to agree to divide the property.

As for the second mode of transmission, by law, this is explained at length in nn. 33 ff. of this article, but the essential point is just this:

> Man, as to his person, belongs more to the republic than to himself, and consequently with better reason this could be held as to his things and his goods, that they belong more to the republic than to man. This is clear from natural Right and from the work of Aristotle (*Politics* II). From here it follows that as much as man can dispose of his things, so can the republic, *with just cause.*[280]

And from this principle, Vitoria extracts the consequence that the republic can establish laws that regulate the transmission and acquisition of property.

Among these laws, and bearing in mind our present purpose, we must now highlight those that establish essential solemnities for the validity of contracts. Let us examine Vitoria's teaching on the consequences of entering into a solemn contract without complying with the formalities required by law, because it will allow us to understand that he does not separate the goal or end of morality, divine Right and natural Right, which is the salvation of souls, on the one hand, from the goal or end of positive Right, on the other, unlike Ockham, Marsilius of Padua, or Locke.[281] As Vitoria tells us elsewhere, "the

---

[280] Ibid., n. 33. The italics are mine.

[281] Locke's case is obvious: according to this author, the purpose of the positive law is to protect property, a merely secular purpose. Natural law, on the other hand, whose purpose is to save the soul, does not exist according to Locke, because authentic "law" is only a proposition whose violation brings an effective punishment sufficient to deter the agent from violating it (*An Essay Concerning Human Understanding* in *The Works of John Locke in Nine Volumes* [London: Rivington, 1824 12th ed.], Vol. 1, book 1, chapter 3 §13. We discuss this point amply in footnote of chapter 4). Ockham holds that the goal or end of divine or natural Right is to save the soul, and he clearly separates this Right from positive (human) Right, since the emperor or any prince has full freedom to establish as positive Right whatever he pleases, without papal interference (see, for example, *Breviloquium de principatu tyrannico*, IV, 6, lines 6–15; in the same sense, IV, 8; 13, lines 1–8; and VI, 2, lines 90–2. In: *Opera politica*, Volume IV, The British Academy-Oxford University Press, 1997, 97–260). Finally, Marsilius explicitly states that divine

intention of the law is to make men good."[282] Indeed, according to the Salamanca theologian, if a contract whose validity has been subjected by law to an essential formality is concluded, and that formality is omitted, the contract is ineffective to bind not only in *foro externo* (the courts), but also in conscience. In this Vitoria opposes the jurists of his time, according to whom a sort of obligation of conscience does arise. Against them, Vitoria says that they are not competent to determine whether or not obligations of conscience arise, but rather whether obligations arise in the contentious forum,[283] and argues theologically thus:

> If this were true, undoubtedly the rights of men would respond to bad deliberation and would be established badly. It is proved: because the allegation in the contentious forum of the defect of solemnity would be useless and very dangerous, if it were not valid in the forum of conscience. For it is absurd to say that a right is given in the contentious forum with which men are condemned, when the laws [indeed] provide more for the health of the soul than for that of the body [...].[284]

Note that Vitoria is not denying that sometimes, when someone cannot prove before the judge that he has a right against or over another person, the other person is nevertheless obliged in conscience to satisfy it. What he is saying is that when the law establishes an essential formality, it cannot be that, if that formality is not fulfilled, the legally non-binding contract nevertheless obliges in conscience. He is talking about that particular case. And it seems to me that he is correct.

---

laws seek the good that man can attain *in the other world*, while human laws seek the good that man can attain *in this world* (*The Defender of the Peace* [*Defensor pacis*], Discourse I, chapter 10; *Defensor minor*, chapter 1; chapter 13, 3), in Marsiglio of Padua, *Defensor Minor* and *The Translatione Imperii* (Cambridge: Cambridge University Press, 1993), 1-64.

[282] *Fragmento sobre si es lícito guerrear a los pueblos que comen carnes humanas* cit. n. 13, 118.

[283] See Commentary on *S. th.*, q. 62, a. 1, n. 38. But he does not hold the same thesis as Ockham does, that jurists know only positive Right, since, according to Vitoria, jurists determine what corresponds in the contentious forum by taking into account positive and natural Right.

[284] Commentary on *S. th.*, q. 62, a. 1, n. 41.

(b) Reflection on the Vitorian doctrine of dominion, in light of the criteria for determining nominalist bend

From this brief presentation of Vitoria's teachings on the nature and emergence of dominion and the modes of its transmission, we can reflect more carefully on a handful of points that will allow us to judge whether Vitoria is, in fact, a nominalist author or not. The exact operation that we are going to perform is to apply the already established criteria to the notion of right that we have seen unfolding in section 1.a, unless the examined materials force us to add a new criterion. The issues I have selected in order to apply the criteria are the following:

(b.1) From our previous exposition it has clearly emerged that Vitoria does not hold that the courts can protect only positive rights or pronounce their decisions based just on positive Right. Thus, Vitoria does not meet this important criterion for considering his conception of rights as nominalist. However, he has held that natural Right is immutable, and that sounds strange to Aristotelian ears. So, we must now explore whether perhaps his understanding of the expression "natural Right" forces us to classify him among the nominalists for a reason different from those previously established. The second point selected is (b.2) whether dominion or rights-as-faculty are conceived in an individualist way (abstracted from political society) or inserted by nature in political society and a juridical network; the third, (b.3) whether rights are inserted in the context of distributive justice; and the fourth, which is really a special aspect of the third, is (b.4) the connection between the dominion by individuals and the restrictions that the republic may impose on them due to their being subject to the common good.

(b.1) We have seen that, following the *Decretum Gratiani*, Vitoria states that natural Right is immutable. This poses a small problem for us, because this statement is both contrary to the teachings of Aristotle and Aquinas and seemingly false. Vitoria draws from the main sources of the tradition in which he is inserted. In it, natural "law" and natural "Right" are occasionally treated as interchangeable, precisely because law is the reason for Right.[285] Vitoria does so as well, even though he is

[285] See, for example, *Summa Theologiae*, I-II, q. 94, a. 5, ad 3m.

certainly aware of the difference between law and Right.[286] For this reason, he calls "natural Right" not only what is just in a concrete relationship, but also the principles with which the problems posed by concrete situations are solved. These principles, especially the logically first ones, are immutable.[287] As for their immutability, Vitoria holds that it is such that no creature can change them.[288] There remains, therefore, an ambiguity: could God change those same principles arbitrarily, as Ockham claimed? To this question two answers must be offered: (1) undoubtedly, there are aspects of the divine-positive law that could be changed. But:

> By the negative precepts of the Decalogue those things are forbidden which are evil in themselves. And concerning this, pay attention to what the Philosopher teaches in books V and VI of *Nicomachean Ethics*: some things are evil because they are forbidden, so that before they were forbidden it made no difference whether they were done thus or thus, as, for example, eating pork under the Old Law and eating meat during Lent are evil things because they are forbidden. Before the law forbade them, it made no difference whether one ate or did not eat those meats. Other things are forbidden because they are evil, so that before they were forbidden they were evil, such as perjury and hatred of God. You know this difference. Therefore,

---

[286] Commentary on *S. th.*, II-II, q. 57, a. 1, n. 7.

[287] See the distinction between primary and secondary precepts in St. Thomas, *Super Sent.*, lib. 4, d. 33, q. 1, a. 1, c, ad 2; a. 2, c; *Summa theologiae* I-II, q. 94, a. 5, co; a. 6 c, for example. However, the theological problem of the licenses or commands given by God in the Old Testament to act apparently against some of these principles, forces the scholastics to classify the primary principles, and to distinguish them from the secondary, and sometimes from the tertiary: God can give licenses in relation to the secondary principles, not in relation to the primary. With these same distinctions in mind, the problem of whether or not there can be inculpable ignorance of the law is also solved. See q. 57, a. 2, nn. 4 et seq. Vitoria's audience considered the topic of whether or not the prohibition of fornication and usury belong to natural Right as a problem, to be solved, because such prohibitions do not follow directly from evident principles (see commentary to q. 57, a. 2, n. 4). The question is strange for an Aristotelian, since according to Aristotle (and St. Thomas), what is of natural Right is what is just independently of the determination of the authority, regardless of whether it is known directly from evident principles or not. But the Aristotelian criterion is clearly adopted by Vitoria as well.

[288] Commentary to q. 57, a. 2, n. 3: "tota natura simul non posset illud tollere sine auctoritate divina".

> I say that the precept, *Thou shalt not kill*, forbids only that killing which is evil in itself, and all killing that is such [...].[289]

This text could not be clearer: it is the nature of things that makes certain actions evil, and, therefore, forbidden by the Decalogue. From that single observation one could infer that Vitoria, unlike Ockham, does not think the will of God constitutes a power detached from every rule, including divine wisdom. Vitoria, undoubtedly, is not a nominalist.

And the second thing to be answered is: (2) Does the fact that natural Right is not an arbitrary imposition of the will of God imply that there cannot be licenses or exceptions? It seems that it does not. For, just as natural laws can be suspended by miracles, without, however, suspending the basic principles of rationality, in the same way, the so-called secondary or tertiary principles can have exceptions of divine origin because their necessity is not as great as that of the primary ones and because, in general, ethics and physics are subjects in which there is not as much necessity as in mathematics (or metaphysics or logic, we might add).[290] This distinction about the degrees of necessity already brings Vitoria quite close to Aristotle[291] and St. Thomas.[292] From there Vitoria can return gradually to the Aristotelian and Thomistic view according to which natural Right is mutable (regarding what is accidental, not regarding what is of the essence of justice),[293] as we have seen that he does when he says that the transmission of ownership by the will of the owner belongs to natural Right. (In the beginning the

[289] Commentary to q. 64, a. 2, n. 10.

[290] Commentary to q. 57, a. 2, n. 3. Anselm Spindler holds that, according to Vitoria, there cannot be divine exceptions to the precepts of the Decalogue, which are principles of natural law. He holds that this is so because Vitoria has a view of law as a matter of reason and not of the will. See "Law, Natural Law, and the Foundation of Morality in Francisco de Vitoria and Francisco Suárez," 185-6, in *The Concept of Law (lex) in the Moral and Political Thought of the "School of Salamanca,"* eds. Kirstin Bunge, Marko J. Fuchs, Danaë Simmermacher and Anselm Spindler (Boston: Brill, 2016), 172-97. He is right on both theses. The second one is true of the primary precepts, which are those explicitly contained in the Decalogue, but not of the secondary or tertiary, only implicitly contained in the Decalogue.

[291] Recall the famous passage in Book I of the *Nicomachean Ethics* on the difference in precision between mathematics and ethics (2, 1094b20–1095a1).

[292] Saint Thomas explicitly makes the distinction between primary and secondary principles of natural law, and states that the secondary can change. See *S. th.* I-II, q. 94, a. 5, c. In this context Aquinas himself sometimes uses interchangeably the expressions "natural law" and "natural Right."

[293] See St. Thomas's commentary on book 5, chapter 7, of the *Nicomachean Ethics*, lecture 12, nn. 12–14.

community of goods was of natural Right, but what is of natural Right might change.)

(b.2) In the Vitorian doctrine of dominion, the right is always understood as existing within relations between at least two persons, one of whom has the duty to respect the other's dominion and the obligation to make restitution in case damages are caused to it. Moreover, a right always gives legal standing to set in motion the judiciary through a legal action;[294] there are no rights as such that cannot be protected by the courts. Additionally, any right (i) turns licit the action enacting it, and (ii) exists in accordance with reasonable laws, which implies that there can be no opposition between positive Right and natural Right in the establishment of subjective rights; there cannot be a right based on positive Right such that its exercise is illicit according to natural Right.[295] And, lastly, as is clear from Vitoria's observations according to which contracts that are void due to the omission of an essential solemnity do not bind in conscience, (i) the end pursued by reasonable laws is not to protect life or property (as according to Hobbes or Locke),[296] but the salvation of the soul, which is how Christians understand what Aristotle expressed as "happiness," life according to virtue; and, furthermore, (ii) there is no separation (although there is distinction) between human and divine Right (while according to the works of Ockham or Luther there is a sharp separation).

From all the above, it follows that the doctrine of Vitoria on dominion is neither nominalist nor individualist. Dominion as he conceives it is not a "power" that the isolated individual has, but the active side of an actual or potential juridical relationship, always

[294] See Francisco de Vitoria, Commentary on the *Summa theologiae* I-II, q. 62, a. 1, n. 6.
[295] Consequently, it follows that there can be no conflict of rights.
[296] According to these authors, individuals consent to form a government so that it will protect their secular interests. Thus formulated, the intention of the founding covenant coincides with that attributed to it by Ockham and Luther as well. Note in Luther's work a very early antecedent of Hobbes: "[God established two governments, one, the spiritual] and [the other] the temporal, which restrains the un-Christians and wicked [i.e., in short, everyone (or, in this early work) almost everyone: "all the world is evil"] to keep the peace and be quiet externally so that –no thanks to them– they are obliged to keep still and to maintain an outward peace." *Temporal Authority, to What Extent It Should Be Obeyed (1523)*, 55-56. In: Martin Luther, *Selected Political Writings* (New York: University Press of America, 1974), 51-69. He is even more explicit a little further on, in the same work: "the temporal government has laws that extend no further than to life and property and all external affairs on earth, for God cannot and will not permit anyone but himself to rule over the soul" (61).

susceptible to judicial protection.[297] Already in Roman Right this same type of subjective right existed, because real rights (rights over *res*, things) and actions for compensation for personal injury[298] belong to the type.[299] Thus conceived, the doctrine of the right-as-faculty can be perfectly compatible with classical and Thomistic legal philosophy.

But a special problem must be considered now. Professor Felipe Widow, in his critique of the Finnisian theory, has pointed out that one

---

[297] Ockham (see *Opus nonaginta dierum* 4, lines 192–207) and Locke hold that there are some natural "powers" or "rights" which subsist within political society, but which cannot be judicially protected. On the other hand, in the nominalist metaphysics of Ockham and Locke, either relations do not exist or we cannot know them with natural reason. Vitoria, on the other hand, thinks that relations are real, as is evident when he says that "Right" is, in the first place, what is just, a certain equality in things (see Commentary to q. 57, a. 1, nn. 7–10); that is, a real relation. On Ockham, see *Quaestiones in II librum Sententiarum I-XX*, Q. 1, 9 (in *Opera philosophica et theologica. Opera theologica* V [St. Bonaventure, New York: Saint Bonaventure University, 1981]). This source is cited by Annabel Brett, *Liberty, Right and Nature* (Cambridge: Cambridge University Press, 1997), 44. See also Marilyn McCord Adams, *William Ockham* (Notre Dame: University of Notre Dame Press, 1987), Vol. I, 215–76 (concerning the reality or knowability of relations). Annabel Brett explains that John Mair (early 16th century) conceives the rights as "powers," *dominia*, because in the nominalist metaphysics that he subscribes relations are not real (see ibidem, 43-44). According to Locke, relations do not exist in reality, and we only have ideas of moral relations because certain mixed modes (which exist only by the work of the understanding: *An Essay Concerning Human Understanding* , book 2, chapter 25; and bk 3, chapter 5), types of action, are linked to the prohibitions and sanctions of a law, whence their criminal or innocent character. What moves the human legislator, moreover, is the idea of "good" and "evil," that is, of what produces pleasure or pain. See Locke. *An Essay Concerning Human Understanding* book 2, chapters 20-21 and 28, n. 4 et seq.

[298] See Gaius's Fourth Commentary on actions. These could be real or personal. Among the personal ones were, for example, that of *damni injuriae.* See Title 1, §§ 1–3 and 5–9. *La Instituta* (Madrid: Typis Societatis Litterariae et Typographicae, 1845).

[299] Annabel Brett claims that *dominium-ius* as understood in Vitoria's commentary to q. 62 is a power of beings made in the image of God (i. e., the ones that have intellect and will) over persons, objects, actions or faculties. However, such power would be separate from any juridical connection. See *Liberty, Right and Nature*, 129. Here she does not sufficiently consider the context: Vitoria is dealing with the subject of restitution. Moreover, Brett claims that although Vitoria starts off in q. 57 seemingly upholding Aquinas' conception of objective Right, he later shifts to a totally subjective conception (see 127-129). But this does not match the way in which Vitoria uses *ius, iustum, dominium* and *usus* in his commentary to *secunda secundae*, taken as a whole. Indeed, in q. 78, on usury, for example, it is clear that Vitoria never abandons the sense that *iustum* is something due in the context of a concrete relationship which can be subject to a court's pronouncement. So, usury breaks the required equality of commutative justice because the consumable thing (money) and its use cannot be distinguished in their exchange value. So, the quantity owed (the thing owed) by the recipient of the loan cannot be greater than the capital borrowed (plus any damage that the lender might have suffered by lending). See Idoya Zorroza, "Francisco de Vitoria y Domingo de Soto: respuestas a una problemática común,"125.

could not find a right in the subjective sense in all juridical relations. He gives two examples: criminal punishment and self-defense. In these cases, the *ius* attributed to the person is a punishment, in one case; and, in the other, the *ius* is suffering that his attack be repelled by force, which can hardly be considered a right in subjective sense, since it is, rather, a *debitum*.[300] However, Vitoria's work teaches us that there can be a doctrine of subjective rights that is not nominalist and that can integrate even these examples. Thus, in the case of self-defense, Vitoria teaches that the attacked person is the holder of a right-faculty to defend himself: even if he kills the attacker, he would do so by using his right, making use of a faculty granted by reasonable laws.[301] As for punishment, I do not know if Vitoria considers this kind of relation in this light, but, applying his insights, one could state that the political society as a whole, acting through whoever represents it, has the right to punish the offender:[302] that is, the republic has a power over the offender by which he is deprived of liberty or life; this power is granted by reasonable laws and can be exercised "with just cause."[303]

(b.3) Regarding the relationship between commutative justice and distributive justice, it must be said that Vitoria's teaching is, thanks to Cajetan's influence, at odds with that of Aristotle and St. Thomas. Indeed, in his Commentary to *Summa theologiae* II-IIae, q. 61, a. 1, n. 2, considering the meanings of *justice* and *what is just* [Right] that Aristotle distinguishes in *Nicomachean Ethics* 5.1–5, Vitoria holds that in general justice the whole (the republic) is compared with the whole; in

[300] *Autonomía de la razón práctica y derecho subjetivo en la filosofía jurídica de John Finnis*, 357. Finnis takes up the problem of punishment in *Aquinas, Moral, Political and Legal Theory*, 134 (cited by Widow). It should be noted, however, that Felipe Widow's objection is directed at those who consider that the fundamental sense of "ius" is subjective. Professor Widow recognizes that a doctrine that holds that the most basic notion of *ius* is "what is just," while also positing that *ius* can be understood in a subjective sense, can indeed account for the objection. Such is the case of the Vitorian doctrine.
[301] See q. 64, a. 7, n. 8: "ego habeo jus ad defendendum me et vitam meam cum moderamine inculpatae tutelae."
[302] As we have said, the power of one person over another would also be a right-as-faculty, according to Vitoria, if it is exercised in conformity with reasonable laws. See Commentary, q. 62, a. 1, n. 10. It is called, in fact, *ius gubernandi*, in the *Relectio de potestate civili* [*y Estudios sobre su filosofía política*] (critical edition and other materials prepared by Jesús Cordero Pando) (Madrid: CSIC, 2008), § 10.
[303] See Commentary, q. 62, a. 1, n. 33.

commutative justice the part with the part; and in distributive justice the part with the whole.

This is very confusing. According to Aristotle, in each of the senses of what is just [Right] the whole and the part are present: in fact, particular justice is an aspect of general or legal justice, since the latter embraces all that is commanded or ought to be commanded to persons by law, that is, the acts of all the virtues (including justice in the particular sense) insofar as such acts have relation to another person.[304] How could a relation of the whole to the whole (general justice) be at the same time a relation of the whole to the part (distributive justice) or of the part to the part (commutative justice)? Commutative justice, moreover, exists in exchanges where each part must receive what is equal, but this "equality" *presupposes distributive justice, which is the rule that allows us to compare heterogenous things.*[305] For example, it is generally established that such and such a crime deserves such and such punishment, and another crime such and such different punishment. This belongs to distributive justice. But, if someone commits a crime, commutative justice requires that the punishment established for this crime be imposed on the criminal according to the rule established in the law and not by comparison with other crimes. Vitoria is in doubt about which type of justice the imposition of punishment belongs to[306] because he does not understand well the relationship between the various meanings of "Right" and justice that Aristotle lists in the relevant chapters of the *Nicomachean Ethics.*

The text that served as the basis for Cajetan to introduce his distinction between the meanings of Right is probably *Summa theologiae* II-IIae, q. 61, a. 1, c. But when St. Thomas teaches there that distributive justice relates the whole to the part, while commutative justice relates the part to the part, he is taking the terms in a precise sense, necessitated by the objection. In this context, "the whole" means the goods and burdens that result from political cooperation; and "the part" means the goods that correspond to each of those who concur in an exchange. But even in this text the fundamental distinction between distributive and commutative justice, according to St. Thomas, is the

[304] See *Nicomachean Ethics* 5.1, 1129b25–27.
[305] See *Nicomachean Ethics* 5.5.
[306] See Commentary, q. 62, a. 4, n. 2.

same as that pointed out by Aristotle. Distributive justice consists in a proportional equality, in which at least four terms are considered, two persons and two things. For example, two criminals and two punishments. Commutative justice, in turn, is an arithmetical equality in which two things are compared, for example, the punishment asked by the prosecutor for a criminal and the punishment established in the rule of law. This becomes clear in q. 62, a. 1, ad 3m, where Aquinas teaches that the correction of an unjust act of distribution already belongs to commutative justice, because in it one thing is compared with another: one party received less according to the proportion used as a rule; therefore, the distributor should compensate that party granting the difference between what he received and what he ought to have received. If this teaching surprises Vitoria,[307] it is precisely because of the confusion that he suffers regarding the conception of distributive and commutative justice.

Vitoria, however, seems to conceive correctly that private property presupposes distributive justice, since he holds that it proceeds from the division of what is common.[308] But it must be recognized that the texts in which Vitoria argues that private property proceeds from the division of common goods have a different meaning from the texts in which Aristotle argues that in the political community goods and burdens produced or incurred in common must be distributed. In effect, Vitoria is speaking of the original community of dominion that men had over all the appropriable goods of the cosmos, a community that was divided after the original sin by the tacit consent of men, as we have seen. According to Vitoria, therefore, private property, as we have also pointed out, could exist before the political community came into existence.[309]

---

[307] See Commentary, q. 62, a. 1, n. 54.

[308] See "Cuestión sobre el Derecho de gentes," 306, in *El pensamiento político hispanoamericano. Vitoria* (Buenos Aires: Ediciones Depalma, 1967), 293–310.

[309] This point is debatable, for it could be said that, since Vitoria holds that the political community is of natural Right, any community prior to the formation of the perfect society, such as the tribe, nevertheless fulfills the functions of the perfect society. Vitoria expressly says, however, that a man can acquire property even if there is no positive (human) Right, but only natural Right (see Commentary, q. 62, art. 1, n. 29), provided he does not do so *against* positive (human) Right. Vitoria is right in this. Property can be acquired before the perfect society is articulated, or in tribal contexts, as happened with Abraham. Of course, in some of

Thus, Vitoria presents property as a right that exists before the political community both (i) because of the historical consideration of the origin of property (Abraham, for example, was an owner while belonging to a pre-political community) and (ii) because of his basic nominalist formation. However, thanks to his conscious return to Aristotelian and Thomistic philosophy and the close attention he pays to the reality and nature of things, Vitoria knows that property, even that which arose before the political community, changes its nature once it is integrated into the heart of the republic. For within the polis, everything is subordinated to the common good and is inserted in the order of distributive justice.[310]

Despite the confusion surrounding the name and nominal definition of distributive justice, Vitoria continues to deal with the same nature of things that Aristotle so clarified in Book 5 of the *Nicomachean Ethics*. Indeed, as we have seen, Vitoria teaches that in the political community, private property, even if it existed before the community was originated, suffers a transformation in its nature because man is part of the polis, and the polis is natural. Therefore, if we transcend the names and fix our attention on the nature of the things with which the writings of Vitoria deal, we can perceive that he places rights-as-faculties (in Commentary to *Summa theologiae*, II-IIae, q. 62, a. 1, n. 54) within the consideration of the problem of restitution, which belongs to commutative justice; and moreover, he places restitution in the context of legal justice and distributions. This fact is crucial for the assessment of the most essential aspect of Vitoria's work in relation to whether such work is nominalist or not.

One point must be added. Vitoria confronted the problem of the contact of the Spaniards with the "Indians" of America. He had to apply the Thomistic and Aristotelian principles, and the Roman Right principles, to this new problem. He declared that the Spaniards had to respect the rights the Indians had acquired, according to natural Right, since the Indians were subject neither to the king's nor to the pope's authority. These rights were born, of course, outside the Spanish and

---

those contexts at least, it could not be protected by the courts, but there would still be a demand of justice directed to all, to respect the real right, the right over *res*.

[310] We could add something to what Vitoria says: in reality, the polis is a cooperative enterprise and, therefore, once it exists, property arises precisely in the bosom of that cooperation.

even the Christian Commonwealth and, in those cases in which conquest had been accomplished, they had to be incorporated to both commonwealths.[311] But the acknowledgment of these rights prior to the incorporation is not nominalist. Those rights were born in the context of the Indians' commonwealths and in the context of the universal community of Adam's children. All individuals must be understood as existing within these two communities, their own commonwealth and the ecumene or the cosmos. In this way Vitoria departs from nominalist doctrines in general because he held that these two communities are real, not just an aggregate of individuals. He is, moreover, in sharp contrast with John Locke's particular strand of nominalist doctrine, which did not acknowledge rights outside the commonwealth, precisely because of two concurrent reasons. Locke held that the civil communities in their mutual relations find themselves in the state of nature: "the whole community is one body in the state of nature, in respect of all other states or persons out of its community."[312] It is easy to imagine the enormous importance that the contrast between these two authors must have even in our days: foreigners are considered by Vitoria, as members of the same community of humankind, deserving just treatment; but they are considered by Locke as completely alien and potential enemies.

Thus, we can conclude this section by stating that Vitoria does not hold a nominalist conception of rights-as-faculties, since he truly

---

[311] See David Lantigua, *Infidels and Empires*, 100-101 (where he cites the 1534 letter by Vitoria to Miguel de Arcos) and, especially, 144 ff. The second passage is very illuminating: "The junta at Valladolid was a defining moment in the history of Christian-infidels relations, and therefore international legal thought in the West. [...] Amidst an intercontinental crisis of conscience culminating at the junta, Spanish theologians generated an inclusive, flexible, and reflexive regime of law based on common humanity and universal society to morally recognize the worth, and juridically protect the rights, of non-European individuals and peoples confronted with European colonialism. [...] What emerged was an enduring normative commitment to the idea and practice of world order with legal ramifications for protecting the subjective rights of non-European unbelievers from foreign and domestic tyranny." The doctrine of Vitoria and of the Junta inspired the measures that were later taken by Francisco de Toledo, Vice-king of Peru, first commanding Polo de Ondegardo to elaborate a study on the acquired rights of the Indians, and then applying the conclusions and thus founding the actual structure of the Spanish American republic. See Carlos A. Casanova, *El republicanismo español en América*, 45-86.

[312] *Second Treatise of Government*, chapter 12, § 145. This is connected with Locke's teaching that there is no real obligation or duty if there is no law sanctioned with effective punishment establishing it. Of course, on this point Ockham held a very different doctrine. However, he paved the way to the Lockean doctrine by conceiving divine law as the imposition of an arbitrary will, disconnected from the nature of things (see chapter 1).

places them in the context of distributive justice, the commonwealth, and the universal community of the children of Adam. This is so despite his lack of full understanding of the classical teaching about distributive justice.

(b.4) In the previous section, we demonstrated that Vitoria's *rights* exist in the context of distributive justice. This implies that their connection with the whole shapes the moral powers of the individuals, even if they were acquired before the individuals became members of the political society. But it should also be emphasized that, according to Vitoria, although the republic can make decisions that affect rights because these are subject to the common good, it can only do so *for just cause*. That is to say, the decisions of the political authority are not sovereign in the sense of having no limits of natural Right. There is a natural just order that the republic and its laws must respect. Literally, Vitoria holds that also "the king, who has authority in the republic, can *for just cause* distribute the thing of another, that is, he can transfer the dominion from one to another."[313] This small qualifier (*for just cause*) shows that Vitoria, unlike Hobbes or Locke, recognizes the subjection of positive law and the sovereign to natural (objective) Right and ethics.

Some could reply that Hobbes and Locke defend the existence of a certain natural Right within the constituted community.[314] But it seems to me that this is inaccurate. First of all, what can be opposed to the sovereign power is *rights* in subjective sense, which is not the same. Second, even regarding those rights these authors defend the following: if an individual consents to obey a *sovereign* political authority for the protection of his life and property, and if that authority is exercised in a way that does not guarantee the goods on which obedience is based, then the subjects have no reason to obey. In fact, they are compelled to

---

313 Q. 62, a. 1, n. 33

314 See, for example, H. L. A. Hart, *The Concept of Law* (Oxford: Oxford University Press, 2012), 193–94 and 303. Hart refers rather to Hobbes, *Leviathan*, chaps. 14–15; and Hume, *Treatise of Human Nature*, III, part 2, parags. 2 and 4–7. But this interpretation could also apply to the *Second Treatise of Government*.

disobey because there is a reversal to the state of nature.[315] This is what the Lockean tradition calls the *right* to rebellion.[316]

Vitoria clearly escapes the Lockean nominalist scheme: if the prince or any supreme authority establishes laws without regard to justice, he endangers his soul, because he is in contempt of an authority above him, God, who has established natural Right and ethics.[317] Besides,

---

[315] Hart perceived this aspect of Hobbesian, Lockean and Humean political conception. See the same passages cited in the previous note. To understand the real metaphysical meaning of the Lockean rejection of the authority that fails to protect property, see *Second Treatise of Government* (Hollis, London, 1689, available at: http://oll.libertyfund.org/titles/222, date accessed: 9 September 2014), §§ 27, 32, 40–45, 149, 155, 168, 207–10, 220–31, 241–43; and *An Essay Concerning Human Understanding*, book 1, chapter 1, §§ 5-13; Bk 2, Chapters 20, 21, especially §§ 24–31, 41, 68–69, 73–75; 28, §5; and book 3, chapter 5), in the light of Leo Strauss's interpretation of Hobbes and Locke (see *Natural Right and History* [Chicago: The University of Chicago Press, 1953], especially, 169–170 and 227). Today, Lockean rights are interpreted as Leo Strauss understands them. But it is generally believed that this way of understanding them is a reinterpretation, since they were originally conceived in a metaphysical context that accepted natural law and God-given rights. See K. Flikschuh ("Reason, Right and Revolution: Kant and Locke," 381, *Philosophy and Public Affairs*, n° 36/4 (2008): 375–404) and his source, J. Dunn ("What Is Living and What Is Dead in John Locke," in: *Interpreting Political Responsibility*, [Cambridge, Cambridge University Press, 1990], 9–25.) It seems to me that those who interpret Locke in this other way fail to take into account the above cited passages form the *Essay*.

[316] In the classical and scholastic non-nominalist view, there is no right to rebellion. If an authority exercises its power in a systematically unjust way, it becomes a tyrant and thus a rebel. In that case, the republic or a representative part of the republic could punish the rebel by killing or overthrowing the tyrant. St. Thomas expressly says that in such a case those who overthrow the tyrant are not seditious because the seditious one is the tyrant: see *Summa theologiae* II-II, q. 42 a. 2 ad 3. A superficial reading of the chapters on tyranny and on the dissolution of government in the *Second Treatise of Government*, in which Locke responds to his more perceptive contemporary critics, has led some to suppose that Locke is merely defending the same scholastic thesis of tyrannicide (see §§ 226–28: the rebel is the tyrant). But, while the scholastics teach that, under certain conditions the tyrant can be killed because he is rebellious against the divine order, Locke instead states that, when the executive or Parliament fails to fulfill the end of the covenant on which the community is founded, society is dissolved and returns "to the state of nature, or pure anarchy" (where there is no law at all: see *Second Treatise of Government*,§ 225), and the people can therefore, by any means at their disposal, declare war on those in power and establish a new community and a new government (§ 222). Notice that in the Lockean text (§ 240-2) the judge of the government is "the people" as the set of those individuals subject to power, not the republic as a whole or a part representative of the republic as a whole. Hobbes' position is found in *Leviathan*, part I, chapter 14.

[317] In his *Relectio de temperantia*, Vitoria reinforced the theological foundations for the Council of the Indies and the entire prudent administrative structure that was to watch over the welfare of the Indians in America until the nineteenth century. His argument, addressed to Emperor Charles V, manifests the Vitorian spirit and doctrine on this point: "Thirteenth conclusion: it is not enough for a prince to give good laws to the barbarians, but he is obliged to appoint such ministers as will enforce them, and until this is achieved the king (or, rather,

because above the political order and encompassing it, stands the divine order, which is a real order that preexists and transcends the civil order, (a) if the political ruler becomes a tyrant there is no "reversal to the state of nature" (which actually equates the state of war).[318] The legal order still exists along with the republic,[319] which can get rid of the tyrant in a way regulated by law and Right. Moreover, because the order is real and conceived as such, (b) Vitoria was able to confront Charles V and tell him that there were real questions of justice that arose from the conquests in the Indies, but that the jurists were not competent to solve them, since the conquered barbarians were not subject to the laws of Spain. They were rather protected by the divine order. For this reason, it was the theologians, and not the jurists, who had to judge about the very real requirements of justice in the new lands.[320]

In total fairness it must be stated that William of Ockham also holds that God is above the political ruler and that the latter is subject to natural law.[321] But we must quickly add that he understood "natural law" as the imposition of the arbitrary will of God, not as a subalternating order that animated from within the juridical structure of political power.

Let us now move on to the second part of this chapter, where we will study the right or power of government.

---

those on whose advice things are managed) is (are) not immune from blame." *Fragmento sobre si es lícito guerrear a los pueblos que comen carnes humanas* cit. n. 13, 131.

[318] See David Schindler, *Freedom from Reality* (Notre Dame: Notre Dame University Press, 2019), 76.

[319] See *De potestate civili*, § 23, 64.

[320] See "Acerca de los indios recientemente descubiertos," 172, in *El pensamiento político hispanoamericano. Vitoria* (Buenos Aires: Ediciones Depalma, 1967), 167–224. Carlos A. Casanova, "The Influence of Christianity on the Spanish Conquest of America and the Organization of the Spanish-American Empire," 127, *Logos* 15:4 (2012): 125-144. David Lantigua cites this Vitorian passage in *Infidels and Empires*, 126.

[321] See Janet Coleman, "Ockham's Right Reason and the Genesis of the Political as 'Absolutist'," 55: "public authority may only be retracted in very extreme circumstances, as when a ruler commits egregious sins or crimes." She then cites *Breviloquium* IV, 13. See also Coleman, 51.

2. The republic and its authority

We have seen that Vitoria considers that dominion [*dominium*] in the broadest sense encompasses the power or rights over other persons, including political power. Therefore, after having reviewed his conception of powers over bodily and external goods, material or immaterial, we must examine whether his conception of society and authority is nominalist or not. This subject deserves a separate section.[322]

We must recall that we identified two central criteria to discern between a nominalist and a non-nominalist conception of political authority: (a) whether political society is conceived as a conventional entity or a natural entity; and (b) whether political authority is conceived as an essential integral part of society or as a structure added to the already existing society by the consent of the latter's members.

A preliminary warning is that, since Vitoria underwent a strong nominalist influence in his youth, we are forced to use an important historiographical principle: we must transcend Vitoria's words and consider the natures of things he is trying to express. He often uses language with a contractarian appearance (as if the legitimacy of government were based on consent) because of his basic training in nominalism, but, as we shall determine, the substance of his doctrine ultimately reflects his fidelity to Aristotelian and Thomistic teaching in much greater measure than other scholastics, such as Francisco Suárez, for example.

(a) Does society have a merely conventional existence?

We have already noted in the previous section that Vitoria holds that the individual really is a part of the political community.[323] So it is clear

[322] I have dealt with it in a previous article, of which I will make extensive use here, but which I will correct because I have at hand the critical editions and the Latin texts of the works cited. See "Nominalismo jurídico, escolástica española y tradición republicana," *Dikaiosyne* VIII/15 (2005), 59–74.

[323] But we have also seen that the individual retains his individuality. Authority cannot affect the rights of the individual without just cause, for example. In this he differs from both the utilitarians and the Hegelians, whose doctrines either do not acknowledge the separability of persons (see H. L. A. Hart, "Between Utility and Rights," in *Essays on Jurisprudence and Philosophy*

that he cannot conceive of the latter as a conventional artifice. Undoubtedly, Vitoria teaches that the community is something real and natural by virtue of its end: the community arises from nature itself for the defense and preservation of mortals, and to turn feasible the good life, the exercise of virtue, friendship, as he holds in the beautiful passage with which he begins *De potestate civili*, which ends thus:

> It is evident that the source and origin of cities and republics is not in mere convention or human invention, nor is it something that can be included among artificial things, but must be considered as *coming from nature itself, which suggested to mortals this solution for their defense and preservation.*[324]

However, we must consider now two passages which undoubtedly sound nominalist in the commentary to *Summa theologiae* II-II, qq. 57 et seq. The first passage is cited by Alejandro Guzmán Brito, and it deals with the authority of the prince to modify property. I will follow the version Ex Cod. Ottob. Lat. 1015, because it seems to me a polished text:

> The prince is elected by the people. And his authority is given to the prince so that he can dispose for just cause of the property of individuals. Therefore, even if now the owner of the particular thing is reluctant, he has nevertheless implicitly consented.[325]

[Oxford: Oxford University Press, 1983], 198-222) or absorb the individual in the collective (see J. Bochenski, *Philosophy: An Introduction*, 98-100).

324 Francisco de Vitoria, *Relectio de potestate civili* cit., §§ 3–5. Annabel Brett takes this passage to imply that Vitoria is "locating the formation of the *civitas* in the world of natural causality and necessity: of science, rather than of the history of peoples" (*Liberty, Right, and Nature*, 136). She opposes it to the Commentary to the *Summa theologiae*, where supposedly Vitoria would have adhered, according to her, to the politics of consent (131-32). However, in the *Relection* Vitoria is not using "nature" in the sophistic sense (see Plato, *Laws* 10, 889a-e) but in the Aristotelian one. "Natural" means necessary for the flourishing of human beings (see *Politics* 1.2). Necessity moves the human wills to form political communities. So, there is full continuity between the *Relectio* and the commentary to the *Summa*. Thomas Osborne has responded competently to Brett's claim, and in a way similar to the one used in this note. See "Francisco de Vitoria on the Nature and Source of Civil Authority," *The Review of Politics* 85 (2023): 1-22. See, specially, 1-2 and 8-11.

325 Commentary, q. 62, a. 1, n. 33. Anabel Brett mentions this passage but, taking it at face value, she assumes that it upholds the contractarian view of political authority. See *Liberty, Right and Nature*, 131-132.

The second passage states that political law is a pact:

> And this kind of what is just is sometimes established by private human pact, sometimes by public pact, and this latter case is called 'law'.[326]

Do these passages mean that Vitoria was a contractarian, and implicitly accepts the worst consequences of contractarianism and/or voluntarism, such as that no rights can be opposed to the decisions of the representative government because no one suffers injustice voluntarily and the decision of the representatives are everybody's decisions, as Kant states?[327] To answer this question, let us first place the two passages cited above in their context. And then let us undertake, briefly, to study the Vitorian conception of political authority.

As for the first passage, it must be said from its context that Vitoria does not mean that the authority of the prince comes from the people *qua* subject to government, as Ockham,[328] Marsilius of Padua,[329] and Luther[330] had claimed, and as Locke[331] and Kant would claim after them. Vitoria does not deny that the government of some men over others can derive from natural Right. A few lines before the passage cited by Guzmán Brito, he had said that "all authority comes from the Lord God, according to Paul's letters and I Pet. 2."[332] This is Vitoria's true thesis: all authority comes from God, through the political community. When he holds that the prince is elected by the people, what he means is that the prince has been appointed according to the procedures established by the republic, so that the prince represents the republic

[326] Commentary, q. 57, a. 2, n. 2.
[327] See *Metaphysics of Morals* (Cambridge: Cambridge University Press, 2008), Doctrine of Law, §§ 46 and 49, 313–14 and 319 of the Berlin Academy edition. David Schindler proves that this very problem is already present in Locke: "[...] the social contract theory implies that entry into political relations is a relinquishing of the state of nature. When we consider this fact along with Locke's theory of tacit consent, it means that every inhabitant of a commonwealth is taken for all intents and puroposes always already to have wholly surrendered his natural liberty." *Freedom from Reality*, 105.
[328] See *Breviloquium* III 7, lines 72–6; 13, lines 43–6; IV 10, lines 55–64 and 75–76.
[329] See *Defensor pacis*, Discourse I, chapter 12; *Defensor minor*, chapter 12.
[330] *To the Christian Nobility of the German Nation Concerning the Reform of the Christian Estate (1520)*. In *Selected Political Writings* (New York: University Press of America, 1974), 37-49.
[331] See *Second Treatise of Government*, §§ 171, 175 and 180, for example.
[332] Commentary on II-II, q. 62, a. 1, n. 33.

as a whole (not the people *qua* subject to government).[333] We will buttress this interpretation below.

It must be admitted, however, that a certain confusion persists in Vitoria's work: the reason why the owner is obliged to obey an order concerning the thing subject to his property right is not that he has implicitly consented to the order, as this Vitorian text seems to state; the reason is instead that the particular good of the owner is subject to the common good with the result that the authority, *with just cause*, can affect his property. The position of the authority in political order and the justice of the cause are sufficient reasons for the owner to be bound to obedience. The consent of the owner is not necessary. But does not this confusion (to think that the ground for mandatory obedience is the previous consent of the owner) give rise to the other, to think that one cannot oppose rights against the prince in Kantian style? It does not seem so because Vitoria does not hold that the prince can do anything he wills, but instead that he must act with just cause. Whether the private individual can sue the king in a court of law is another matter, but such a matter in a monarchy probably can be reduced to the question, "*quis custodit custodem?*" that affects every regime and not just monarchies. In Christendom, however, the prince fears God's punishment and this constitutes an effective guarantee of his subjection to justice.

As for the second passage, a distinction is being made precisely between natural Right and positive Right. In this context, as is often the case today among people who are certainly not nominalists, Vitoria says that positive Right is "conventional." He does not really mean that it is literally the fruit of a pact, but he wants to oppose "conventional" to "natural." That is why he says in the same place that natural Right is necessary, while positive Right "depends on the will and pleasure of men."

It is, therefore, clear that Vitoria's political conception is not nominalist according to the first criterion established above. He holds

[333] J. A. Fernández-Santamaría interprets this passage in precisely this way. See *The State, War and Peace. Spanish Political Thought in the Renaissance 1516-1559* (Cambridge: Cambridge University Press, 1977), 77.

that political society is natural and not conventional. This conclusion will be reinforced in the next section.

(b) Is the will of the people the foundation of the concrete hierarchical authority existing in society?

It is not difficult to find the answer to this question in Vitoria's writings. According to him, not only political society is natural, but the hierarchical structure of political society is natural as well:

> From this principle it follows that the end and the need for the public authorities is identical to that of the community. If the assemblies and congregations of men are indispensable for the preservation of mortals, and if no society can subsist without some force and power that rules it and provides for its common good, the need and utility of both the public power and society itself are entirely the same. *Indeed, if all men were equal, without being subject to any power, each tending to different objectives, according to his own will and criterion, the disintegration of the republic would be inevitable*; and the city would be annihilated if there were no one to look after the common interests and promote the public good.[334]

Vitoria, like Aristotle, sees that political order and justice naturally demand inequality and understands that, therefore, real political freedom can only consist in the subjection of political power to truth and divine order. Aristotle, in fact, stated that in a republic, a just political community, three conditions concur: (i) there is distributive justice, but this consists not in arithmetic equality but in proportional equality; (ii) there is freedom, but in the sense that citizens obey the laws because these are reasonable; and, finally, (iii) not all the members of society are active citizens, but some are in one sense or another *alieni iuris*.[335] One can immediately perceive the immense distance that separates Vitoria from the nominalist principles that Ockham held

---

[334] *Relectio de potestate civili*, cit. § 5. The italics are mine.
[335] See *Nicomachean Ethics* 5.6.

concerning political authority,[336] which were received by Hobbes and Locke, and are clearly present in the 1789 Declaration of the Rights of Man and the Citizen. These sources (1) hold that among all members of society there must exist a kind of equality that is not realistic, and (2) aspire to a kind of freedom that consists not in subjection to truth or reasonable laws, but in acknowledging as legitimate only that government that is self-government or emanates from the consent of the subjects.

So, how does the concrete hierarchical structure of political society arise in history? According to Vitoria, God is the efficient cause and the author of political society and public power, just as he is the author of natural Right, because he inserted in human nature the natural tendency to form societies.[337] Vitoria encounters enormous difficulties in explaining the origin of power and Right in God, not only because of his initial nominalist training, but also because (i) it did not occur to him to formulate the problem of political articulation,[338] and because (ii) he was not sufficiently aware of the important role that fortune plays in the marvelous event of articulation. With this limitation, however, the sense of his teaching is quite transparent.

So, God is the efficient cause, while the republic itself would be, according to Vitoria, the material cause of power, because it is incumbent upon it as a whole to rule itself and to direct all its powers to the common good.[339] Again, he is not saying that the government should be self-government of the people *qua* subject to government, but that, although it is natural Right that there is and there must be civil power, human reason must nevertheless determine (i) the regime, (ii) who must rule, and (iii) who must obey. This is the case because before political societies were formed, no one was superior to the others and "by natural Right each one has the power and the right to defend and protect himself, since nothing is more natural than to repel force with

---

[336] Remember Ockham's teaching, presented above in chapter 2: "all mortals, who are born free and in no way subject to anyone by positive (human) right, have from God and nature the power to spontaneously establish for themselves a ruler, as any people and any city can constitute Right for itself." *Breviloquium* IV 10, lines 55–64 and 75–6.

[337] See ibid., § 6.

[338] "Political articulation" is the historical event by which a conglomerate of individuals or of families or tribes become a political entity able to act in history. Orestes Brownson and Eric Voegelin are perhaps the authors that most lucidly have studied this historical phenomenon.

[339] Ibid., § 7.

force."[340] By this latter statement he does not mean that the only legitimate regime is democracy, nor, like Suárez, that the natural regime is democracy.[341] It can be seen that the formulae chosen are not perfect. It is true that a human conglomerate that becomes politically articulated is the material cause of the political community, but it is not true that the community that rules itself is the material cause of political power. There is no community without government, and the material cause cannot include government. The difficulty here is similar to that encountered by Aristotle when he defined the soul as "act of the natural body that has life in potency."[342] There is no body without the soul, therefore, this "body that has life in potency" is an abstraction. It seems to me that Vitoria means something similar: the "not-yet-organized-community" is the material cause, and it is an abstraction. That there is no substantive or conceptual—but only linguistic—limitation here is clear from what he adds next:

1) Monarchical power comes ultimately from God, not from the community, for several reasons. First, because the republic as a whole can administer the political *potestas*, which comes from God, neither by itself nor by the multitude, so that the establishment of an authority is necessary. Moreover, the multitude cannot "establish laws, propose edicts, settle disputes, restrain transgressors, or determine and give to each his right." The community as a whole transfer to political authority (and, in this case, the king) its own authority, which comes from God, so

[340] Ibid. This is exactly the Thomistic and Aristotelian doctrine. Only if there were someone who notably exceeded all others in virtue and wisdom would monarchy be of natural Right; but this not being the case, the determination of the regime corresponds to human reason and will, since all regimes can be just. See Aquinas, *Sententia Libri Politicorum* III, Lesson 5, nn. 1–7, concatenated with *S. th.* II-II, q. 57, a. 2, ad 2m, for example. Both, if there was a natural monarch and if reason and will establish a different regime, authority is said to come from God. Perhaps this is the reason why Vitoria states that the community with its authority and power is the matter that the efficient cause uses: to resolve the problem of the divine origin of government and the mediation of positive Right to establish the regime. The best way to solve this is to say that God acts through second causes, so that power and authority come from him and exceed what the wills of the citizens in coalition can produce.

[341] See Francisco Suárez, *Defensio fidei*, Book III, *Sobre el poder y superioridad del Sumo Pontífice sobre los reyes temporales*, chapter II, "Utrum principatus politicus immediate a Deo sit, seu ex divina institutione", nn. 7–9 (20–22, in: *Corpus hispanorum de pace* II, Consejo Superior de Investigaciones Científicas, Madrid, 1965).

[342] See *De anima* II 1, 412a27–28. See also Aquinas' *Sentencia de anima*, l. 2, lec. 1, n. 12.

that the king can use the power of the republic.[343] And, thirdly and above all, because

> No power of this kind can be abrogated by the agreement of men. [...] Therefore, if all the citizens were to agree on this: that all should enjoy such power and liberty that they should not be subject to the laws of anyone, nor obey any authority, such a pact would be null and void, as contrary to natural Right, which the republic cannot renounce.[344]

This is the key point. Suárez states that democracy is the natural regime and all other regimes are stablished by men, although not against natural law, because the multitude is allowed to transfer its authority to the king and/or the aristocracy. Suárez also states that the power of the king is based on the principle *pacta sunt servanda*, while that of the community—on the other hand—comes from God. Vitoria, instead, avoids two fundamental confusions. It is true that the authority of the king comes from the community as a whole and is established *qua* authority by natural law, and *qua* monarchical regime according to the law of peoples. The community as a whole, however, is not the same as the "people" understood as the set of those subject to power. The "people" and/or "the multitude" are equivocal terms, they might mean the set of those subject to power or the republic as a whole.[345] Vitoria, unlike Suárez, follows Aquinas in a right understanding of the terms "people" and "multitude."[346] For this reason he does not claim that democracy is the only natural regime. Moreover, according to Vitoria, there is a moral necessity of "transferring" authority, so that the foundation of authority is natural Right.[347] This means that the reason

---

343 *Relectio de potestate civili* cit., § 8.

344 *Relectio de potestate civili*, cit., § 10.

345 See Eric Voegelin, *The New Science of Politics*, 40. Concerning Lincoln's famous statement describing "democracy," the "government of the people, through the people and for the people," Voegelin observes that "the symbol 'people' in this formula means successively the articulated political society, its representative, and the membership that is bound by the acts of the representative." Thomas Osborne interprets Vitoria in exactly the same way in 3 of "Francisco de Vitoria on the Nature and Source Civil Authority," cit.

346 See *Summa theologiae* I-II, qq. 90, a. 3; and 97, a. 3, ad 3m. That Aquinas understands rightly the terms can be inferred from the fact that he does not state that democracy is a natural regime while monarchy or aristocracy are not.

347 Vitoria states that the republic cannot manage political power by itself, without authority. He also states that the republic can transfer authority and not power. But this is because the government, based on the received authority, uses the power of the community when

for obedience is not the inherent strength of a pact or of any other kind of act of the human will. From this follows the next point.

2) The authority of the republic and of princes and magistrates exists by divine Right, which is the only reason why there can be death penalty. For the Decalogue forbids us to kill human beings; not only the innocent man, but also the guilty, except in legitimate defense, in war, or in the exercise of public authority.[348]

3) Authority is something "licit" from the point of view of natural Right and, therefore, the power of kings is not opposed to evangelical freedom, "such as these ignorant and seditious men whisper to the uneducated ears of the plebs."[349] The modern *democratist* doctrines had already been born in Europe in general and were already trying to act in Spain in particular (as even today, under new forms like "direct democracy," they continue to cause revolutions and tyrannies in many places, such as Venezuela), but the most enlightened Spanish intellects were able to defeat them, at least until the nineteenth century.

Vitoria teaches that there is no more freedom in democracy or aristocracy than in monarchy, although the regime most free of dangers is the mixed of the three forms of government, "as it seems to be the one existing in Spain."[350] In the monarchical regime there is true

---

representing it. (See *Relectio de potestate civili* cit., § 8. See also Thomas Osborne, "Francisco de Vitoria on the Nature and Source Civil Authority," 14. Bellarmine gives exactly the same argument. Cited by Yves Simon, *Philosophy of Democratic Government* [Notre Dame: University of Notre Dame Press, 2017], 166.)

[348] *Relectio de potestate civili* cit., § 7. The twentieth century at the same time both (1) lost the notion that only legitimate authorities (which ultimately proceed from God) may licitly condemn to death, and (2) witnessed the most massive mass murders and executions in history. It seems to me that there is a strong connection between these two facts.

[349] *De potestate civili* cit., § 8.

[350] *Relectio de potestate civili* cit., § 11. In his commentary to *Summa theologiae* I-II, q. 105, a. 1, *De legibus* (Salamanca: Ediciones Universidad de Salamanca and Università degli studi di Genova, 2010), 258, Vitoria explains that the regime in Spain is mixed because there is a Council, Chancery, Corregimiento, and so on. In truth, European regimes (and also Spanish and Anglo American) with their assemblies, parliaments, courts, councils, and town halls were traditionally mixed regimes. Only very late they tended to become "absolute monarchies," first in France and later in Spain, under the Bourbons. (Although Simon Schama describes eighteenth-century monarchical France as a society where there is subsidiarity, a variety of decision-making centers, and a good measure of respect for the courts' independence. See *Citizens: A Chronicle of the French Revolution*, 105 and 114.) The composition and influence of the

authority and government because the people as a whole (not as the set of those subject to authority) give their power [*potestatem*] to the king without reserving it for themselves,[351] so that he is placed above each citizen and above the whole set of them. But (a) in Christian states the regime is always mixed to some extent, because there is not one man who outstrips all in virtue and wisdom;[352] (b) if the king becomes a tyrant, "there always remains in it [in the community] the natural right to defend itself and, if such defense is not possible in any other way, it can get rid of the king"; (c) the king cannot grant dispensation concerning natural Right because "what goes against natural Right, generally and ordinarily, cannot [really] be expedient to the republic";[353] and (d) although the king cannot be punished for transgressions of the laws he himself gives,[354] he is bound in conscience to obey them both because he is part of the republic and because he is subject to natural Right and does injury to others if he does not submit to the law (implicitly, then, because there is distributive justice and burdens must be shared equitably).[355]

---

councils and parliaments were very different in the West (due to the influence of classical philosophy) and in the East, as Max Weber has very ably demonstrated. See "The types of legitimate domination", 280-282, in: Guenther Roth y Claus Wittich (Eds.), *Economy and Society* (Berkeley: University of California Press, 1978) Volume 1, 212-307.

[351] See *De legibus* cit., q. 105, a. 1, 260. It is easy to perceive how this doctrine, in the light of the abdication of the Bourbons after the Napoleonic invasions, could have been the basis for Francisco Xavier Yáñez in Caracas to pronounce on June 25, 1810 that power had returned to the community. See Mario Briceño Iragorry. *Tapices de historia patria* (Caracas: Cultural Venezolana, S. A., 1978), 186.

[352] See *De legibus* cit., q. 105, a. 1, 259. Monarchy is better when there is one who excels in virtue and wisdom, but, when this is not the case, the mixed regime is better and safer. Vitoria adds that the elective monarchy is better than the hereditary one, although the hereditary one can be defended in a concrete case with four or five reasons that he gives and that we do not reproduce here (see 261). I will point out just that it avoids the quarrels that are typical of elective monarchies. He gives no example, but the Polish case easily comes to mind.

[353] *De legibus* cit., q. 105, a. 2, 264 (I deviate from the translation of the edition used). I imagine that when he says "generally and ordinarily," Vitoria has in mind examples such as polygamy in the Old Testament, which St. Thomas taught were exceptions to non-first principles of natural Right that God permitted for the good of the People of Israel. I doubt very much that Aristotle would have held that it was possible to dispense from natural Right, which require a miraculous or supernatural intervention of God. Equity is not a case of a dispensation from natural Right, but a dispensation from a general law, in order to find the natural Right, which is mutable.

[354] This is the famous problem "*quis custodit custodem?*"

[355] See Vitoria's commentary on II-II, q. 60, a. 5, n. 1.

An important corollary that flows from Vitoria's theological-political conceptions is that he does not think that political power emanates from individual rights. On the contrary, individual rights exist in the society of human beings, be it the universal community of Adam's children or be it political community. Subjective rights, moreover, in sharp contrast to Ockhamist doctrine, may be individual or collective (like the right of the republic to get rid of the tyrant), and they can limit political power and any other power of action. On this point the foundational act of the United States seems to be closer to Francisco de Vitoria than to John Locke. The 1789 Declaration of the Rights of Man and the Citizen, instead, seems to be closer to John Locke. Because, as Hannah Arendt explains, the Founders of this country were too well acquainted with the classics to attempt what the French Revolution attempted—namely, to establish the Rights of Man understood in nominalist way as the source of all political power and the foundation-stone of the body politic. The Founders, instead, understood the Bill of Rights as "permanent restraining controls upon all political power, and hence [the Founders] presupposed the existence of the body politic and the functioning of political power."[356] But this will be the subject of the next chapter.

From all the above, it follows that Vitoria is not a nominalist, according to the second criterion having to do with political authority and established in the introduction to this third chapter. Not only the political community is natural, but its authority is an integral, natural part of the polis.

3. Conclusion

We see that Vitoria meets all the standards we identified at the beginning to measure whether a doctrine is in continuity with the classics (it is not nominalist). Indeed, as we have seen, Vitoria subjects the rights-as-faculties to distributive justice; he holds that the judge must determine the Right, with its positive and natural aspects. Consequently, Vitoria conceives the rights-as-faculties as the active side of actual or potential juridical-commutative relations in the Aristotelian

---

[356] Hannah Arendt, *On Revolution* (New York: The Viking Press, 1973), 104.

sense, more or less like the real (rights over *res*) and personal rights of Roman Law. But, in addition, Vitoria defends the idea that political society and authority are natural, and that natural Right depends on the nature of things. On the latter point, it should be remembered that he holds that the negative precepts of the Decalogue prohibit actions that are evil in themselves; they do not transform actions that would otherwise be indifferent into evil actions. These precepts are established, therefore, because the good of the creature or the nature of things demands them, not because of God's arbitrary decision. In light of all these results, it can be confidently concluded that Vitoria is not a nominalist and that, in consequence, in the sixteenth century, he represents the continuity of the classical political and juridical wisdom that was handed on to the following centuries by means (among others) of the Thomistic School, which has lasted to this day.[357]

[357] Therefore, Mariano Fazio and Horacio Rodríguez-Penelas are wrong when they evaluate Vitoria well because, supposedly, "he anticipated the Modernity that was germinating," and he can be considered "a revolutionary." See Horacio Rodríguez-Penelas, "Francisco de Vitoria: la cuestión del dominio en la primera Relección *de indiis*," 165, in: Juan Cruz Cruz (Editor), *Ley y dominio en Francisco de Vitoria* (Pamplona: EUNSA, 2008), 165–73. Vitoria was not a revolutionary; and "Modernity" is neither an agent nor an age in which classical philosophy loses its force or its relevance.

CHAPTER 4

The 1789 Declaration of the Rights of Man and the Citizen as an attempt to build a political society on the basis of the nominalist version of rights

Having established the criteria to distinguish between a nominalist version of subjective rights and a version that is in continuity with the classical conception of law and Right, we are now going to apply these criteria to a particular political concretization of the notion of rights. The [French] Declaration of the Rights of Man and the Citizen of 1789 (from now on, the Declaration) is presented as a canon by which, on the basis of "simple and indisputable principles," every government and every regime can be evaluated in relation "to the purpose of any political institution." A detailed analysis of it, coupled with the testimony of Abbé Augustine Barruel,[358] reveals that some of its main immediate sources were the works of John Locke, François-Marie Arouet (Voltaire), René-Louis de Voyer de Paulmy (D'Argenson), Charles de Montesquieu, Jean-Jacques Rousseau, Claude-Adrien Schweitzer (Helvetius) and Cesare Beccaria. It is in the light of these authors that it should be understood.

The gathering of all these materials makes it possible to establish a clear understanding of the principles received in the text of the Declaration and their connection with the nominalist version of *rights*.[359] Actually, it will allow us to make clear that the French Revolution, by proclaiming this *Declaration of Rights* as its main foundation and its goal, is the event in which the nominalist version of

[358] Augustine Barruel, *Memoirs Illustrating the History of Jacobinism* (New York: Hartford, 1799), volume II.

[359] Of course, Locke, Montesquieu, and Rousseau introduced changes in the nominalist version, but their works cannot be understood except as holding precisely that version of rights. As Tierney stated, "the philosophes retained more than they acknowledged of the scholastic culture." See "Response to S. Adam Seagrave's 'How Old Are Modern Rights? On the Lockean Roots of Contemporary Human Rights Discourse,'" 463, *Journal of the History of Ideas*, Volume 72, Number 3 (July 2011): 461–68.

rights burst into the position of power. For this reason, a brief study of the Declaration and its sources sheds additional light on the subject of this book.

The criteria already established in order to distinguish between a nominalist understanding of subjective rights and an understanding that is in line with the classical conception of Right allow us to perceive that the 1789 Declaration, as well as both Locke and Rousseau, held a nominalist conception of subjective rights. Indeed, Locke and Rousseau clearly held that there are rights that are prior to political society and distributive justice, and that such rights are the measure of the government's legitimacy and of the people's freedom. The last point implies, as we shall see, that the government (and especially the legislator) must count with the will, the consent, of "the people," understood as the set of human beings subject to political power and not as the whole republic.[360]

There is another very important criterion the application of which must be highlighted: nominalism leads one to think of society as an artifact, a conventional entity without an intrinsic order. The rejection of the classical principles of order (the direction towards the common good prescribed in the laws) leads to replacing them with a construction the main bricks of which are the "rights" understood in subjective way and according to the nominalist version. This trend can be clearly discovered both in the 1789 Declaration of the Rights of Man and the Citizen and in its philosophical sources. Let us focus initially on John Locke in order to illustrate this point.

Locke denied that there is law without effective sanction, and he stated that natural laws do not have effective sanction. On this there is a clear difference between Ockham's nominalist doctrine and Locke's. However, there is a deep connection between the two views. Indeed, although Ockham holds that there is divine, natural law, he also argues that such law is imposed by an arbitrary will and is not connected to the nature of things. This in turn implies that "natural law" (a) can consist only in a set of *a priori* principles and (b) obliges only through the

[360] See, for example, John Locke, *Second Treatise of Government*, §§ 22, 54, 190, in *The Two Treatises of Civil Government* (London: Hollis ed., 1689); and Jean Jacques Rousseau, *The Social Contract and Discourses* (New York: Dent and Sons, 1761), book 1, chapter 1. Both works have been made available to the public by the *Liberty Fund*.

promise of reward or punishment (see chapter 1).[361] However, if someone holds as Locke did both that there is no law without effective sanction and that the threats of punishments in the afterlife do not qualify as factors able to dissuade men from violating laws, then that author must be led to the conclusion that there are no innate principles which actually compel us to conform to them (because there is no effective sanction of those supposed principles). This implies immediately, of course, that there is no innate natural law. The only way to defend natural law would be by arguing that it is a set of principles that we come to know when we assess what actions are adequate to the nature of things. However, if one holds, like Ockham, that the law has nothing to do with the nature of things, then one cannot find laws that flow from the nature of things. A careful reading of the relevant passages of *An Essay Concerning Human Understanding* , book 1, chapter 3, allows us to conclude that this inference is applicable to John Locke as much as to William of Ockham. In fact, in § 12 the scope of Locke's arguments against innate principles of natural law clearly can be applied not only to innate principles, but to all natural laws. If there is disparity of laws in different countries, that means that no rule is natural:

> "parents, preserve your children," is so far from an innate truth, that it is no truth at all; it being a command, and not a proposition, and so not capable of truth or falsehood. To make it capable of being assented to as true, it must be reduced to some such proposition as this: "it is the duty of parents to preserve their children." But what duty is, cannot be understood without a law; nor a law be known, or supposed, without a law-maker, or without reward and punishment: so that it is impossible that this, or any other practical principle, should be innate; i. e. be imprinted on the mind as a duty, without supposing the ideas of God, of law, of obligation, of punishment, of a life after this, innate: For that punishment follows not, in this life, the breach of this rule; and consequently, that it has not the force of a law in countries,

[361] In the classical, Platonic and Aristotelian view, what is naturally right leads to our real happiness by its very nature. Sanctions only serve to help the young and the ill-educated to obey reason. See, in particular, *Nicomachean Ethics* 10.9.

where the generally allowed practice runs counter to it, is in itself evident.

Notice well that the argument encompasses the proposition "it is the duty of parents to preserve their children" both as an innate principle and as a learned principle. The same thing happens in §14, with the observation, "The difference there is amongst men in their practical principles, is so evident, that I think, I need say no more to evince, that it will be impossible to find any innate moral rules by this mark of general assent." No moral principle has a natural punishment that restrains men from violating the duties implied by that principle.

Even clearer is *Essay*, book 2, chapter 28, §5:

> Good and evil, as hath been shown, b. ii. chap. 20. § 2. And chap. 21. § 42. are nothing but pleasure or pain, or that which occasions or procures pleasure or pain to us. Moral good and evil then is only the conformity or disagreement of our voluntary actions to some law, whereby good or evil is drawn on us by the will and power of the law-maker; which good and evil, pleasure or pain, attending our observance, or breach of the law, by the decree of the law-maker, is that we call reward and punishment.

The situation in the state of nature is such, precisely, that there is no law, according to the *Second Treatise of Government*: "for the *law of nature* would, as all other laws that concern men in this world, be in vain, if there were no body that in the state of nature had a *power to execute* that law, and thereby preserve the innocent and restrain offenders" (§ 7). And, finally, nothing guarantees that in the state of nature the supposed "law of nature" could be enforced. Locke astutely postulates that "*in the state of nature every one has the executive power* of the law of nature." But he immediately shows how absurd that is and, therefore, how necessary the "civil state" (ibidem, § 13).[362] This is the reason why

[362] David Schindler presents both (a) the tensions existing between the letter of *An Essay Concerning Human Understanding* and the *Second Treatise of Government*, and (b) the debate existing among the scholars concerning the connections between the two works. He, very judiciously, concludes that "whatever Locke's own intentions may be, we will show in this chapter that the two texts are quite evidently compatible." *Freedom from Reality*, 382, note 2. And, more concretely, concerning the Lockean state of nature, he rightly concludes that, after many distractions in the presentation, "we [...] end up in a situation scarcely different from

Locke explicitly claims that the States are in their mutual relations in a state of war of all against all, in a state of nature (see chapter 12, § 145). That is to say, there is no valid law among them, because there is no sanction that guarantees or makes effective any duty.[363]

Hobbes: a state of nature as total war, which therefore necessarily gives rise to the social contract." Ibidem, 76.

[363] The clearest Lockean text in this regard is *An Essay Concerning Human Understanding* , book 2, chapter 28, §5, read along with book 1, chapter 1, §§ 5-13; and book 3, chapter 5. But he states the same thing less clearly in book 2 chapter 21, § 37. David C. Schindler (*Freedom from Reality,* 37-50) takes *The Reasonableness of Christianity as Delivered in Scripture* (London: C. And J. Rivington et al., 1824), 150, at face value to claim that, according to Locke, by the promises of rewards and the threats of punishment in the afterlife contained in natural and divine laws, we are really moved to veto some of our desires. We are moved in such way, according to Schindler, that our "freedom of the mind," and the conception of the will as a paradigmatic power depends entirely on this. This is a very subtle and ingenious interpretation of Locke (and in some points that I cannot expound here, correct), but, in my opinion, it does not reflect Locke's real mind. The reasons are the following: (1) Locke is explicit even in the last edition of the *Essays* in stating that those threats and promises do not move us; (2) the very structure of the state of nature, so essential for Locke's political philosophy and anthropology, depends on those promises and threats being ineffective. (3) In 41, 50 and 52 Schindler does not realize that, when Locke states that the determination of reason "abridges not the power wherein liberty consists," he is holding the definition of freedom that he has given previously in chapter 21 of book 2 of the *Essays*, not the concept that Schindler has formed in his mind of a will that is a power that moves itself, an "unmoved mover." The Lockean definition of freedom does not include the freedom of the will itself. (4) It is true that Locke asserts that the power of the will is the paradigm of power based on which we understand all other powers. But the point is that Locke will implicitly deny the existence of metaphysical powers. I think that Hume does nothing more than just to make explicit what is implicit in Locke, when he states that our will is the power through which we acquire the idea of all other powers, and then denies that there is any real power, including that of the will (see *Enquiry Concerning Human Understanding* [Oxford: Oxford University Press, 1999], I, 7). Locke and Hume reduce experience to sensation (and feeling). Since causal powers are sensible only *per accidens* (see Aristotle, *De anima* 3.1, 425a24-27, 30-b4; 3.4, 429b10-18; 3.8, 431b20-432a8; *Metaphysica* 1.1, 981a5-b6), Hume and Locke must conclude that causal powers are outside of our experience. (5) Finally, Schindler is aware that there is much deception in Locke's work, *The Reasonableness of Christianity*. Schindler, first, cites approvingly Michael Zuckert (376, note 93), who states that the defining characteristic of Locke's "way of writing" is "to give the [false] appearance of not straying too far from the classical tradition" (*Launching Liberalism. On Lockean Political Philosophy* [Lawrence, Kansas, University Press of Kansas, 2002], 187-197. Zuckert basically develops a Straussian reading of Locke). And then, second, Schindler states that *The Reasonableness of Christianity* "does not deny divine authority and the normative status of scripture," but "maintains that '*reason must be our last judge and guide in everything*" (376, note 99. Italics in the original).

The early *Essays on the Law of Nature* are different from the *An Essay Concerning Human Understanding* , but Locke never published them and his mature mind was fixed in the moral doctrines of the *An Essay Concerning Human Understanding* , not in the earlier *Essays on the Law of*

These observations confirm the connection that both John Lamont[364] and Francis Oakley[365] perceived between Locke and Ockham, the doctrines of both on *subjective rights* belong to the nominalist version. And they also demonstrate that Locke went beyond Ockham, of course, because, as noted, Ockham did think that the threats of afterlife punishment were sufficient to grant the existence of a divine, natural law.

Now, if this is so in the works by Locke, the only way to devise some kind of order according to the Lockean view is to build it by using the bricks that nominalism allows us to use. Such bricks are the "rights." That is why Locke must imply that the only canon and measure of political regimes are the rights nominalistically, individualistically

---

Nature. See Wolfgang von Leyden's Preface to John Locke, *Essays on the Laws of Nature* (Oxford: Clarendon Press, 1958), V-VII.

I am aware of the extensive controversy on these points but have chosen to base my argument on direct sources and on a philosopher who has reflected deeply on them and on the secondary literature (David Schindler). Anyways, the reader can find alternative interpretations, here: (1) Elliot Rossiter, "Hedonism, and Natural Law in Locke's Moral Philosophy," *Journal of the History of Philosophy*, 54/2 (2016): 203-226. This paper is very much based on the early and unpublished *Essays on the Law of Nature* and on its intended conclusion plus some Diary entries that were written years prior to the *An Essay Concerning Human Understanding* . It cites the latter work, of course, but overlooks the key point that Locke states in it: moral good is the pleasure derived from the rewards of actions offered by the legislator; and moral evil the pain derived from the punishment. Moreover, the rewards and punishments of the natural law efficaciously motivate neither to act nor to forbear from acting. (2) Adam Seagrave ("Locke on Natural Rights and Natural Law," in *The Foundation of Natural Morality* [Chicago: the University of Chicago Press, 2014], Chapter One, 27-51) purports to demonstrate that Locke harmonizes a morality based on natural law with a politics based on rights. In such task he, by the way, demolishes Brian Tierney's thesis according to which Locke's conception of *dominion* is in continuity with the main medieval tradition. However, the attempt to demonstrate the main thesis fails because Seagrave does not take sufficiently into account that Locke's mature conception of law requires an effective sanction and Locke denies that natural law possesses such sanction. I suspect that in reality Seagrave is instantiating an exercise of Straussian writing in layers of meaning. Indeed, after a painstaking apparent demonstration of the said thesis, he adds that "Locke's political philosophy [...] appears to begin and end with natural rights rather than the natural law." That is so because all societies are really concerned with natural rights instead of natural laws. In order to explain this, besides explicitly citing Strauss' interpretation of Locke approvingly, he uses two very typical Straussian categories: although natural laws are "nobler", rights are "more urgent." These categories appear in Leo Strauss, *Natural Right and History* (Chicago: University of Chicago Press, 1974), specially 142, 161 and 162-163.

[364] "In Defense of Villey on Objective Right," 184-185, in *Truth and Faith in Ethics* (Charlottesville: Virginia: Imprint Academy, 2011), 177-198.

[365] See *Natural Law, the Laws of Nature and Natural Rights* (London: Continuum, 2005), 94.

conceived.[366] This is, moreover, why Locke must hold, as he clearly held, that the courts cannot protect other rights than those derived from positive laws.[367]

These points appear undoubtedly in the Declaration or are derived immediately from its statements. However, the principles of the Declaration, although nominalist, exert an undeniable attraction over the spirit. Such attraction has seduced even so sober an author as Eric Voegelin—the apparent pretension of incorporating into the regime on an equal footing every last member of political society, so that the community represents itself and each one of its members through its authorities:

> [...] when articulation expands throughout society, the representative will also extend until the limit is reached where the membership of the society has become politically articulated down to the last individual and, correspondingly, the society becomes the representative of itself. [368]

In this chapter I am interested in examining the principles of the Declaration understood as the canon by which societies and political regimes were judged during at least two centuries. The first step will be to show the connection between the Declaration and some of the philosophical works that influenced it. The second will be to demonstrate that these "natural, inalienable and sacred rights" depend on a very peculiar conception of man and political society and are connected with particular political events. So much so that the rights appear not as universal, but as profoundly parochial. In particular, the separation of powers, parliamentary approval of taxes and the Rousseauian direct democracy will be considered. The third objective of this chapter is to unveil the subversive background of the notions of "liberty" and "equality" contained in the Declaration, connecting it to

---

[366] Felipe Widow made this observation in *Autonomía de la razón práctica y derecho subjetivo en la filosofía jurídica de John Finnis (Estudio crítico y confrontación con Tomás de Aquino)*. Doctoral dissertation submitted to the Faculty of Law of the Pontificia Universidad Católica de Chile, and approved on July 6, 2016, 368-75. John Lamont makes the same observation in "In defence of Villey on Objective Right," 183.

[367] See *Second Treatise of Government*, § 136.

[368] *The New Science of Politics* (Chicago: University of Chicago Press, 1952), 40, chap. 1, 5.

ancient tyrannical movements. The fourth will be to contrast this canon with some of the central tenets of classical political wisdom and to bring to light the originality of its lawlessness as rebellion against God.

We will use the reasoning and testimony of Abbé Augustine Barruel (1741–1820). The reasons to use them are the following: i) This French priest and essayist is an exceptional witness of the events that took place during the French Revolution or that prepared them; ii) his work allows us to perceive that he possessed great penetration and was quite honest; iii) this honesty was demonstrated by the confirmation of his testimony given by other contemporary witnesses and by his answers to objections; iv) the depth and extent of his studies put him in contact with important documents and witnesses on which he made excellent reports and which without him would have been lost.

Barruel's work has been little studied recently and his person has been subjected to severe criticism by some authors. However, the solidity of his research and argumentation is undeniable. As William Fanning states:

> The Freemasons of France, Germany and England angrily contested his assertions and a voluminous literature was the consequence. While some are of the opinion that Barruel's work attributes to the secret societies many evil deeds for which they are not responsible, all admit that his exposition of their [secret societies'] principles and the logical consequences flowing from them is the work of a powerful mind.[369]

Today, some authors, such as Elisa D'Annibale, accuse him of attributing to a Masonic-Luminist-Voltairean conspiracy what was due to the structural problems of "bourgeois society." Unfortunately, this author does not attend to a single one of Barruel's arguments and sources, but makes a summary and, perforce, superficial judgment. In fact, she makes serious errors even with regard to important aspects of Barruel's life and the chronology of his work.[370] She also claims that the

---

[369] William Fanning, "Agustín Barruel", *Catholic Encyclopedia* (New York: The Knights of Columbus' Catholic Truth Committee, 1913), volume 2, 310. I am aware that this source is old. But I have not found a better succinct presentation of this aspect of Barruel's work in English. The *New Catholic Encyclopedia* contains important historical mistakes concerning Barruel.

[370] Thus, for example, she describes him as a "Jesuit" (like almost all recent literature), when Barruel did not manage to formally enter the Society of Jesus. He wished to do so, and entered

argument with which Barruel proved that the Voltaireans manipulated public opinion in order to destroy the existing allegiance to God and to the monarchy is all based on the edition of the *Encyclopaedia*. This claim, however, is demonstrably false. In fact, a good part of Barruel's argumentation is based on the existence and activity of the D'Holbach Club, which D'Annibale completely overlooks.[371] In these pages we will not enter into this discussion and will use Barruel as a philosophical critic or as a witness to particular historical events, aspects of his work which the literature on the Abbé usually does not sufficiently address. Let us turn, then, to the matter we propose to study.

A final warning seems necessary first, however. This chapter is not an attempt to present a factual history of the French Revolution.[372] It is instead a philosophic-critical judgment on the sources that inspired the Declaration of Rights of Man and the Citizen. I do not claim that there is a direct connection between these sources and the horrors of revolution, because the free agents who committed such horrors could have acted in many different ways, even if they held the same views that they did. However, there is a connection between the fact of revolution and the ideas here examined in a different sense. *Ideas* are final, exemplary, and/or formal causes of actions. For example, the prevalence of a theory that denies any place to Aristotelian distributive justice (such as the postulate that all men are equal and equally free) is not the action of destroying non-arbitrary distinctions, but it is often a necessary presupposition. Augustine Barruel did an excellent job in

---

the Novitiate, but the Jesuits were expelled from France before he had professed any vows (see Jean-Joseph Dussault, "Notice sur la vie et les ouvrages d'Augustine de Barruel," pp. IV–V, in *Les Helvetiennes* [Paris, Librairie de la Société Typographique, 1823]). This is what explains why such a truthful man as he was speaks of the Jesuits as third persons in the very text of his *Memoirs Illustrating the History of Jacobinism* (see Barruel, *Memoirs Illustrating the History of Jacobinism*, *op. cit.*, Vol. II, 209). Another example of D'Annibale's inaccuracies is found in that, according to her, the *Memoirs* have five volumes (although she never cites the fifth), and the fourth was published in 1803, which is impossible, since the English translation of it appeared at the latest in New York in 1799 (see Barruel, *Memoirs Illustrating the History of Jacobinism* (New York: Isaac Collins, 1799), volume IV. Also, Elisa D'Annibale, "Memorie di un gesuita: Augustin Barruel e la teoria del complotto in Italia," in Gianluca Paoluci [ed.], *Illuminatismo tra Germania e Italia nel tardo Settecento* [Roma: Instituto Italiano di Studi Germanici, 2019], 139).

371 See Barruel, *Memoirs Illustrating the History of Jacobinism*, *op. cit.*, volume II, 87 ff.; and D'Annibale, "Memorie di un gesuita: Augustin Barruel e la teoria del complotto in Italia," *op. cit.*, 142–3.

372 For such a history, see Simon Schama, *Citizens: A Chronicle of the French Revolution* (New York: Alfred A. Knopf, 1989).

demonstrating the causal, though mediate, influence of ideas over revolutionary action. In this chapter we will try to confirm his philosophical insights with factual observations taken from Simon Schama's more recent historical study of the *French Revolution*. I think that to a reflective reader, this chapter will provide a new perspective to reconsider the facts described and told by pragmatic historians.

1. The Declaration of the Rights of Man and the works of John Locke, Charles de Montesquieu, and Jean-Jacques Rousseau

The Declaration of 1789[373] bears the imprint of Montesquieu and Rousseau and—through them—of John Locke. Voltaire, D'Argenson, Beccaria, and Helvetius, among others, had considerable influence as well. But we will focus on the first three authors, which are the most important sources for the Declaration, and on the most important articles that bear their imprint.

Article 1 states: "Men are born and remain free and equal in rights." We could understand this formula as standing partially in harmony with the Aristotelian notion of distributive justice,[374] if we read it as an affirmation (i) that no unjustified distinctions, no arbitrary discriminations, can be made among human beings; and (ii) that laws and commands must tend to meet the requirement of being rational and reasonable. This kind of reading of similar constitutional texts did become frequent in juridical doctrine and jurisprudence later and was adopted in the interpretation of the Fourteenth Amendment of the Constitution of the United States.[375] However, originally this is not what

[373] I have used the English text published on the web by the Avalon project of the Yale Law School, https://avalon.law.yale.edu/18th_century/rightsof.asp (date of consultation: November 7, 2023). I correct it in the light of the French text, published by the French Conseil Constitutionnel: https://www.conseil-constitutionnel.fr/le-bloc-de-constitutionnalite/declaration-des-droits-de-l-homme-et-du-citoyen-de-1789

[374] "[...] whenever equals receive unequal shares, or unequals equal shares, in a distribution, that is the source of quarrels and accusations." *Nicomachean Ethics* 5.3, 1131a23–24. (Indianapolis: Hackett Publishing Company, 1999.)

[375] The very text of the Fourteenth Amendment (see https://www.archives.gov/milestone-documents/14th-amendment) manifests a spirit profoundly different from the revolutionary spirit of the French declaration. I think that a careful reading of the Virginia Declaration of Rights of 1776 (see https://www.archives.gov/founding-docs/virginia-declaration-of-rights) also demonstrates much classical influence and much less influence from enlightened authors

was meant.[376] In order to unveil the exact original meaning, we must turn our attention to the works of both John Locke and Jean-Jacques Rousseau.

John Locke interpreted the classical qualities "free and equal" as existing in all men, and in a very particular way. "Free" would mean, in the state of nature, being subject to no power;[377] and in the civil state, being subject only to the laws given by the legislator constituted by the consent of the people understood as the total set of those subject to government.[378] In the family, Locke has to "confess" that young children are not equal,[379] but, he argues, the government over them exists exclusively in order that they can arrive at the state of equality as soon as possible. And, because of this,[380] as soon as they can fend for themselves, they are disengaged from all obedience to parents, *unless they wish to inherit them.*[381]

---

than the French declaration of 1789. Hannah Arendt perceives the deep difference between the mind of the US Founders and the French revolutionaries, and she states accurately what characterizes the case of the Founders: "[they] remained committed to the foundation of freedom and the establishment of lasting institutions, and to those who acted in this direction nothing was permitted that would have been outside the range of civil law"; moreover, they construed "the rule of government over the governed according to the age-old model of the rule of reason over passions." Finally, they understood their Constitution as a true Law, imposed over even the majority of the people due to its being an "embodiment of essential and unchanging justice." *On Revolution* (New York: The Viking Press, 1973), 87, 91 and 156 (with note 31, in 306). See also 104, 146–48, 152 and 163–64. One can see these traces of the mind of the Founding Fathers referred to by Yves Simon in his *The Philosophy of Democratic Government* (Notre Dame: University of Notre Dame Press, 2017), 149 and 169. The second clause of the same article 1 of the 1789 *Declaration* may receive very different interpretations as well: "Social distinctions may be founded only upon the common utility." "Utility" can be understood in a utilitarian way or can be reduced to the classical notion of the common good, or could be understood as the Rousseauian "general interest," or in many other ways.

376 Hannah Arendt perceives the novelty here very well, *On Revolution*, 33, 79 and 146–47. Simon Schama describes the festivals of the Supreme Being in which Robespierre appeared as founder of "freedom." See *Citizens*, 835.

377 See *Second Treatise of Government*, §§ 22, 54, 190.

378 See ibidem, §§ 22, 190.

379 See ibidem, § 55.

380 There is a further, deeper, reason: Locke claims that relations are fictional, that only substances, individuals and their powers are real. So, there is no filiation or paternity. There are only individual human beings, and, among them, some that are dependent on others for a while.

381 See ibidem, §§ 72–73, 191.

According to Rousseau in *The Social Contract*,[382] "man is born free and everywhere he is in chains";[383] or "every man being born free and master of himself, no-one, under any pretext whatsoever, can make any man subject without his consent."[384] In Book I, chapter 2, the phrase "all are born free and equal" appears literally. But in Book II, chapter 8, Rousseau gives the key definition for understanding "liberty" as understood in the Declaration of 1789: "the mere impulse of appetite is slavery, while obedience to a law which we prescribe to ourselves is liberty." This is why, according to chapter 7 of the same book, the citizen who does not obey the general will, the will of the legislator, will be forced to be free because only the citizen who surrenders to his country is safe from all dependence. This definition is made more explicit in Book IV, chapter 2: only he is free who obeys his own will; and this is possible because popular sovereignty is recognized, and the people constituted as legislator form the general will,[385] which is my own will as a citizen, the will from which the laws emanate.[386] Pierre Manent has demonstrated that this longing for equality and liberty, so understood, is precisely the inextinguishable revolutionary flame that Rousseau was to breathe into the West,[387] and that, by attempting to eliminate all private interest in order to produce the identification of all with the general interest [and by defining "virtue" as that

---

[382] Simon Schama implicitly acknowledges the influence of Rousseau on this kind of declaration: see his observations on Marivaux in *Citizens, A Chronicle of the French Revolution* (New York: Alfred A. Knopf, 1989), 108–9.

[383] See Book I, chapter 1.

[384] See Book IV, chapter 2. These citations demonstrate clearly that in the sources of the French revolutionaries, the existence of the 1789 *rights* is proclaimed as "independent of and outside of the body politic." Hannah Arendt, *On Revolution*, 147. David Schindler pervceived this fundamental problem quite lucidly. See *The Politics of the Real* (Steubenville, Ohio: New Polity Press, 2022), 117.

[385] Maritain gives a fine metaphysical explanation of Rousseau's "general will": "We might call it the myth of general pantheism. The *General Will* (which must not be confused with the sum of the individual wills) *is the Common Self's own will, born of the sacrifice each has made of himself and all his rights on the altar of the city*." See *Three Reformers* (London: Sheed and Ward, 1928), 134. He proceeds later to compare this General Will with the Will of God in Christian prayer: I ask for something, but submit to God's Will, because that is best for me. In a similar way, according to Rousseau, the General Will is my true will even if I voted against the will of the majority and such will is imposed upon me as the General Will (see 135).

[386] See, in a similar sense, Book II, Chapter 6.

[387] See Pierre Manent, *An Intellectual History of Liberalism* (Princeton: Princeton University Press, 1994), 74–79.

identification], Robespierre was striving to realize the Rousseauian ideal.[388]

These two doctrinal influences, not entirely compatible with each other, are what lead to the denial that men are free who live in a regime in which the government is not grounded on the consent of those subject to it. Such consent must be given either directly (as Rousseau demands) or through representatives (as is sufficient for Locke). These two doctrinal influences also lead to the abandonment of the important Roman distinction, consistent with Aristotelian principles, between persons *sui iuris* and *alieni iuris*; and to the assumption that every contract is just, because *volenti non fit iniuria*. This view will thus become the theoretical ground for justifying both the abusive labor contracts that the English Parliament had to modify through the labor laws promulgated during the nineteenth century, and the legalization of usury.[389]

Article 2 of the Declaration of 1789 states: "The aim of all political association is the preservation of the natural and imprescriptible rights of man. These rights are liberty, property, security, and resistance to oppression." It should be understood in connection with *Article 17*, which establishes that property is an inviolable and sacred right. Here the Declaration subscribes to the Lockean view of the civil state, which denies that the main purpose of political society is cooperation to turn life possible through the division of labor, and to turn life good through the exercise of virtue. *Article 3* enshrines popular sovereignty, although it does not speak of the people, but of the nation as being sovereign, which is a vocabulary more Rousseauian[390] than Lockean.

Articles 4 and 5 are corollaries of the acceptance of Lockean views, perhaps complemented by Montesquieu's and Beccaria's observations on the principle of legality in criminal law ("*nullum crimen,*

---

[388] *Ibid.*, 75. In similar sense, see Hannah Arendt, *On Revolution*, 74.

[389] As Pierre Manent notes, Rousseau, in fact, sees the rise of the state (according to Lockean theory) as the protection of the property of the rich with the force of the poor (see *An Intellectual History of Liberalism*, *op. cit.*, 76).

[390] See *Social Contract*, Book I, chapter 4.

nulla poena, sine lege"), on the reasons that ground the justice of diverse punishments and on the just proportionality of any punishment.

Article 6 states: "Law is the expression of the general will. Every citizen has a right to participate personally, or through his representative, in its foundation." This article is mainly of Rousseauian descent, but the acceptance of representatives is closer to Locke or Montesquieu than to Rousseau. In any case, it presupposes the reception of the doctrine of popular sovereignty and implies that the majority of the governments existing in 1789 were supposedly illegitimate.

Articles 7, 8 and *9* have aspects of classical ancestry, and others come from Beccaria or Montesquieu, or even Rousseau, but we will leave them aside now. Articles 10 and 11 establish freedom of religion, freedom of opinion, and freedom of the press, and we will leave them aside as well. *Articles 12, 13*, and *15* are of Lockean descent, and their analysis would add nothing to the analysis of article 2 regarding the philosophical roots of the Declaration.

Article 14 expressly establishes that taxes cannot be just if they are not approved by the body of citizens or their representatives. This requirement existed in ancient Christian-Latin law, but was exacerbated by the main revolutionary writers during the eighteenth century, and is the subject of an interesting analysis by Augustine Barruel. For this reason, we will examine it briefly below.

Article 16 holds that a society that does not establish the separation of powers has no Constitution—that is, it is subject to despotic government. This aspect of the Declaration comes from Montesquieu (and contradicts Rousseau) and has also been subjected to a fine analysis by Barruel. Montesquieu embraced the dream of "political science" that aspires to supersede political philosophy[391]—

[391] This transition to "social science" in Montesquieu was also perceived by Durkheim, although he interpreted it in a very different way. See Émile Durkheim, *Montesquieu and Rousseau, Forerunners of Sociology* (Ann Arbor: University of Michigan Press, 1960), 51–57. Pierre Manent points out that Montesquieu was the first to consider power as a thing (see Manent, *An Intellectual History of Liberalism*, *op. cit.*, 55). Eric Voegelin, in his study of Helvetius, characterizes this transition excellently: "the growth of the soul which is nourished through communication with transcendental reality is replaced by the formation of conduct through

that is, the hope of achieving a perfect system, which does not require men to be good. The main passages of *The Spirit of the Laws*[392] in which the presence of this dream may be perceived are the following:

Where one power does not restrain the other, there is despotism.[393]

For there to be political freedom, government must be so constituted that no man need fear being oppressed by another man. This fear can only disappear if the legislative, executive, and judicial powers are clearly separated.[394] Thus, for example, "there would be an end of every thing, were the same man, or the same body, whether of the nobles or of the people, to exercise those three powers";[395] and "if there were no monarch, and the executive power should be committed to a certain number of persons, selected from the legislative body, there would be an end of liberty, by reason the two powers would be united."[396] It is very symptomatic that the chapter in which this appears is entitled "The Constitution of England."

But the aforementioned separation is necessary by the very nature of things, states Montesquieu. And here is the central passage, which places this author at a great distance from all classical and scholastic wisdom:[397]

> Political liberty is to be found only in moderate governments; and even in these it is not always found. It is there only when there is no abuse of power: but constant experience shows us that every

---

external management." Eric Voegelin, *From Enlightenment to Revolution* (Durham: Duke University Press, 1977), 70.

392 In Montesquieu, *The Complete Works of Montesquieu* (London: Evans and Davis, 1777), vol. 1.

393 See Book V, Chapter 14, 80.

394 See Book XI, Chapter 6, 198 ff. Montesquieu is here under strong Lockean influence, just as in Book I, Chapter 3, in the passage where he claims both that men cannot live in society without some kind of external constraint, and that they transition from the state of war to the political state, which is where laws have force. G. Klosko does not perceive this point. See 167–168 of his "Montesquieu's Science of Politics: Absolute Values and Ethical Relativism in *L'Esprit des lois*," *Studies on Voltaire and the Eighteenth Century*, 189 (1980): 153–77. Klosko's texts is transcribed in David Carrithers (ed.), *Charles-Louis de Secondat, Baron de Montesquieu* (New York: Routledge, 2009), 159–83.

395 Montesquieu, *The Spirit of the Laws*, 199.

396 *The Spirit of the Laws*, 205.

397 Montesquieu here is distancing himself from all the scholastic tradition, including the nominalist one.

man invested with power is apt to abuse it, and to carry his authority as far as it will go. Is it not strange, though true, to say that virtue itself has need of limits? To prevent this abuse, it is necessary, *from the very nature of things, power should be a check to power.* A government may be so constituted that no man shall be compelled to do things to which the law does not oblige him, nor forced to abstain from things which the law permits.[398]

According to these passages, all the governments existing at the time when Montesquieu wrote, except England, were despotic and in them liberty had met its end.[399] But a few decades later, English liberty too would have met its end, for, as is well known, at least since the time of the Pitts, the English Executive is effectively an emanation of Parliament.[400] This observation takes us gently to the next step of this work.

---

[398] Book XI, Chapter 4, 197. I added the italics.

[399] Daniel Mansuy perceives that, in *The Spirit of the Laws*, Montesquieu uses three different criteria when evaluating political societies: the kinds of regime, which is a criterion of classical origin strongly modified by Montesquieu; moderation or lack of moderation; and liberty or lack of liberty. But, curiously, unlike D'Alambert, Mansuy seems not to realize that part of the display of these criteria intends to conceal the true meaning of the work. On pages 262–3, for example, Mansuy states that Montesquieu sharply differentiates monarchy from despotism, and does not point out that this could be a rhetorical device to conceal the true meaning of the work, so as to being able to publish it in France (Daniel Mansuy, "Liberalismo y regímenes políticos: el aporte de Montesquieu," *Revista Internacional de Pensamiento Político* I Época, 10 (2015): 255–71). Yet, in note 29 he states that "in later developments Montesquieu will greatly qualify the supposedly radical distinction between monarchy and despotism." In the latter sense, see also 265.

[400] Already in *The Federalist* (Indianapolis: Liberty Fund, 2001) Madison made similar observations. See No. 47, 250 ff. Pierre Manent explains that this happened because the principle of legitimacy based on popular sovereignty ends up being imposed in such measure that it abolished all or almost all counterweight emanating from the monarchical principle (see Manent, *An Intellectual History of Liberalism*, *op. cit.*, 54–5). But he tries to save the "spirit" of Montesquieu's liberalism, which supposedly offers us a "state of satisfaction," arguing that the dynamic vision of the division of powers that appears in book XIX, chapter 27, allows to transfer the separation of powers between the executive and the legislative powers to the peaceful coexistence within the legislature of the political parties of government and opposition. According to him, this opposition would turn the compromise between the parties into the true sovereignty within the liberal system, which can be classified as a "state of nature [because there is no real coexistence or cooperation], but safe" (54–5 and 61–4). This conception would not be able to withstand the Marxist critique, because it is simply blind to the true nature of political societies. There is an effective cooperation for a common good, which consists in the good life, even if Manent does not perceive it. If England has been able to survive up to this moment in the face of the Marxist onslaught, it was because the classical and Christian tradition, which is conscious of this cooperation, was still alive and inspired the

2. The parochial character of part of the Declaration of the Rights of Man or of its sources: the separation of powers, parliamentary approval of taxes, and Rousseau's direct democracy.

It is not possible in this section to make a complete philosophical critique of these enlightened "principles." I wish to limit myself in this section, with the help of Abbé Augustine Barruel, to showing their "parochial" character; that is to say that they are, on the one hand, conceived in the light of particular societies and political regimes and, yet, on the other hand, postulated as the universal measure of humanity. In this respect, they also present a considerable contrast with classical political theory, which is classical precisely because it has endeavored to discover the permanent measure which underlies all particular regimes or societies as much as they are true to their nature.[401] The nominalist version of subjective rights cannot grasp the permanent measure because such measure is immersed in the essential nature of things, which the nominalist rejects. I shall confine myself to studying three points: a) the parochialism behind the demand for separation of powers; b) the parochialism behind the demand that taxes be approved by Parliament; and c) the Rousseauian parochialism of demanding direct democracy.

a) It is known that Locke wrote his treatises on government to refute Robert Filmer and to promote and justify the so-called Glorious Revolution. Many of the arguments in the *Second Treatise* are aimed at undermining the legitimacy of James II, the last English Catholic king, and justifying a parliamentary rebellion. Similarly, much of what Charles de Montesquieu intends to do in his work *The Spirit of the Laws* is to propose the English constitution resulting from that revolution as a model for all mankind, as the paradigm to which all must conform

reaction of Michael Thomas Sadler and Lord Ashley. See André Maurois, *A History of England* (London, Jonathan Cape LTD., 1937), 437-441.

[401] One must keep in mind that the Platonic-Aristotelian reflection on politics is not limited to the Greek *polis*, although, of course, it starts from the observation and experience of the *polis*, because it was there that their earliest immediate experience was constituted. But they also studied the Persian Empire, the Macedonian kingdom, the Carthaginian republic, Egyptian society and other forms such as the Thracian and Scythian.

through revolutionary action. I would like to illustrate this second point with some brief but very relevant reflections by Augustine Barruel.

The abbé notes that Montesquieu wants to adopt the English system of division of powers. He observes that such a system was proper to a nation enjoying, perhaps, a "boisterous liberty," "more celebrated for its civil broils in quest of liberty, than for the wisdom of its constitution, which, at length fixing every mind and every heart, had scarcely terminated a long struggle between the Monarch and the People." (The Glorious Revolution took place in 1688, and Montesquieu was writing *The Spirit of the Laws* in the 1740s.) Barruel adds:

> Without doubt we may admire, as much as Montesquieu, the wisdom of that nation that has known to model its laws according to the experience it had acquired during those struggles. Laws, indeed, congenial to the manners that characterized it, to its local situation, and even to its prejudices. But is that constitution, the most perfect perhaps existing for a nation surrounded by the ocean, to be equally perfect when transplanted to a continental State? [...] Are men, so heterogeneous in their characters, men that may be viewed from so many different points, are they, in order to attain happiness and freedom, to be reduced to one only mode of government? No; it would have been madness to adopt the English constitution in France.[402]

Further on, Barruel points out that Montesquieu's discourse is an incitement to rebellion in most republics where, as he himself notes, the powers are not separated according to the principles laid down in his work:

> The whole universe was then in a state of slavery, and Montesquieu was the apostle sent to teach men to break their chains, chains so light that few were even sensible of their existence! A general revolution was then necessary, that mankind might assert its liberty![403]

[402] Barruel, *Memoirs Illustrating the History of Jacobinism*, *op. cit.*, volume II, chapter 2, 39.
[403] *Ibid.*, 40.

It is not obvious that the legislative and executive powers should be separated, and rather there are good reasons to think of the inexpediency of this separation.[404] However, as Rousseau well understood,[405] once both popular sovereignty and self-government are postulated as the only legitimate form of government, the separation becomes a necessity. For the necessity of magistrates or rulers is something that does not escape even some of the most ideologized visions (aside from the anarchists). The way to defend that government could be self-government was to declare that those magistrates had to submit to the laws imposed upon them by the sovereign people,[406] either gathered in assembly, as Rousseau wanted, or through representatives, as Locke and Montesquieu proposed.[407]

Note in any case that, although contemporary constitutionalism reveres the principle of separation of powers, the way in which Montesquieu conceived it in *The Spirit of the Laws*—a clear separation between the legislative and executive powers—is ignored today by England or Canada, for example, which does not imply that freedom cannot exist today in those countries. We could make the same point regarding all the regimes existing in the middle of the eighteenth century, none of which was organized in accordance with that principle, with the exception of the England of that time.[408] This reflection is

[404] In fact, it has been a long time since the executive started invading the legislative power by issuing all sorts of regulations on the most diverse matters and by being the origin of most of the projects that the so-called legislative power passes as laws.

[405] See *The Social Contract*, Book III, chapter 15.

[406] This point is acutely observed by Durkheim in his *Montesquieu and Rousseau*, *op. cit.*, 116–118 and 123 ff. David Schindler finds this point already in Locke: see *Freedom from Reality*, 108.

[407] This claim that political liberty demands that government be self-government is clear in Montesquieu. That David Lowenthal does not perceive that this very claim is the dividing barrier between Montesquieu, on the one hand, and the classics, on the other, is surprising. See "Montesquieu and the Classics: Republican Government and *The Spirit of the Laws*," in Joseph Cropsey (ed.), *Ancients and Moderns. An Essay Concerning the Tradition of Political Philosophy in Honor of Leo Strauss* (New York: Basic Books, 1964), 258–287. (Transcribed in David Carrithers [ed.], *op. cit.*, 187–216). Disinterested knowledge of truth is paramount in order to have good government. This knowledge alone, according to the classics, is capable of showing to reason the divine rule or measure, subject to which alone, law can be the guarantee of true political liberty. Thus, truth, and not an impossible self-government, is the source of political freedom.

[408] Madison in *The Federalist*, n. 47, 250-254, demonstrates that not even England at the time conformed to a strict separation of powers. These pages contain a subtle critique of Montesquieu and demonstrate that his principles must be adapted to political experience because otherwise they are just utopian.

enough for me in the present context to confirm that Montesquieu's work is parochial, as I have explained.

Rousseau's work contains a strange paradox, to which I must briefly attend to avoid a possible objection: According to Rousseau, the sovereign people must give themselves the laws, because the source of legitimacy is the will of those subject to government. However, Rousseau stated that it is possible for a law established by the vote of the majority of the members of the sovereign people to be illegitimate, because, supposedly, there is a general interest at which the will of the sovereign people must aim, and the majority could deviate from that interest (interest that is identified with "the general will"). It would seem, then, that knowledge about the good, the general interest, should be the source of the law's legitimacy, and not the will of the majority of the sovereign people. But Rousseau does not draw this consequence. One might wonder why.

I think the reason above all is because his "general interest" is not the same as the common good of the classics. Indeed, the common good of the classics, on the one hand, is identical with happiness [*eudaimonía*], which they identified in turn with acting in accordance with virtue. Acting in accordance with virtue is nothing else but acting in accordance with the order that the truth about the good produces in love, in actions and in character. On the other hand, according to Rousseau, virtue is nothing but the conformity of the individual will to the general will; and truly the voice of the people is the voice of God.[409] There is no place for practical knowledge in the classical sense (the truth about the good), nor, therefore, for a legitimacy founded on anything other than a "will" of the people, real or hypothetical.[410] In

---

[409] See Jean-Jacques Rousseau, *Le citoyen ou Discours sur l'economie politique* (Geneva: 1756), 14 and 27.

[410] All that refers to Rousseau in the last two paragraphs is very well presented by Emile Durkheim in *Montesquieu and Rousseau*, *op. cit.*, 92–234.

Jason Canon has tried to solve the paradox with which we deal in the last two paragraphs, the connection between the general interest or common good, on the one hand, and the general will, on the other. It seems to me, however, that he does not clearly perceive the deepest tension, which is the appearance of postulating a real knowledge of the good while at the same time emphatically postulating a voluntarist thesis. Canon rightly points out that Rousseau holds that the good is unknowable by the individual man (358), that in the *Social Contract* Rousseau suppresses any reference to a rational natural Right or to an objective law (360, 362, 367), that in the same work he rejects all epistemic authorities (362), but then adds that each citizen must "discern" within himself what pertains to his private will from what pertains to

other words, the "general interest" is not an order present in the reality of being, but whatever the hypothetical "general [revolutionary] will" commands.

That the judiciary should be separate from government is a proposition more susceptible of being defended and embraced with success as it was in the Constitution of the United States.[411] But Barruel shows at some length why this is not a necessary condition for there to be a good administration of justice. What is necessary in a monarchy, says Barruel, is that the monarch should not be both judge and party,[412] and that he should not violate customary forms. But in France, these principles were observed because it was recognized that the monarch was subject to the law of nature, which forbids him to be a judge in his own case. Moreover, a case could be brought against the king before the courts, and it was recognized that the monarch was bound by the laws, as were his subjects. "Hence nothing could ever have made the French unite the idea of despotism to that of a monarch the judge of his subjects." And he adds, "what constituted the despotic power of the Sultan was [not the lack of separation of powers, but] the power of capriciously and instantaneously pronouncing on all points, following no other guide but his passion and his momentary interest."[413]

Barruel does not go into political-constitutional details, but I suspect that something analogous to what Palacios Rubios said about the Spanish monarchy could be said about the French monarchy: one

---

his "general will" (363 ff.). And then Canon further adds that, although this discernment has some epistemic conditions, they have nothing to do with knowledge but with the "good organization" of society (364). He fails to see the circle there and the danger it entails. See "The General Wills in Rousseau," *The Review of Politics* 84 (2022): 350-371. Fernando Atria has perceived this point in Rousseau's thought and has tried to use it to promote a radical revolution in Chile, radical revolution that is precisely the danger I am referring to. See "La Verdad y lo político II. Democracia y ley natural," 59-64, *Persona y Sociedad* XXIII/2 (2009): 35-64. Atria holds there that if the decisions made by majority rule after public deliberation are perceived as radically unjust, then the right course of action would have to be not to persuade the people about the injustice of their decisions, but to promote a radical revolution that changes the whole structure of social relations, so that a good social organization can be established in which the majority conforms to the authentic general will, and the authentic general will becomes law.

[411] See Alexander Hamilton, *The Federalist*, n. 78, 402–408.

[412] Simon Schama points out the independence of the courts or *parlements* in the *ancient régime*. See *Citizens*, 105.

[413] See Barruel, *Memoirs Illustrating the History of Jacobinism*, *op. cit.*, volume II, 41–43.

thing is the king and another the Crown. The Crown is the republic, what Palacios himself called "the kingdom" and we call the state.[414] And, we could ask, additionally, is a fundamental principle of justice by any chance violated because the state has the three powers, executive, legislative, and judicial? The Crown was the center of legality and activity in France, but the king, unlike Rousseau's sovereign, was bound by divine law, natural law, and the laws of the realm.

b) Another area in which the parochialism of the *enlightened* authors can be noted is in their postulate that every tax or public burden must receive the consent of the subjects in Parliament to be just. Barruel masterfully shows that such a demand is but a residue of that feudalism which the *enlightened* authors claim to hate. Orestes Brownson rightly directs a similar but more general accusation against John Locke.[415] But let us limit ourselves here to the point made by Barruel:

> Mably and his disciples, or more properly the adherents of Montesquieu, detested the feudal laws; but they did not reflect that it was to those very laws the States General owed their former existence. When Philip Le Bel and some other Princes had found themselves under the necessity of applying to those

[414] Alfredo Cruz Prados, based on J. H. Elliot, cites Palacios Rubios as follows: "the king is entrusted only with the administration of the kingdom, but not with the dominion over things, because the goods and rights of the State are public and cannot be the private patrimony of anyone" (Alfredo Cruz Prados, *Ethos y polis* [Pamplona: Eunsa, 1999], 310). The quotation is taken, in a mediate way, from José Cepeda Adán, *En torno al concepto del Estado en los Reyes Católicos*, and supposedly comes from the *De donationibus*. However, the original does not say this exactly, but rather: "the king has been entrusted with the sole administration, not the ownership of things, as is said in the Gloss [...] because the goods and rights of the kingdoms are public and, therefore, are not in anyone's patrimony [*in nullius bonis sunt* ...]. 'King' [*rex*] is said for 'rule' [*regere*], because he must rule the things and rights of the kingdom [...]." And then he continues: "Therefore, if he rules badly, he already loses the name of 'king' [...], he is called a tyrant rather than a king [...]. And, therefore, if he does not rule well, the subjects are no longer obliged to render their services" (see Juan de López y Palacios Rubios, *Commentaria et Repetitio in rubricam et Cap. Per vestras, de donationibus inter virum et uxorem*, in *Opera varia* [Antwerp: Ioannem Keerbergium, 1616], 1–468, 334). A little earlier, in the same place, a doctrine even closer to that of the text is held: "*loca et iura regni non sunt regis, sed dignitatis regalis.*" An analogous doctrine can be inferred from other passages of the same work, which came either from the pen of Palacios Rubios or from that of Juan Bernardo Díaz de Luco. Thus, for example, it is held there that the force of law emanates from the king's chest (insofar as he represents the Crown or the republic, I interpret), but that in contracts the king acts as a private person and must, therefore, be subject to them (see 210, column 2; and 211, column 1).
[415] See *The American Republic* (New York: P. O'Shea, 1865), chap. 4.

> States for subsidies, the reason was, because under the feudal system the King, like the Counts of Provence, Champagne, and Toulouse, or the Dukes of Brittany, had their fixed revenues and particular desmenes which were supposed to suffice for the exigencies of the state. And in fact wars of the longest duration could be carried on without it being necessary to augment the revenues of the Sovereign. Armies at that time were composed of the Lords and Knights serving at their own expence and, defraying that of their vassals whom they led after them into the field. Neither Mably nor his disciples would reflect that at a period when France had acquired so many new Provinces, when the armies, general officers, and soldiers, waged war solely at the King's expence, it was impossible for the ancient crown lands to supply the wants of Government. They could not conceive, that in the new system of politics, it would have been the height of imprudence for the Monarch in France to be dependent (every time he found it necessary to repel or anticipate an attack of the foreign enemy) on the great and jealous Lord, on the seditious tribune, or on the surly deputy, perhaps even in the interest of the enemy, for the necessary subsidies on so pressing an occasion. Such reflections as these never occurred to the minds of our Sophisters.[416]

c) I would like to end by pointing out an aspect that is perhaps not as well-known as the previous ones. Just as Montesquieu adopted the post-revolutionary pre-Pitt England as the universal rule to measure humanity, Rousseau transferred the rule to his beloved Geneva.[417] According to the Genevan author, representation is the end

[416] Augustine Barruel, *Memoirs Illustrating the History of Jacobinism*, volume II, chap. 7, 124. "Sophisters" is how Barruel called the *enlightened* authors, especially those of the school of Voltaire. Under the dynasty of the Austrias, the Spanish "confederation" of Castile and Aragon had enormous difficulties to fund the wars required for the Spanish attempt to preserve the ancient order of Christendom due to the need of approval of the taxes by the *Cortes* of Aragon, Barcelona and Valencia. In the United States this was solved by eliminating the need that the States' legislatures approve of all new taxes or contributions to the federal government. See *The Federalist* (Indianapolis, Liberty Fund: 2001), n. 30, 147; n. 34, 164, and by creating the National Bank. See Alexander Hamilton, *Report on the National Bank*. In *Official Reports on Public Credit, National Bank, Manufactures and a Mint* (Philadelphia: William McKean, 1821), 59-110.

[417] See *The Social Contract*, Book IV, Chapter 1. In this sense, see Emile Durkheim, *Montesquieu and Rousseau*, 120.

of the sovereignty of the people,[418] and, therefore, the ideal is for the republic to be a city-state or, at most, a confederation of city-states without a fixed capital, in which the people gathered in assembly exercise their sovereignty.[419]

3. The subversive and anomic [lawless] character of the notions of "equality" and "liberty" contained in the Declaration of the Rights of Man of 1789

From the vision that Augustine Barruel gives us, it can be stated that the Declaration of the Rights of Man of 1789, with the ideologies that inspire it, was originally above all a subversive weapon, similar to that of the partisans of Greek tyranny, who used slaves to destroy constitutions. Let us examine, for this purpose, if only briefly, the examples given by Barruel of the application, *prior* to the French Revolution, of the principles of ideological liberty and equality. The first and perhaps most interesting example was that of the revolutionary agitation carried out by Voltaire in poor Geneva, the homeland of Rousseau.

In this republic established by Calvin there were four classes of inhabitants: the citizens who had a vote in the General Council and could be magistrates; the natives; the simple inhabitants; and the subjects. All of them were protected by the republic and enjoyed a quiet and prosperous life. There were no major disputes or rifts. But the faith in Christ was in crisis there and, partly because of that, and partly because of the proximity to Ferney, Voltaire's lair, the ideologues chose it to test the establishment of their new "liberty and equality."

As Barruel states verbatim in a passage of his *Mémoires pour servir à l'histoire du jacobinisme*:

> However odious such distinctions [between the four classes of inhabitants of Geneva] may have appeared to the Sophisters, nevertheless the man who appeals to sound judgment and real principles will easily agree, that a Republic, or any State enjoying Sovereignty, has a right to admit new inhabitants on

[418] In the 15th chapter of Book III of *The Social Contract* Rousseau states: "sovereignty is not susceptible of representation."
[419] See Jean-Jacques Rousseau. *The Social Contract*, book III, chaps. 12, 13, 15.

> certain conditions which may be just and oftentimes necessary, without establishing on that account a perfect equality between the real and the adoptive children of the State. He who asks to be admitted knows the conditions of his admission, and the exceptions he is exposed to. He was perfectly free to accept, to refuse, or to seek an asylum elsewhere; but certainly, having once accepted and admitted of these exceptions, he has no farther right to create disturbances in the Republic, on pretence that, all men being equal, the adoptive child is entitled to the same privileges as the ancient children of the State.[420]

Barruel adds that he has not been able to find

> [...] what species of oppression the people of Geneva suffered under their magistrates; I have found that it was not possible for a people to be more fondly or more justly attached to their government; that the union between the magistrates and the subjects resembled that of a numerous family with its Chiefs. The Sophisters knew this too well [...]. They presupposed discord, that they might create it where it did not exist, and add to it where it already began to spread.[421]

The *philosophes*, then, according to Barruel, possessed neither a serene judgment nor true principles. What mattered to them was not justice, nor human dignity, but the anomie that threw political power into their hands. That is why they caused a bloody revolution in Geneva, which was extinguished in 1782 by French troops, but which was consummated once France itself was bathed in its own blood under Robespierre.[422]

After having shown the deleterious effects of Voltairean ideologies on a republic, Barruel goes on to show their effects on Bohemia and Transylvania. Both cases are interesting for different reasons.

In Bohemia, the agents of the *philosophes* first attempted a revolution by the simple expedient of infiltrating thousands of armed

---

[420] Barruel, *Memoirs Illustrating the History of Jacobinism*, Vol. 2, chap. 6, 113–114.
[421] *Memoirs Illustrating the History of Jacobinism*, Vol. 2, 21, note.
[422] *Memoirs Illustrating the History of Jacobinism*, Vol. 2, 122.

men, and then stirring up the masses against the nobles by means of inflammatory rhetoric. One of the interesting things about Barruel's narrative is that it shows that the political regime in Bohemia, although to all appearances despotic, was actually quite humane. Let us transcribe a brief passage:

> [It is easy to imagine that such inflammatory rhetoric] must have made a strong impression on men who, for the greatest part, cultivated lands which they only held at the pleasure of the Lord, in consideration of so many days' work every week, employed in the culture of the Lord's lands. [...] It was [...] difficult for the traveller accustomed to other governments not to be persuaded, that these men were very unhappy. I was of that opinion, when an unexpected light nearly reconciled me to that mode of administration. It was an immense granary belonging to the Lord. In the middle of a large hall were vast heaps of corn; around the place as many divisions as there were families in the village, and each division contained the corn belonging to one family. An overseer attended at the distributions, which were made once a week. If the stock of any particular division was exhausted, the necessary quantity was taken from the Lord's heap for the family in need, who were to replace the corn so taken at the ensuing harvest. By this means the poorest peasant was certain of his sustenance. Let the reader decide, whether such a government may not be as good as others, where the poor man may often starve in the possession of perfect Liberty. I know what might be wished for under every administration; but it is not the part of true Philosophy to overthrow existing governments in the chimerical idea of reducing, some day or other, every thing to its own plans.[423]

They failed the first time but, later, the same ideologues tried a much more subtle method, and succeeded in deceiving even Empress Maria Theresa and Joseph II. It was a kind of "agrarian reform" which would transfer idle, uncultivated land to the most industrious peasants. Everything was covered with a cloak of justice and moderation that concealed the real purpose of disorder, anarchy, and destruction of the

[423] *Memoirs Illustrating the History of Jacobinism*, Vol. 2, ch. 8, 134–5.

existing elites.[424] But this time the revolutionaries again failed in Bohemia, because the empress, along with her neighbor King Frederick II, realized the true purpose in time and acted with great energy to punish the rebels in an exemplary manner.

However, under Joseph II, a new scheme did work in Transylvania. I will not narrate here the details of the fraudulent scheme, but only the results presented by Barruel, guided by the authors of the memorials on which his narrative is based:

> Among the castles which were reduced to ashes the most remarkable were those of the Counts D'Esterhazy and Tekeli; and of the Noblemen who were murdered the most distinguished were the two Counts and Brothers Rebiezi. The eldest was spitted and roasted; many others of the same family, men, women and children, were cruelly massacred. The unfortunate Lady Bradisador, with whom I had spent a few days (says Mr. Petty) also fell a melancholy victim. —These barbarians seized her, cut off her hands and feet, and then left her to linger in that state till she expired.[425]

Barruel then connects these scenes with some of the most horrible scenes of the French Revolution, such as the one in *Place Dauphine*, on September 3, 1792, in which women were being killed, and their roasted meat was given as food to the victims who would later suffer the same fate.

In the face of all these aberrations, Barruel concludes:

> These statements I know will make my reader shudder with horror, but it is a salutary tremor. At length perhaps they will cease to hearken to those Sophistical Apostles of an Equality and Liberty less chimerical than atrocious, and whose systems assimilate man to the ferocious beasts of the forest. The error

---

[424] Simon Schama adds an interesting observation to Barruel's: Beaumarchais and his *Marriage of Figaro* were two powerful symptoms and causes of the rebellion of the masses against the nobles and against all social hierarchy, despite the existence of wide social mobility in eighteenth century France. See *Citizens*, 140-4.

[425] *Memoirs Illustrating the History of Jacobinism*, Vol. 2, ch. 8, 140–1.

is too fatal; let us therefore guard against the delusions of pride by the remembrance of deeds humiliating to nature itself.[426]

What underlies all these examples is the rejection of what the Greeks called geometric or proportional equality (distributive justice), and of the political wisdom drawn from experience and capable of ordering the most diverse regimes to justice and the common good. The rejection of due hierarchy and degree, which are necessary in every society and which are good as long as they stay within due proportion.

To achieve a better and deeper understanding of what we have been saying, we will proceed to establish a clear contrast with the classics' conception of the end and canon of a just society.

4. Contrast between the Declaration and the classics

As is well known, the classics teach that the end of action is the principle of practical knowledge, that the purpose of the political community is the common good consisting in happiness—that is, a life according to virtue, both of the individual and of society as a whole. That the city should be happy translates into the concretization of two things, civic friendship and justice, both general and particular: a government and legislation that are ordered to total virtue and that respect equality, both proportional in distributions and arithmetical in transactions. From here are drawn the canons by which political regimes and societies are assessed.

Chapter 6 of Book 5 of the *Nicomachean Ethics* is perhaps the passage in which the essential criteria for the assessment of political regimes and societies are condensed in the most summary and clearest way.[427] In reviewing this passage, we should keep in mind that Aristotle has repeatedly stated that in political matters, because they are always practical and their measure is concrete, theory can only establish

---

[426] *Memoirs Illustrating the History of Jacobinism*, Vol. 2, ch. 8, 142. He then goes on to show the carnage caused by the previous systems of freedom and equality, those of the Cathar heretics, Waldensians, Albigensians, Hussites, etc., who in the 11th-16th centuries bathed Europe in human blood.

[427] Aristotle, *Ethica Nicomachea* (Oxford: Oxford University Press, 1962). I will use the English translation by Irwin, published by Hackett, already cited.

outlines as guidance for action, and can never rightly dictate minute prescriptions as to the best course to be taken in the infinite variety of situations that a political agent must face. With this in mind, let us review this chapter.

According to Aristotle, in the well-ordered city there is political justice and there is domestic justice, because not all members of society are free and equal like the Roman *patres familias*. The Modern authors who claimed to be enlightened denied this distinction and, in doing so, gave rise to many disorders and unjust situations, such as considering in the first part of the nineteenth century that labor contracts were always fair, regardless of schedules, wages, working conditions, (i) because the workers, who were free and equal, consented to such contracts and (ii) by application of the principle *volenti non fit injuria.* As is well known, the English Parliament, persuaded by Michael Thomas Sadler and Lord Ashley, returned to classical wisdom on this point and gave birth to Labor Law which, abandoning the Enlightenment's assertion of total equality in freedom of self-determination, recognized that workers were not free in entering into labor contracts, nor equal, that an inequality of bargaining power between employer and employee existed.[428]

But political justice exists between free and equal people, and not all people are so. This equality, moreover, may not be arithmetical, but only proportional. The measure or rule or canon of proportionality will vary from regime to regime, but it should not be forgotten that there is no universal "best regime" to be adopted by all societies. There is, yes, a "best regime" as a standard concept or canon of judgment, as seen in chapter 7 of the same book 5 of the *Nicomachean Ethics* (1135a4–5), as a paradigm with which the rulers of the various regimes can orient themselves in order to legislate.

Political justice exists, then, among those to whom the law principally refers. Among these (the equivalent in various regimes and cultures to the Roman *patres familias*) we do not allow a human being to become the rule of government, but we require that reason be the rule. For if the ruler is not subject to reason, we consider ourselves oppressed,

---

[428] Neo-Marxists are causing even more serious problems by denying that children are *alieni iuris*, subject to parental authority.

"because man does that [to rule without the guidance of reason] in his own interest and becomes a tyrant."[429] In Book 10, chapter 9, and elsewhere, Aristotle states that we do not allow man to become the rule, but law. This formula is equivalent to that in book 5.6 because being ruled by law is equivalent to being ruled by reason, since the law in the Aristotelian conception is a rule of right reason, of prudence (see 1180a22–4 and 1180a18.21–2). The contrast with the Enlightened authors, the *philosophes*, could not be greater. These latter ones claim that the basis for the legitimacy of law is the will or consent of those subject to government. But legitimacy thus conceived is an anti-utopia or dystopia, because it is impossible to achieve, especially in the current vast states, and because if achieved it would be harmful, since the mass of the people, when too often consulted, acts from passion and not from reason, as *The Federalist* so ably explained.[430] In contrast, the classics hold that the foundation of the legitimacy of the law is reason, that the law really constitutes an opinion of the art of government, of general justice.[431]

Chapter 6 of book 5 of the *Nicomachean Ethics* teaches as well that,

> [...] the ruler is a guardian of the just, and if of the just, also of the equal. He is considered to have no more [than others], if indeed he is just (because he does not attribute to himself more than to others of what is good absolutely speaking, unless more corresponds to him proportionally [...]).[432]

---

[429] 1134a35–1134b1. I do not use here Irwin's translation but my own.

[430] See James Madison, n. 49.

[431] See *Nicomachean Ethics* 10.9, 1180a22–24 and 1180a18.21–22; and 5.1, 1129b14–27. Daniel Mansuy states that "[Montesquieu's] political liberalism rejects [...] the classical science of regimes (which seeks human perfection rather than individual freedom). What is proper to Modernity, then, says Mansuy, is political freedom, and philosophy must assume this new criterion, with its costs and benefits: such is the task that Montesquieu undertakes in *The Spirit of the Laws*" (Mansuy, "Liberalism and Political Regimes," 270). However, the real difference between the classics and Montesquieu lies in the fact that Montesquieu attempts to establish freedom by means of a "mechanism" (Mansuy sees this in op. cit., 266 and 269), because he rejects classical virtue as the end of politics and the best safeguard for a reasonable regime. Like the democratic man of Plato's *Republic* 8, he seeks "freedom" as the end but does not understand by "freedom" the rule of truth over passions (Mansuy, 269).

[432] 1134b1–4. My translation, although contrasted with Irwin's.

There can, therefore, be inequality, and it is reasonable that there should be inequality, greater or lesser according to the regime. This is no obstacle to good government and to liberty, as long as this inequality is proportional and the laws are subject to reason. Of course, to accept that a reasonable law could be the criterion of freedom and legitimacy, one presupposition must be accepted: the rule according to which a law is assessed as true. And what is such rule? According to Aristotle, it is practical truth or, as John Paul II formulated it, the truth about the good.[433] Aristotelian philosophy taught that in order to achieve a just regime it is indispensable to recognize the existence of practical truth, which embraces natural Right and natural moral law.[434] How, then, can there be freedom in a political society founded on a doctrine that replaces practical truth, natural Right, and natural law, on the one hand, with the consent and expression of the will of the majority of those subject to government, manifested directly (according to Rousseau) or through Parliament (according to Locke), on the other?

When the law and proportional justice are respected, Aristotle continues, the ruler

> [...] toils for other, and this is the reason why it is said that justice is a good for the other, as we remarked before. Hence some payment [for ruling] should be given, and this is honor and dignity; those who are not content with this become tyrants.[435]

To all these observations, Cicero adds a crucial one: for there to be a republic (which can be monarchical, aristocratic, democratic, or mixed) it is decisive that a Right be recognized that is at the disposal of no one: neither of the rich, nor of the powerful, nor of the majority. If

---

[433] See *Nicomachean Ethics* 6.2, 1139a26–27; and John Paul II, Encyclical *Veritatis splendor*, August 6 1993, n. 30, available here: https://www.vatican.va/content/john-paul-ii/en/encyclicals/documents/hf_jp-ii_enc_06081993_veritatis-splendor.html.

[434] See *Nicomachean Ethics* 5.7. Some claim that Aristotle postulates natural Right but not natural law. However, Aristotle undeniably postulates the general formulation of natural Right and that is precisely natural law (see *Nicomachean Ethics* 5.7, 1135a5–15). See also Carlos A. Casanova, "La verdad práctica como piedra angular de la ética," *Cuadernos salmantinos de filosofía*, XXXIV (2007): 402–434.

[435] *Nicomachean Ethics*, 5.6, 1134b4–8. The translation is my own, but I follow Irwin's in one phrase.

this Right is not recognized, there can be no republic, but tyranny, even if it is the tyranny of the mobs.[436]

According to the classics, what is essential is to always keep in mind that the regime of the city is a reflection of the character of the most influential citizens. It is absolutely ridiculous to try to legislate with the aim of obtaining a perfect regime without counting on virtue. And this is so for two reasons. First, because the good regime is precisely that in which the citizens are virtuous, since that is the end of politics, as we have seen. And, secondly, because the citadel of both the soul and of institutions consists in wisdom and prudence, since the character can only be defended with wise reasons, as Plato teaches in *Republic* books 8 and 9. The designs of the aspiring political scientist, who tries to build a system of perfect separation of powers to secure freedom, are useless if afterwards, for example, despotic parties or clubs conquer the three powers. Manuel García Pelayo knew very well that there is an insoluble problem for those false sages who

> [...] constantly try to escape/ From the darkness outside and within/ By dreaming of systems so perfect that no one will need to be good.[437]

The insoluble problem is, *quis custodit custodem?* "Who will watch the watch-man?" And García Pelayo also knew that the Christian-Latin solution is perhaps the best ever found for this problem: the "mirrors of princes" in which Christ, King of the Universe, is proposed to the rulers as a model, while they are reminded that, when they die, they will be judged by that Judge.[438]

One discovers at the root of the Enlightenment forsaking of classical knowledge a repudiation both of the hierarchy that is necessary and appropriate for any political society and of the political-philosophical knowledge that recognizes the structure that each society needs for achieving its common good. Such repudiation of knowledge (and even of the most elementary experience) would seem inexplicable

---

[436] See Cicero, *On the Republic* 1.25.39; and 3.33.45, in *De re publica, De legibus* (Cambridge, Mass. and London: Harvard University Press and William Heinemann Ltd., 1970), 2–285.

[437] See T. S. Eliot, *Choruses from "the Rock,"* VI, in *The Complete Poems and Plays, 1909–1950* (New York: Harcourt Brace and Company, 1980), 106.

[438] I refer to the work *El Reino de Dios, arquetipo político* (Madrid: Revista de Occidente, 1959).

if the Declaration of the Rights of Man and the Citizen of 1789 did not betray the influence of ideologies of Voltairean or similar filiation that include in their constitution an intra-worldly eschatological hope, masking a voracious will to power, just like the utopianism of Marx, Lenin,[439] or Mao, although in a lesser degree. The *philosophes'* was a movement, according to Barruel,[440] that started with the Cathar and Albigensian heresies, passed through the Hussites, continued with the anabaptists of Müntzer, went underground with other egalitarian European movements, and openly reappeared on the European continent from the eighteenth century onwards. Shakespeare probably had experience of such movements and witnessed it in a fragment of his *Troilus and Cressida*: [441]

> O, when degree is shaked,
> Which is the ladder to all high designs,
> Then enterprise is sick! How could communities,
> Degrees in schools and brotherhoods in cities,
> Peaceful commerce from dividable shores,
> The primogenitive and due of birth,
> Prerogative of age, crowns, sceptres, laurels,
> But by degree, stand in authentic place?
> Take but degree away, untune that string,
> And, hark, what discord follows! each thing meets
> In mere oppugnancy: the bounded waters
> Should lift their bosoms higher than the shores
> And make a sop of all this solid globe:
> Strength should be lord of imbecility,
> And the rude son should strike his father dead:
> Force should be right; or rather, right and wrong,
> Between whose endless jar justice resides,

---

[439] Eric Voegelin, in his study of Helvetius (one of the figures who had the greatest influence on the Declaration of 1789), analyzes the nature of this intramundane eschatology and its satanic character. He also establishes an explicit connection with Lenin (see Voegelin, *From Enlightenment to Revolution*, *op. cit.*, 51–52, 59, 60, 70 and 73). In his own way, Ernst Bloch makes exactly the same point (see Ernst Bloch, *The Principle of Hope* [Cambridge, Mass., The MIT Press, 1996], volume I, 152): "what the citoyen promised is a promise which can certainly only be kept in socialism."

[440] See Barruel, *Memoirs Illustrating the History of Jacobinism*, Vol. 2, 131–143 and 224 ff. for example. I have added the English Puritans.

[441] *Troylus and Cressida* was written in 1602.

Should lose their names, and so should justice too.
Then every thing includes itself in power,
Power into will, will into appetite;
And appetite, an universal wolf,
So doubly seconded with will and power,
Must make perforce an universal prey,
And last eat up himself.[442]

This tendency of the will to power to devour everything and finally swallow itself is precisely what Barruel shows us in his very sharp critique of the philosophers who inspired the Declaration, although in them the tendency appears masked as the yearning for a utopia of freedom and equality.

But we can now go a step further in the analysis of this phenomenon. The rejection of the political hierarchy contains within itself a rebellion against legitimate human authority (legitimized by history and distributive justice), and, consequently, against the God from whom all legitimate authority comes.[443]

Barruel precisely demonstrates the deep and real connection that exists between submitting to God and submitting to legitimate authority; and between rebellion against God and rebellion against legitimate authority.[444] Plato had seen in books 4,[445] 8, and 9 of his *Republic* the profound connection that exists between the temperance of the soul, the harmony between concupiscence and reason, on the one hand, and political temperance, the harmony between the people and their rulers, on the other. But the experience that Barruel gathers allows us to explore the very sources of the temperance of the soul. Just as Adam and Eve experienced the rebellion of their passions and

---

[442] William Shakespeare, *Troilus and Cressida*, 276–77, in *Complete Plays in Nine Volumes* (London: William Pickering, 1825), Vol. 6, 259–348.

[443] See Juan Antonio Widow, "Non est potestas nisi a Deo," in *Sobre las relaciones y límites entre naturaleza y gracia* (Santiago: UST-Ril Editores, 2016), 645–57.

[444] Perhaps the classical text that comes closest to Barruel's insight on this point is Book 10 of the *Laws*, where Plato observes that atheism arises from considering that nature and chance are prior to the soul and intelligence, which leads to denying that God exists and, at the same time, denying as well both that law is the fruit of a knowledge of truth on the part of reason and that justice is an intellectually cognizable reality. Law, in this perspective, would be a pure convention and truth would require rebelling against the established order with the goal of dominating others (see 888b–890a).

[445] In particular, 430c-432b.

realized that they were naked after disobeying the divine command themselves,[446] so too, the kings who tolerated or embraced rebellion against the divine order later experienced the disobedience of the people.

Let's review a couple of Barruel's remarks:

First, the physical and economic means used to destroy piety were the same as those used to promote rebellion, and they were used by the same people:

> Nothing proves this with more certainty than the care with which they combined their attacks against the Throne with those against the Altar, in that inundation of Antichristian writings which we have seen flowing like a torrent through every class of society. This second inundation of Antimonarchical writings, by which the Sophisters were in hopes of perverting that sentiment of confidence and respect, which the people had for their Sovereign, into hatred and contempt, was only a continuation of those means which they had employed against their God. These writings are issued from the same manufactory, composed by the same adepts, recommended and reviewed by the same chiefs, spread with the same profusion, hawked about from the town to the village by the same agents of Holbach's Club, sent free of cost to the country school-masters, that all classes of people from the highest to the most indigent might imbibe the venom of their Sophistry.[447]

By this identity of means and authors, Barruel proves that the same *philosophes* who had conspired against God had also plotted against kings.

Secondly, a penetrating magistrate, Mr. Seguier, Advocate General of the Parliament of Paris, shows us in his denunciation of

[446] See Gn 3:7; and John Paul II, *Man and Woman He Created Them. A Theology of the Body* (Boston: Pauline Books and Media, 2006), § 28:1-3, 242-244.

[447] Barruel, *Memoirs Illustrating the History of Jacobinism*, volume 2, chap. 5, 87. Simon Schama does not even mention d'Holbach. But he does mention the distribution of slanderous pamphlets against the monarchy *via* Marie-Antoniette. See, for example, section "i Uterine Furies and Dynastic Obstructions," in Part 2, Chapter 6, "Body Politics," 203 ff.

August 18, 1770, the deep connection between the rebellion against the Altar and the rebellion against the Throne, which explains why the same persons used the same means. These are his words:

> An impious and daring sect has raised its head in the midst of us, and it has decorated its false wisdom with the name of Philosophy. [...] Government should tremble at tolerating in its bosom such an inflammatory Sect of unbelievers, whose sole object appears to be to stir up the people to rebellion, under pretence of enlightening them. [...] From these different productions [...] a system of the most flagitious doctrine may be collected, which invincibly proves, that their proposed object is not to destroy the Christian Religion only—Impiety has not limited its plan of innovation solely to its dominion over the minds of men. Its restless and enterprizing genius, averse to all dependence, aspires at the overthrow of every political institution, and its wishes will only then be fulfilled when it shall have thrown the Legislative and Executive Powers into the hands of the People, when it shall have destroyed the necessary inequality of ranks and stations,[448] when it shall have reviled the Majesty of Kings, and have rendered the authority precarious and dependent on the caprice of a blind multitude; when, in fine, by these astonishing changes, it shall have immersed the whole world in the horrors of Anarchy with all its concomitant evils.[449]

This is the keen insight contained as a pearl in Hannah Arendt's book *On Revolution*:

> The specific sanction which religion and religious authority had bestowed upon the secular realm could not simply be replaced by an absolute sovereignty, which, lacking a transcendent and transmundane

[448] It is a sarcasm of history that those who promoted or tolerated rebellion against God suffered the rebellion of their subordinates in the social scale, as did those who promoted rebellion against the king. Simon Schama points out the connection between the rejection of monarchy and the rejection of all social hierarchy in *Citizens*, 140-44.
[449] *Ibid.*, 103–5.

> source, could only degenerate into tyranny and despotism. [...] The enormous significance for the political realm of the lost sanction of religion is commonly neglected in the discussion of modern secularization [...]. [...] The numerous difficulties and perplexities, theoretical and practical, that have beset the public, political realm ever since the rise of the secular, the very fact that secularization was accompanied by the rise of absolutism and the downfall of absolutism followed by revolutions whose chief perplexity was where to find an absolute from which to derive authority for law and power, could well be taken to demonstrate that politics and the state needed the sanction of religion even more urgently than religion and the churches had ever needed the support of princes.[450]

Barruel seems to have written with the same phenomenon in view as Shakespeare. And so it was, for Shakespeare met the beginnings of the first great modern revolution, that of the English Puritans. And that revolution was already infected, in a surreptitious way, by the virus of rebellion against God, manifested in the rebellion against all hierarchy, political or ecclesiastical.[451] That is the virus that affects Western society. The West cannot heal except by a restoration of political wisdom among the heirs of classical republicanism to avoid falling

[450] *On Revolution*, 158, 159, and 160. And in 161 she adds this most interesting observation: "This was the reason why even Blackstone had maintained that 'an absolute power must in all governments reside somewhere,' whereby it is obvious that this absolute power becomes despotic once it has lost its connection to a higher power than itself. That Blackstone calls this power despotic is a clear indication of the extent to which the absolute monarch had cut himself loose, not from the political order over which he ruled, but from the divine or natural-law order to which he had remained subject prior to the modern age."

[451] In the preface to his book, *The Laws of Ecclesiastical Polity*, Hooker identifies the revolutionary tactic that has been used since Puritan times: denounce the vices always existing in any regime (which are due to human frailty), generalize them, blame them on the institution one wishes to abolish, and go on the offensive to effectively abolish it, while, by the denunciation, the denouncer gains a reputation as wise and virtuous, though in reality he is neither one thing nor the other. See Richard Hooker, *The Laws of Ecclesiastical Polity* (London: printed for John Walthoe, George Conyers, James Knapton, Robert Knaplock, J. and B. Sprint, Dalt. Midwinter, Bernard Lintot, Benj. Cowse, William Taylor, W. and T. Innys, John Osbome, Ranew Robinson, Sam Tooke Tho Wotton, 1723), LVIII (in the dedicatory epistle), LXVII–LXVIII (in the preface).

under the various kinds of despotism whose genealogy goes back to Robespierre and Rousseau.[452]

5. Conclusions

In the Declaration of the Rights of Man and the Citizen of 1789, the direct influence of Voltaire, Charles de Montesquieu, and Jean-Jacques Rousseau, and the indirect influence of John Locke, can be detected without much difficulty.

An analysis of the conceptions and proposals of these authors concerning the legitimacy of government, equality, liberty, the division of powers, and the need for Parliament to approve taxes, together with an examination of the historical-political situations in which these proposals were put into practice, lead to two initial persuasions: (a) that the attempt to ground political order on subjective rights is a crystallization of the nominalist version of rights, which is in sharp contrast with the 18th century constitutional movement of the United States; and (b) that the said conceptions and proposals are parochial. That is to say, they are not based on the true universal measure of political regimes, but instead they attempt to turn a concrete political experience into the universal measure. And this is so because the nominalist disconnection between the laws and the nature of things prevents the authors holding the nominalist version of rights from grasping the essential nature of things.

Such analysis and examination also lead us to perceive (c) that the conceptions and proposals of the enlightened authors were at the time, in reality, a call for universal revolution and universal rebellion against the established authorities in all countries. Of course, there were in many places enormous inequalities that offend our modern sensibilities, but: (i) we have seen how Barruel explores a couple of those systems and demonstrates that they were not as unjust as we imagine; and (ii) it is clear that what has come from the revolution worldwide is

[452] Yves Simon observes that Rousseau "supplied tyranny with a new vindication of unprecedented efficaciousness." See *The Philosophy of Democratic Government*, 149.

often far from being a system as perfect, or even as egalitarian as we imagine.

On the three points, nominalism, parochialism and rebellion, the Enlightenment differs profoundly from classical philosophy. In particular, the classics did not propose universal recipes, but they identified principles that can be put into practice in very different ways, contexts, and regimes. Among these principles are: 1) in every political society there is need to observe distributive justice ("treat equally those who are equal and unequally those who are unequal in relevant ways"); 2) an objective Right exists that can be known and may not be violated by anyone, not even by majorities; 3) there is a distinction between human beings who are fully free and equal, and human beings who are not (either because they have not reached the full use of reason or because an inequality of bargaining power must be recognized, so that the weak party is protected as in Labor Law); 4) that political freedom consists not in an impossible self-government, but in the government making its decisions according to reason, according to political knowledge, normally embodied in the law; and, furthermore, 5) that the exercise of virtue is the end-goal of the republic and also its best defense.

It is also shown in these pages that the rebellion against established authority on the part of the eighteenth-century Revolution leads to a dangerous destruction of the political and social hierarchy, driven, according to Shakespearean and also Voegelinian intuitions, by the will to power. Behind the destruction of the hierarchy lies, moreover, a rebellion against the ultimate source of political order, which is none other than God. Barruel illustrates this with precious observations and data, which fit in with the ancient Platonic analyses, although at least in one point they possess greater penetration.

At this point, we can add two final reflections. First, it is difficult to explain both 1) the rebellion against all authority of some men over others (only the government is legitimate that is based on the will of those subject to it), and 2) the repudiation of classical political knowledge. The only way to make sense of these two aspects of the eighteenth-century Revolution is to regard them as the concretization of a new type of intramundane eschatological hope, as Eric Voegelin and Ernst Bloch have understood. I think this is what Hanna Arendt is aiming at when she holds that modern "revolutions" have an element that is very different from the ancient *mutatio rerum* or *metabolaí*, and that element is the attempt to establish a new kind of freedom.[453]

Second, today, the constitutional rhetoric that uses the symbol "human rights" is nourished by at least three different ways of understanding them, classical-Christian, liberal (nominalist), and neo-Marxist.[454] With the present chapter I hope to have contributed to the understanding of the moment in which one of these versions of rights, the nominalist, burst forth as the main structuring force of political power in the West. But in order to adequately clarify the rhetorical-constitutional landscape, we must keep in mind, in addition, (a) what we have accomplished in the previous chapters, pointing out the remote origin of that nominalist version of subjective rights in William of Ockham, and (b) the splitting off from this way of understanding "subjective rights" of a different version that is faithful to the classical and Roman heritage.[455] Besides, we must keep in mind, (c) the transformations that the nominalist/liberal version has undergone in the last two hundred fifty years, and the interaction of these transformations with the other versions of subjective rights. The study of these transformations is already outside the scope of the present book.

---

[453] See *On Revolution*, 27–28, 35. Schama tells a very interesting story about concrete messianic aspirations that saw Robespierre as the actual messiah of the new freedom. See *Citizens*, 839.
[454] Concerning the classical-Christian and liberal, see Gustav Zagrebelsky, *El derecho dúctil* (Valladolid: Trotta, 1997), 75–92. As was said in a note at the introduction to this book, by "Neo-Marxism" I understand the cultural movement that promotes a Marxist revolution not mainly through class struggle but mostly by creating new social divisions or sharpening old ones. Herbert Marcuse's *Repressive Tolerance* is perhaps the most important founding document of this movement. There he rejects "bourgeois tolerance" and proposes the implementation of intolerance against reactionary movements and pockets in society. In my experience, the most powerful means of coercion existing in societies that still have some republicanism in their institutions are the new "rights" through which Christian professors, students, hospitals, doctors, lawyers, parents are coerced to abandon their moral standards as "reactionary" and "discriminatory." The note at the introduction substantiates this claim.
[455] I have dealt with this *supra*, in chapters 2 and 3.

CONCLUDING REFLECTIONS

Both in Aristotelian philosophy and in Roman Law it was understood that there is a real order, cosmic[456] and political[457], that the human will must respect, that such order included natural Right, and that within that context things, actions and acts of refraining were owed to all human persons.[458] In scholastic philosophy and theology that was not fundamentally affected by the nominalist turn, such basic classical insights on the structure of the cosmos were assumed and illuminated with the light of faith.

Already in the works of Aristotle, the existence of a sphere of wisdom which must be exempt from the dictates of politics was discovered.[459] In Latin Christendom, such a sphere, which was shattered by the barbarians who took over political power in the West, was protected by the Church in a way that ultimately led her to the foundation of the universities. But the Church had, besides, a spiritual authority based not on the power of arms but on the respect that the politicians who controlled the arms had for the natural and divine order from which political authority received its own legitimacy. With the end of illustrating this type of respect, we can turn to Alexander Hamilton. The judiciary authority inherited from Christendom the science concerning an important aspect of the traditional order, i. e., the science of Law. Hamilton understood very deeply the situation of this authority, *vis- à -vis* the executive and the legislative powers, which, in modern times is similar to the situation of the Church respecting secular power in Latin Christendom:

> The executive not only dispenses the honours, but holds the sword of the community; the legislature not only commands the purse, but prescribes the rules by which the duties and rights of every citizen are to be regulated; the judiciary, on the

---

[456] See *Metaphysics* 12.10, 1075a12-24.
[457] See *Nicomachean Ethics* 1.1-2, 1094a1-1094b10.
[458] "Justice is the constant and perpetual will of giving each his own Right," according to the *Institutions* 1,1,1 of the *Corpus iuris civilis* (Berlin: Weidmannos, 1928). Here "Right" is taken in objective sense and it could stand for a harsh punishment due to a criminal, for example.
[459] See *Nicomachean Ethics* 6.13, 1145a6-11.

> contrary, has no influence over either the sword or the purse; no direction either of the strength or of the wealth of the society; and can take no active resolution whatever. It may truly be said to have neither Force nor Will, but merely judgment; and must ultimately depend upon the aid of the executive arm even for the efficacy of its judgments.[460]

Very important political goods depended on the respect commanded by the spiritual power, in a way analogous to the important political goods that depend on the respect commanded by the feeble judiciary power, as stated by Alexander Hamilton:

> The benefits of the integrity and moderation of the judiciary have already been felt in more states than one; and though they may have displeased those whose sinister expectations they may have disappointed, they must have commanded the esteem and applause of all the virtuous and disinterested. Considerate men, of every description, ought to prize whatever will tend to beget or fortify that temper in the courts; as no man can be sure that he may not be tomorrow the victim of a spirit of injustice, by which he may be a gainer to-day.[461]

While Ockham rejected, as we have seen, the guardianship that the hierarchy of the Church exercised over the order of the cosmos, Vitoria accepted such guardianship and actually exercised it by forcing Charles V to reconsider the system imposed in Spanish America and to establish or reform the Council of the Indies. In this system that Ockham rejected and Vitoria accepted, the ecclesiastical hierarchy and the theologians were custodians of the cosmic order of which the political order was just a part or an aspect. This sapiential authority was used in many ways for the common good of each society within Christendom, for the common good of the whole Christendom, and, in the 16th century Spain, for the establishment of a just order in the relations with the "barbarians newly discovered," as Vitoria would put it. All benefited

---

[460] See *The Federalist* (Indianapolis: Liberty Fund, 2001), n. 78, 405. In a similar sense, see n. 81, 420.

[461] See *The Federalist*, n. 78, 406.

from it, especially the weakest and the poorest who had no power other than the invocation of the demands of justice and mercy.[462]

Of course, this system was not perfect, since no human reality is so, and many men did not live up to it. However, it was, in fact, a beautiful reality, more beautiful than the cathedrals that were its architectural expression. It was based on the assumption that there is a common good of each political society and a common good of the cosmos, in which the lesser goods of cities, villages, guilds, families, individuals (all perceptible with reason) participated, forming a network that was the source of law and Right, and therefore the source of authority as well. This is why it was understood that the law was predominantly an act of reason rather than an act of the will.[463] But this order was first weakened, and then came close to being torn to pieces by the negation of the reality of the intelligible goods that were its source.[464]

A major event in the process of Christendom's dissolution was constituted by the rise of political and juridical nominalism mostly in the works of William of Ockham. This Franciscan friar, when denying the reality of intelligible, "universal" dimensions in the sensible world, was stabbing the heart of Christendom's order. If "good" and "just" do not mean any real dimension inherent in things and actions and

---

[462] Jackson's disobedience of the John Marshall's Supreme Court decision regarding the respect of the rights of the Cherokee Indians is a good illustration of this point: the weak are unprotected if there is no institutional respect paid by those with military power to those who cultivate knowledge of the truth. The yeast of this disobedience was summarized in the famous remark that Jackson made (or that at least reflects his attitude towards the ruling): "John Marshall has made his decision; now let him enforce it." There is a good discussion concerning this remark in Mark Sherer's paper "'Now let him enforce it.' Exploring the Myth of Andrew Jackson's Response to *Worcester vs. Georgia* (1832)," *The Chronicles of Oklahoma*, 74/1 (1896): 16-29. Independently of Andrew Jackson's degree of responsibility in this tragedy, it is undisputable that both the government of Georgia and the Federal Government showed a total disregard for the requirements of justice when it came to the *Right* belonging to the Cherokee nation, even after it was pronounced by the Supreme Court of the United States.

[463] See *Nicomachean Ethics* 10.9, 1180a16-24; *Summa theologiae* I-II qq. 90, aa. 1-3.

[464] This has some resemblance to what MacIntyre proposes in "Community Law, and the Idiom and Rhetoric of Rights," 106-110. The doctrine is not exactly the same for several reasons, the main one being that MacIntyre does not distinguish between subjective rights in nominalist sense and subjective rights compatible with the classical tradition. For the same reason he sees the whole structure of the United States since the Independence as incompatible with his proposal, while I highlight in the order of the United States the presence of classical elements that are competing with nominalist elements.

situations, the whole network on which law and Right are grounded comes crumbling down to the dust. It becomes necessary to ground them in some other way, so that the arbitrary Will of God and the will of men had to replace with their acts the void left by the sapiential order. Thus, the law became predominantly an act of the will and God's authority became arbitrary, based solely on His exceeding power.

The political realm was no longer to be conceived as an order under a higher, cosmic order. The system of spiritual authority over political authority, therefore, collapsed; and the political realm became entirely secularized.[465] In other words, Ockham's denial of the natural consistency of morality and Right eroded the ground for the spiritual authority in Christendom.

Moreover, since according to nominalist doctrine only individuals and their powers are real, and particularly relations are not real (they exist only in reason or imagination), political society was to be no longer conceived as real and natural (as Aristotle and Aquinas did conceive it), but as conventional (merely an aggregate of the powers of individuals) and artificial. The legitimacy of political authority was to be no longer based on its submission to what is just and truly good, but instead on the consent of those who are ruled by it. Moreover, since "justice" does not mean anything not determined by an arbitrary will, the rulers are the ones who establish the laws that must be applied by the courts. This led to the first positivistic proposal in Latin Christendom (in the sense that the courts of justice are supposedly subject only to positive law). A corollary is that it is assumed that there is no ground, other than arbitrary divine law, for the existence of secular justice regarding those who lie outside the political contract. So, when the nominalist version of rights became secularized all grounds for such justice disappeared, which is why in Locke's work the different nations find themselves in the state of nature, war regarding their mutual relations.

On these points Michel Villey's theses were correct. Nominalism leads to consider the world as a set of individuals who form

---

[465] Regarding the Lockean system, David Schindler very acutely points out that in it: "the potentializing of religion [...] allows one to neutralize the implications of the existence of God without having to shoulder the burden of responsibility that would come with rejecting God outright." *Freedom from Reality*, 127.

a hierarchy of sheer power, and who through their will establish a cosmic voluntaristic law (God would do this, according to the nominalist perspective) and a political order based on consent. Villey also held that the secularized version of nominalist subjective rights, focused on the political, appears in Hobbes and Locke, and that Locke, in turn, had a prevalent influence on the 1789 Declaration of the Rights of Man and the Citizen. In his *Philosopie du droit*, Villey expressed the connection between the 1789 Declaration and the version of subjective rights that Ockham inaugurated:

> The "rights of men" are precisely the natural subjective rights and they encompass property, which the revolutionary text proclaims as a "sacred, inviolable" right; the accessories of property, the right to use and to enjoy the thing and of disposing of it by contract; and also the right which each possesses over his person; and other freedoms. "The goal of every political association, says the 1789 declaration of rights (art. 2), is the conservation of the natural and indefeasible rights of the individual."[466]

Villey's original theses were the ones just stated. He was correct when he pointed out this deep connection between the 1789 Declaration of rights and the nominalist version of subjective rights. He was wrong in many other points, two of which we have argued here: it is not true that Ockham coined the notion of subjective rights, and it is not true that all uses of such notion are nominalist and/or individualist. Villey ignored that there is a rival version paradigmatically instantiated by Francisco de Vitoria. In this book we have painstakingly demonstrated the existence of these two different versions. We subscribe, however, to the main insights that Villey expressed in the bulk of his work. Such main insights have become more plausible in the light of what has been established in our previous chapters. This will be apparent if we now stress doctrinal similarities between Ockham and Locke, on the one hand, and between Locke and the 1789 Declaration of Rights, on the other. (The exact historical connection between Locke and Ockham has not been established, but Ockham clearly created the first nominalist

[466] *Philosophie du Droit* (Paris: Dalloz, 1978), I, 156 (section 84).

system of subjective rights and the main doctrines contained in such system appear in Locke.)

In a note contained in the Introduction it was shown that, according to Ockham and Locke there are no real relations.[467] This is the ground for conceiving both political society as conventional and rights as powers over things. Moreover, according to both, things and actions are not morally or politically good due to their nature or their intelligible structure, but due to being in conformity with a law, be this God's arbitrary law or be it human, positive law. In Locke's case, since he has defined good and evil as that which produces pleasure or pain, only that law which promises effective pleasure or threatens with effective pain can be the source of moral or political good and evil. But, according to him, only human, positive laws are such. He expresses these ideas brilliantly:

> Good and evil, as hath been shown, b. ii. chap. 20. § 2, and chap. 21, § 42, are nothing but pleasure or pain, or that which occasions or procures pleasure or pain to us. Moral good and evil then is only the conformity or disagreement of our voluntary actions to some law, whereby good or evil is drawn on us by the will and power of the law-maker; which good and evil, pleasure or pain, attending our observance, or breach of the law, by the decree of the law-maker, is that we call reward and punishment.[468]

---

[467] There is even a deeper metaphysical connection between these two authors. We explained in the introduction that Ockham is a nominalist, or a conceptualist. Locke is a conceptualist too, and one that has developed already a detailed explanation of how those "concepts" and "general terms" that do not signify a real essence were formed by our mind. Through sensation and abstraction, we form simple ideas and terms. Concerning these, to have ideas and to perceive are the same thing. However, the general simple idea is an abstraction of sensible similarities, not an intellection of an intelligible essence. By combination of simple ideas and abstraction we form complex ideas and terms. These latter ones have "nominal essence" but no "real essence." See *An Essay Concerning Human Understanding* (Book 3, chapter 7-book 4), in *The Works of John Locke in Nine Volumes*, (London: Rivington, 1824 12th ed.), Vol. 2, 1-299, book 3, chapters 3 and 4; and book 4, chapters 4, §§ 4 and 5; 5; 6; and 7, § 9.

[468] See *An Essay Concerning Human Understanding*, book 2, chapter 28, §5. On Ockham, see chapters 1 and 2. *supra*. On Locke, see as well *An Essay Concerning Human Understanding*, book 1, chapter 1, §§ 5-13; and book 3, chapter 5, on mixed modes. Notice that "adultery" for example is nothing existing in nature, but just in the mind of the legislator, according to Locke.

In chapter 2 we proved that "in order to defend the position of the Franciscans against John XXII, Ockham laid one of the foundations of the Lockean system. In effect, the competence of the court is restricted to declaring positive law." Locke taught this explicitly in his *Second Treatise of Government*, § 136.

As we explained in chapter 4, "John Locke interpreted the classical qualities 'free and equal' as existing in all men, and in a very particular way. 'Free' would mean, in the state of nature, being subject to no power (*Second Treatise of Government*, §§ 22, 54, 190); and in the civil state, being subject only to the laws given by the legislature constituted by the consent of the people understood as the total set of those subject to government (§§ 22, 190)."

It seems to me indubitable, then, that there is a strong similarity between William of Ockham's teachings and Locke's teachings, and that this is a confirmation of Villey's insights. One new aspect of the Lockean doctrines is his strong emphasis that the consent of the people from which political authority emerged was given to protect property over things acquired through work (mostly land) and to protect property over one's own self and life. This aspect may be said to be new and original. We see in the 1789 Declaration of the Rights of Man and the Citizen a reception of the nominalist version, with the addition of these Lockean elements.

Since society is conceived by both, Locke and the French Declaration, not as a natural gathering of men in order to achieve the common good understood as living well in the Aristotelian sense (that is to say, living virtuously)[469], but as an association for the mutual protection of subjective rights understood in a Lockean (or Rousseauian) way, it follows naturally that the Declaration states that the standard to measure the legitimacy of governments is the subjective, human rights defined in it.[470]

From these reflections it can be gathered that our investigation yielded an important philosophical result. It allows us to discover what

---

[469] See *Nicomachean Ethics* 1.5 and 7, 1098a5-18; and 5.1, 1029b15-33.
[470] See, for example, Felipe Widow, *Autonomía de la razón práctica y derecho subjetivo en la filosofía de John Finnis*, 189. Ph.D. dissertation presented at the Pontifical Catholic University of Chile, School of Law, on July 6, 2016.

is behind a particular use of the word "right" today, that use that Bobbio and Zagrebelsky call "right" in "liberal" sense. We can now see that what is behind that use is a philosophical position that we may call "nominalism." Here we can make more explicit what the reasons are behind this statement: (1) nominalism denies the reality of relations. (2) For this reason, it holds that all collective entities are reducible to conglomerates of individuals. (3) For this reason, it holds that political society is not an entity beyond and above the individuals and their powers, and it is forced to state that political society is born from an act of the will of the individuals. (4) For reason (1) it holds that there is not such a thing as a network of relations as that which is needed for distributive justice to exist. (5) For this reason, it postulates "natural rights and powers" that are prior to political society and independent from distributive justice. (6) The use of the power of consent is what originates political societies (see 3), which are, therefore, totally conventional; (7) nominalism also denies that there is a nature "what is just" that is present in all the things that are just (the same can be said of the good). (8) For reason (7) nominalism holds that things are just because of their conformity to a law established by an arbitrary will. (9) For reasons (8), (7), (6) and (3) (and also for contingent historical reasons) it holds that the courts may apply only positive law.

In chapter 4 we have explored some of the problems that this conception of the political order entails. It seems expedient to remember here that the classical tradition was alive at the same time. The presence of this rival tradition crystalized in the 19th century constitutional Law, which was a mixture of "enlightened" positions, on the one hand, and the strength of the Western classical and Christian tradition, on the other.[471] Among the main forces that brought back the influence of classicism and of Christianity over the most relevant political scene were the jurists in the European and the Spanish American scenarios, and Alexander Hamilton and other jurists in the United States.[472] I have come to think that it was mostly Hamilton's

[471] This state of affairs, the simultaneous presence of Revolution and classical traditions, has been the subject of much reflection by Eric Voegelin. See *New Science of Politics* (Chicago: University of Chicago Press, 1952), chapter 6, section 6.

[472] In *The Federalist* James Madison and John Jay wrote as persons versed in the Western juridical tradition and as such they lent strength to the tradition against the stream of revolution. Madison, however, later became very close to Thomas Jefferson, and so was drawn closer to

influence that determined the rise of classical elements in 19th century constitutionalism.

It is unclear if a line of influence from Vitoria to Hamilton can be established. But undoubtedly Hamilton held a view on subjective rights very much influenced by Blackstone in whose works (a) the rights were necessarily concretized in the context of a strong government as expressions of justice and law, and (b) justice and law were conceived as rooted in nature and in the principles of reason. Blackstone even used "right" in the objective, Roman sense occasionally.[473] So, his work was an expression of the version of subjective rights understood within a classical conception of the cosmos, of justice and of rationality. This is the reason why Hamilton held that for the protection of the common good and of the real, not chimerical, political liberty, more important than to have a perfect bill of rights was to establish a strong republican government. In other words, unlike the French revolutionary, he knew that a bill of rights was not the universal standard to measure good government.[474]

Hamilton's continuity with the classics in the aspects commented on in this book and *vis-à-vis* John Locke can be further established. Hamilton, indeed, knew and acknowledged that there is a real order which must first be known and received by reason and then promulgated as a real law. This is why, although occasionally yielding to the prevailing democratic rhetoric of his time,[475] he predominantly

---

the revolutionary camp. See Ron Chernow, *Alexander Hamilton* (New York: Penguin Books, 2004), 391, 433, 436 and 497.

Gianna Englert's book, *Democracy Tamed* (New York: Oxford University Press, 2024), is a very good source to study this conflict between the revolutionary idea of popular sovereignty and the classical, traditional understanding that good government must be directed by reason and knowledge towards the common good. She studies the struggle in nineteenth century France. The most relevant characters in that struggle and in the "conservative" side were François Guizot and Alexis de Tocqueville.

Concerning the main Spanish American authors who tried to oppose the waves of revolution, the reader can see Miguel Ayuso Torres, Camilo Noguera Pardo and Jackson René Valbuena Cure (eds.), *El conservadurismo en el mundo hispánico* (Bogotá: Tirant lo Blanch, 2021), 548 pp.

473 See William Blackstone, *Commentaries on the Laws of England* (Dublin: John Exshaw, Henry Saunders, Samuel Watson and James Williams, 1766), Vol. 1, 8, 12 and 40.

474 See *The Federalist* n. 84, 445-6; and 85, 454-5.

475 See *The Federalist* n. 78, 403-404, where Hamilton holds that the Constitution, emanated from the direct will of the people, is above the laws of the legislature which emanate indirectly from the people. This passage could be read in classical terms as well, however. See *Summa theologiae*

held (1) that the Constitution is a real law that, therefore, imposes its rules even over the will of the majority of the people (unless reformed through the proper channels): "Until the people have, by some solemn and authoritative act, annulled or changed the established form, it is binding upon themselves collectively, as well as individually: and no presumption, or even knowledge of their sentiments, can warrant their representatives in a departure from it, prior to such an act."[476] Hamilton held, moreover, (2) that the judiciary represent the law, and not the people.[477] And, finally, Hamilton also held (3) that the common good must be the standard of good government and that the rulers must be able to withstand the winds of popular passion so that with reason they correct the popular errors concerning the means to achieve happiness.[478]

Since Hamilton succeeded (with much effort and against not small opposition by Thomas Jefferson and others, including James Madison) in consolidating these principles in the republican life of the United States,[479] the two versions of subjective rights coexisted in the text of Western constitutions and in the body of Western constitutional law since the 18th century and up to our days, although now both versions of subjective rights are under heavy attack by neo-Marxist and other post-Modern forces.

I-II, q. 90, a. 3, c: the community as a whole (not as the set of those subject to the law in question) is the ultimate source of political law.

[476] See *The Federalists* n. 78, 406.

[477] See *The Federalist* nn. 51 (by Madison); 78 and 81.

[478] See *The Federalist* n. 71.

[479] See Ron Chernow, *Alexander Hamilton*, 304-305, 321 ff., 350, 354-355, 497. Talleyrand was right, in my opinion, in holding that Alexander Hamilton was the greatest politician of his time, both in Europe and America. See Chernow, ibidem, 466 and 720. A good study on the conflict between Alexander Hamilton, on the one hand, and Thomas Jefferson and (to a lesser extent) James Madison is Carson Holloway's *Hamilton versus Jefferson in the Washington Administration* (New York: Cambridge University Press, 2015). In 209 Holloway demonstrates the loathing that Hamilton felt for the French *philosophes*. Actually the occasion for the conflict with Jefferson becoming very sharp was Hamilton's opposition to the French Revolution, as expressed by him in the *Pacificus* essays. See the essays here: Hamilton, Alexander; and Madison, James. *The Pacificus-Helvidius Debates*, ed. Morton Frisch (Indianapolis: Liberty Fund, 2007).

In the last decades of the twentieth century, moreover, new generations of subjective rights were added, inspired by conflicting philosophies and world views. It is a hard task to keep them apart and to demonstrate their strength and their weaknesses. But such a task is necessary to be able to bring back order and authentic rationality to judiciary decisions. This book had as its goal to contribute to achieving the desired distinctions and critiques by placing apart the nominalist version of subjective rights from a completely different version that stands in continuity with the classics.

BIBLIOGRAPHY

ADAMS, Marilyn McCord, *William Ockham* (University of Notre Dame Press, Notre Dame, 2015).

ADAMS, Marilyn McCord, "The Structure of Ockham's Moral Theory," 15–23, in *Franciscan Studies* 46 (1986): 1–35.

ADLER, Mortimer, "The Doctrine of Natural Law in Philosophy," in *Natural Law Institute Proceedings*, Vol. 1, Notre Dame (1949): 65–84 (available here: http://scholarship.law.nd.edu/cgi/viewcontent.cgi?article=1001&context=naturallaw_proceedings)

ALAND, Kurt et al, *Greek New Testament* (Stuttgart: Württemberg Bible Society, 1968).

AQUINAS, St. Thomas, *Contra impugnantes* (Pamplona: Universidad de Navarra, 2000). Available at: www.corpusthomisticum.org. All of Aquinas works are cited from this edition.

AQUINAS, St. Thomas, *In Psalmos Davidis Expositio.*

AQUINAS, St. Thomas, *Quaestiones disputatae de veritate.*

AQUINAS, St. Thomas, *Sententia de anima.*

AQUINAS, St. Thomas, *Sententia libri Ethicorum.*

AQUINAS, St. Thomas, *Sententia libri Politicorum.*

AQUINAS, St. Thomas, *Summa theologiae.*

ARENDT, HANNAH, *On Revolution* (New York: The Viking Press, 1973).

ARISTOTLE, *Politics* (Leipzig: Teubner, 1894).

ARISTOTLE, *Metaphysica* (Leipzig: Teubner, 1895).

ARISTOTLE, *De anima* (Leipzig: Teubner, 1896).

ARISTOTLE, *Ethica Nicomachea* (Oxford: Oxford University Press, 1962).

ARISTOTLE, *Nicomachean Ethics* (Indianapolis: Hackett Publishing Company, 1999).

ATRIA, Fernando, "La Verdad y lo político II. Democracia y ley natural," *Persona y Sociedad* XXIII/2 (2009): 35-64.

AYUSO TORRES, Miguel; NOGUERA PARDO, Camilo; and VALBUENA CURE, Jackson René (eds.), *El conservadurismo en el mundo hispánico* (Bogotá: Tirant lo Blanch, 2021), 548 pp.

BARRUEL, Augustine, *Memoirs Illustrating the History of Jacobinism* (New York: Hartford, 1799), volume II.

BARRUEL, Augustine, *Memoirs Illustrating the History of Jacobinism* (New York: Isaac Collins, 1799), volume III.

BARRUEL, Augustine, *Memoirs Illustrating the History of Jacobinism* (New York: Isaac Collins, 1799), volume IV.

BASTIT, Michel, *Nascimento da lei moderna* (Sao Paulo, WMFMartinsfontes, 2010).

BASTIT, Michel, "Ockham as a precursor of modern philosophy of law". Lecture delivered at the Universidad Bernardo O'Higgins (Santiago, August 2015).

BLACKSTONE, William, *Commentaries on the Laws of England* (Dublin: John Exshaw, Henry Saunders, Samuel Watson and James Williams, 1766), Vol. 1.

BLOCH, Ernst, *The Principle of Hope* (Cambridge [Mass.]: The MIT Press, 1996), vol. 1.

BOBBIO, Norberto, "I diritti del'uomo oggi." In *L'età dei diritti* (Einaudi, 2014), 184-194.

BOCHENSKI, J. M., *Philosophy: An Introduction* (Springer Science and Business Media, 1964).

BRADING, David. *The First America* (Cambridge: Cambridge University Press, 1991).

BRETT, Annabel, *Liberty, Right and Nature. Individual Rights in Later Scholastic Thought* (Cambridge: Cambridge University Press, 2003).

BROWNSON, Orestes, *The American Republic* (New York: P. O'Shea, 1865).

CANON, Jason S., "The General Wills in Rousseau," *The Review of Politics* 84 (2022): 350-371.

CARROLL, William, "Thomas Aquinas on Creation and Science," in *Investigación científica y fe católica*, Carlos Casanova ed. (Santiago, Chile: RIL Editores-Universidad Santo Tomás, 2016), 89-198.

CASANOVA, Carlos A., *Verdad escatológica y acción intramundana. La teoría política de Eric Voegelin* (Pamplona: EUNSA, 1997).

CASANOVA, Carlos A., "Nominalismo jurídico, escolástica española y tradición republicana," *Dikaiosyne* VIII/15 (2005): 59–74.

CASANOVA, Carlos A., "La verdad práctica como piedra angular de la ética," *Cuadernos salmantinos de filosofía* XXXIV (2007): 402–434.

CASANOVA, Carlos A., "The Influence of Christianity on the Spanish Conquest of America and the Organization of the Spanish-American Empire," 127, *Logos* 15:4 (2012): 125-44.

CASANOVA, Carlos A., *Racionalidad y justicia* (Santiago: Globo Editores, 2013).

CASANOVA, Carlos A., "Ha sido derrotada la teoría clásica del Derecho natural por el argumento de la falacia naturalista?" *Logos, Anales del seminario de metafisica*, Vol. 47 (2014): 37–54.

CASANOVA, Carlos A., *El republicanismo español en América: una evaluación* (Mexico: UNAM, 2015).

CASANOVA, Carlos A., "Guillermo de Ockham y el origen de la concepción nominalista de los derechos subjetivos," *Cuariensia* Volume 11 (2016): 113–140.

CASANOVA, Carlos A., "¿Es voluntarista la ética de Guillermo de Ockham?" *Acta Philosophica*, 1/28 (2019): 113–130.

CASANOVA, Carlos A., "¿Era Francisco de Vitoria un nominalista?" *Scripta Medievalia*, 12/2 (2019): 67–99.

CASANOVA, Carlos A., *A Restatement of the Fifth Thomistic Way to Prove the Existence of God, Rivista Angelicum*, 96/1, (2019): 29-59.

CASANOVA, Carlos A., "¿Son los derechos del hombre el verdadero objeto de la esperanza humana y la medida de las sociedades políticas?" *Díkaion*, eISSN 2027–5366, Año 37 (2023) - Vol. 32 Núm. 1, DOI: 10.5294/dika.2023.32.1.8

CHERNOW, Ron, *Alexander Hamilton* (New York: Penguin Books, 2004).

CICERO, *De re publica, De legibus* (Cambridge, Mass. and London: Harvard University Press and William Heinemann Ltd., 1970).

CLARK, David V., *William Ockham on Right Reason*, in *Speculum*, vol. 48 (1973), No. 1, 13–36.

COLEMAN, Janet, "Ockham's Right Reason and the Genesis of the Political as 'Absolutist," *History of Political Thought*, Vol. XX, No. 1 (Spring 1999): 35-64.

CRUZ PRADOS, Alfredo, *Ethos y polis* (Pamplona: Eunsa, 1999).

CURY, Enrique, *Derecho Penal. Parte General* (Santiago, Ediciones Universidad Católica de Chile, 2005).

D'ANNIBALE, Elisa, "Memorie di un gesuita: Augustin Barruel e la teoria del complotto in Italia," in Gianluca Paoluci (ed.), *Illuminatismo tra Germania e Italia nel tardo Settecento* (Roma: Instituto Italiano d Studi Germanici, 2019), 142–143.

DEBBAUT, Steven, "The legitimacy of criminalizing drugs: Applying the 'harm principle' of John Stuart Mill to contemporary decision-making," *International Journal of Law, Crime and Justice*, 68 (2022), 1-12. Article 100508. https://doi.org/10.1016/j.ijlcj.2021.100508

DE MURALT, André, *L'unité de la philosophie politique. De Scot, Occam et Suarez au liberalisme contemporain* (Paris: Librairie Philosophique J. Vrin, 2002).

DENEEM, Patrick, *Regime Change, Toward a Postliberal Future* (Sentinel: 2023).

DIMITROV, Svetozar A., *Herbert Marcuse's Role in Shaping the New Left: The Reception of the Notions of Repressive Tolerance and Alternative Revolutionary Forces in West Germany (1963-1974) and their Contemporary Legacy*, PhD dissertation presented by Svetozar A. Dimitrov at the Freie Universität Berlin to obtain the PhD degree at the Department of the Sciences of History and Culture in 2021, 348 pp. Available here: https://refubium.fu-berlin.de/bitstream/handle/fub188/39829/Dissertation_Svetozar_Dimitrov.pdf?sequence=3

DUHEM, Pierre, *History of Physics*, in *Catholic Encyclopedia* (New York: The Encyclopaedia Press, 1913) Vol. 12, 47–67.

DUNN, John, "What Is Living and What Is Dead in John Locke". In: *Interpreting Political Responsibility*, Cambridge, Cambridge University Press, 1990, 9–25.

DURKHEIM, Emile, *Montesquieu and Rousseau, Forerunners of Sociology* (Ann Arbor: University of Michigan Press, 1960).

DUSSAULT, Jean Joseph, "Notice sur la vie et les ouvrages d'Augustine de Barruel," in *Les Helvetiennes* (Paris: Librairie de la Société Typographique, 1823).

ELIOT, Thomas Stearns, *Choruses from "the Rock,"* VI, in *The Complete Poems and Plays, 1909–1950* (New York: Harcourt Brace and Company, 1980).

ENGLERT, Gianna, *Democracy Tamed* (New York: Oxford University Press, 2024).

FANNING, William "Agustín Barruel", *Catholic Encyclopedia* (New York: The Knights of Columbus' Catholic Truth Committee, 1913), volume 2, 310.

FERNÁNDEZ-SANTAMARÍA, J. A., *The State, War and Peace. Spanish Political Thought in the Renaissance 1516-1559* (Cambridge: Cambridge University Press, 1977).

FESER, Edward: The Last Superstition (South Bend: St. Augustine Press, 2010).

FINNIS, John *Natural Law and Natural Rights* (Oxford: Clarendon Press, 1980).

FINNIS, John, "Aquinas on *Ius* and Hart on Rights: A Response to Tierney," *The Review of Politics*, Vol. 64, No. 3 (Summer, 2002): 407–410.

FLIKSCHUH, Katrin, "Reason, Right and Revolution: Kant and Locke", *Philosophy and Public Affairs*, n° 36/4 (2008): 375–404.

FREPPERT, Lucan, *The Basis of Morality* (Chicago: Franciscan Herald Press, 1988).

FROHMEN, Bruce P.; and GRASSO, Kenneth L., "Introduction. Rights in a Multicultural Landscape," in *Rethinking Rights. Historical, Political, and Philosophical Perspectives* (Columbia: University of Missouri Press, 2009), 1–33.

GARCÍA PELAYO, Manuel, *El Reino de Dios, arquetipo político* (Madrid: Revista de Occidente, 1959).

GAYO, *La Instituta* (Madrid: Typis Societatis Litterariae et Typographicae, 1845).

GRATIANUS, *Decretum* (Excerptum prepared in Rome, 2007), Æ. Friedberg (Editor), in *Corpus iuris canonici*, Pars Prior (Leipzig: Ex officina Bernhardi Tauchnitz, 1879).

GROSSI, Paolo, "Usus facti", in: *Il dominio e le cose. Percezioni medievali e moderne dei diritti reali* (Milan: Giufffrè Editore, 1992), 123–189.

GUZMÁN BRITO, Alejandro, "Historia de la denominación del derecho-facultad como 'subjetivo'," *Revista de Estudios Histórico-Jurídicos* 25 (2003): 407-443

GUZMÁN BRITO, Alejandro, *El derecho como facultad en la neoescolástica española del siglo XVI* (Madrid: Iustel, 2009).

HAGEDORN, Eric, "On Loving God Contrary to Divine Command: Demystifying Ockham's *Quodlibet* III 14," *Oxford Studies in Medieval Philosophy* 9 (2021): 222-45.

Hamilton, Alexander; *Report on the National Bank*. In *Official Reports on Public Credit, National Bank, Manufactures and a Mint* (Philadelphia: William McKean, 1821), 59-110.

HAMILTON, Alexander; MADISON, James; JAY, John. *The Federalist* (Indianapolis, Liberty Fund: 2001).

HAMILTON, Alexander; and MADISON, James. *The Pacificus-Helvidius Debates*, ed. Morton Frisch (Indianapolis: Liberty Fund, 2007).

HART, Herbert L. A., "Between Utility and Rights," in *Essays on Jurisprudence and Philosophy* (Oxford: Oxford University Press, 1983), 198-222.

HART, Herbert L. A., *The Concept of Law* (Oxford: Oxford University Press, 2012).

HERING, Hiacinthus, "De iure subjective sumpto apud S. Thomam", en, *Angelicum* 16 (1939).

HERNÁNDEZ, Héctor, *Derecho subjetivo. Derechos humanos. Doctrina solidarista* (Buenos Aires: Abeledo-Perrot, 2000).

HOLLOWAY, Carson. *Hamilton versus Jefferson in the Washington Administration* (New York: Cambridge University Press, 2015).

HUME, David, *Enquiry Concerning Human Understanding* (Oxford: Oxford University Press, 1999).

ISLER, Carlos, "Is nominalism necessarily associated with a voluntarist conception of natural law? The case of Ockham and Hobbes," in *Praxis Filosófica* Nueva Serie, No. 38 (January July 2014): 175–200.

JOHN PAUL II, Encyclical *Veritatis splendor*, August 6 1993, available here: https://www.vatican.va/content/john-paul-ii/en/encyclicals/documents/hf_jp-ii_enc_06081993_veritatis-splendor.html.

JOHN PAUL II, *Man and Woman He Created Them. A Theology of the Body* (Boston: Pauline Books and Media, 2006).

JORDÁN DE ASSO, Ignacio; and MANUEL AND RODRÍGUEZ, Miguel de (eds.), *El fuero viejo de Castilla* (Madrid: 1847).

JOHN KING OF ENGLAND, *Magna Carta of 1215*, in MONT, Charles B., *Chartes des libertés anglaises (1100–1305)* (Paris: Alphonse Picard, 1892), 24–40.

JUSTINIAN, *Corpus iuris civilis* (Berlin: Weidmannos, 1928).

KANT, Immanuel, *Critique of Practical Reason*, in *Critique of Practical Reason and Other Writings in Moral Philosophy* (Nueva York, Garland Publishers INC., 1976).

KANT, Immanuel, *Metaphysics of Morals* (Cambridge: Cambridge University Press, 2008).

KEELE, Rondo, *Ockham Explained. From Razor to Rebellion* (Chicago and Lasalle, Illinois: Open Court, 2010).

KELSEN, Hans, *Theorie pure du droit* (Neuchâtel: Éditions de la Baconnière, 1953).

KLOSKO, George, "Montesquieu's science of politics: Absolute values and ethical relativism in *L'Esprit des lois*," *Studies on Voltaire and the Eighteenth Century* (1980), 153–177. (Transcribed in David Carrithers [ed.], *Charles-Louis de Secondat, Baron de Montesquieu*, New York, Routledge, 2009, 159–183).

LAMONT, John, "In Defence of Villey on Objective Right," in *Truth and Faith in Ethics* (Charlottesville, Virginia: Imprint Academic, 2011), 177-198.

LANTIGUA, David. *Infidels and Empires* (Cambridge: Cambridge University Press, 2020).

LEGGE, Dominic, "Do Thomists Have Rights?" *Nova et Vetera*, English Edition, Vol. 17, No. 1 (2019): 127-147.

LEYDEN, Wolfgang von, Preface to John Locke, *Essays on the Laws of Nature* (Oxford: Clarendon Press, 1958).

LOCKE, John, *The Two Treatises of Civil Government* (London: Hollis ed., 1689).

LOCKE, John, *An Essay Concerning Human Understanding (book 1-book 3, chapter 6)*, in *The Works of John Locke in Nine Volumes*, (London: Rivington, 1824 12th ed.), Vol.1.

LOCKE, John, *An Essay Concerning Human Understanding (book 3, chapters 7-11 and book 4)*, in *The Works of John Locke in Nine Volumes*, (London: Rivington, 1824 12th ed.), Vol.2, 1-299.

LOCKE, John, *The Reasonableness of Christianity as Delivered in Scripture* (London: C. And J. Rivington et al., 1824).

LOCKE, John, *Two Treatises of Government* by John Locke, with a Supplement *Patriarcha* by Robert Filmer. Thomas I. Cook (Editor) (Hofner Publishing Company. New York, 1947–reprint of 1964).

LOCKE, John, *Fundamental Constitutions of Carolina*. Available at: https://avalon.law.yale.edu/17th_century/nc05.asp, Accessed November 26th 2023.

LOWENTHAL, David, "Montesquieu and the classics: Republican government and *The Spirit of the Laws*," in Joseph Cropsey (ed.), *Ancients and Moderns. Essays on the Tradition of Political Philosophy in Honor of Leo Strauss* (New York: Basic Books, 1964), 258–87. (Transcribed in David Carrithers [ed.], *Charles-Louis de Secondat, Baron de Montesquieu*, [New York: Routledge, 2009], 187–216).

LUTHER, Martin, *The Bondage of the Will* (Grand Rapids, Michigan: Fleming H. Revell, 1957).

LUTHER, Martin, *Temporal Authority, to What Extent It Should Be Obeyed (1523)*. In: Martin Luther, *Selected Political Writings* (New York: University Press of America, 1974), 51-69.

LUTHER, Martin, *To the Christian Nobility of the German Nation Concerning the Reform of the Christian Estate (1520)*. In *Selected Political Writings* (New York: University Press of America, 1974), 37-49.

MACINTYRE, Alasdair, "Community Law, and the Idiom and Rhetoric of Rights," *Listening: Journal of Religion and Culture* 26 (1991): 96-110.

MANENT, Pierre, *An Intellectual History of Liberalism* (Princeton: Princeton University Press, 1994).

MANSUY, Daniel, "Liberalism and political regimes: the contribution of Montesquieu," *International Journal of Political Thought* I Epoch 10 (2015): 255–71.

MARCUSE, Herbert, “Repressive Tolerance,” in Robert Paul Wolff, Barrington Moore, Jr. and Herbert Marcuse, *A Critique of Pure Tolerance* [Boston: Beacon Press, 1969], 81-123.

MARITAIN, Jacques, *Three Reformers* (London: Sheed and Ward, 1928).

MAUROIS, André, *A History of England* (London, Jonathan Cape LTD., 1937).

MCDONNELL, Kevin, *Does William of Ockham Have a Theory of Natural Law*, in *Franciscan Studies* 34 (1974): 383–92.

MCGRADE, Arthur S., “Natural Law and Moral Omnipotence,” in: *The Cambridge Companion to Ockham*, ed. Paul Vincent Spade (Cambridge: Cambridge University Press, 1999), 273–301.

MCINERNY, Ralph, “Natural Law and Human Right,” *American Journal of Jurisprudence* 36 (1991): 1–14.

MONTESQUIEU, Charles de, *The Complete Works of Montesquieu* (London: Evans and Davis, 1777), vol. 1.

NATIONAL ASSEMBLY OF FRANCE, *Déclaration des Droits de l'Homme et du Citoyen de 1789*, French Conseil Constitutionnel: https://www.conseil-constitutionnel.fr/le-bloc-de-constitutionnalite/declaration-des-droits-de-l-homme-et-du-citoyen-de-1789

NATIONAL ASSEMBLY OF FRANCE, *1789 Declaration of the Rights of Man and the Citizen*, Avalon project of the Yale Law School: https://avalon.law.yale.edu/18th_century/rightsof.asp

NOZICK, Robert, *Anarchy, State and Utopia* (Oxford: Blackwell, 1999).

OAKLEY, Francis, *Natural Law, Laws of Nature, Natural Rights* (London: Continuum, 2005).

OAKLEY, Francis, *The Watershed of Modern Politics: Law, Virtue, Kingship and Consent (1300.1650)* (New Haven: Yale University Press, 2015), third volume of the Trilogy, “The Emergence of Western Political Thought in the Latin Middle Ages.”

OCKHAM, William, *Summa totius logicae* (Oxford: 1675).

OCKHAM, William, *Tractatus contra Benedictum*, in *Opera politica*, Vol. 3 (Manchester: University of Manchester Press, 1956). 165-322.

OCKHAM, William, *Scriptum in I librum Sentetiarum Ordinatio* (St. Bonaventure: Franciscan Institute ed., 1970), in *Opera Theologica*, Vol. 2.

OCKHAM, William, *Opus nonaginta dierum* (chapters 7-124), (Manchester: University Press, 1973), in *Opera politica*, Volume II, 375-858.

OCKHAM, William, *Opus nonaginta dierum* (chapters 1-6), (Manchester: University Press, 1974), in *Opera politica*, Volume I, 292–368.

OCKHAM, William, *Commentary on Porphyry*, in Kluge, Eike-Henner W. (trans.), 1973–1974, "William of Ockham's Commentary on Porphyry: Introduction and English Translation," *Franciscan Studies*, 33: 171–254 and 34: 306–382.

OCKHAM, William, "The Three Modes of Natural Law" (II-III *Dialogus* iii 6), critical edition of the text by H. S. Offler, in "The Three Modes of Natural Law in Ockham: A Revision of the Text," 212-218, *Franciscan Studies* 37 (1977): 207-218.

OCKHAM, William, Scriptum in Librum Primum Sententiarum Ordinatio. Distinctiones XIX-XLVIII (Saint Bonaventure University, Saint Bonaventure [New York State], 1979), in *Opera theologica*, Vol. IV.

OCKHAM, William, *Quaestiones in II librum Sententiarum (Reportatio)* (Saint Bonaventure, New York State: Saint Bonaventure University, 1981), in *Opera theologica*, Vol. V.

OCKHAM, William, *Quaestiones in IV Sententiarum (Reportatio)*, (Saint Bonaventure University, Saint Bonaventure [New York State], 1984), in *Opera theologica*, Vol. VII

OCKHAM, William, *Quaestiones Variae* (Saint Bonaventure University, Saint Bonaventure [New York State], 1984), in *Opera theologica*, Volume VIII.

OCKHAM, William, *Quodlibetal Questions* (New Haven: Yale University Press, 1991).

OCKHAM, William, *A Letter to the Friars Minor and Other Writings*, eds. McGrade and Kilcullen (Cambridge: Cambridge University Press, 1995).

OCKHAM, William, *Breviloquium de principatu tyrannico* (Oxford: The British Academy-Oxford University Press, 1997), in *Opera politica*, Volume IV, 97–260.

OFFLER, H. S., H. S. Offler, in "The Three Modes of Natural Law in Ockham: A Revision of the Text," 212-218. *Franciscan Studies* 37 (1977): 207-218.

OLIVI, Petrus J., "Quaestio '*Quid ponat ius vel dominium*' ou encore 'De signis voluntariis,'" edited by F. Delorme, in *Antonianum*, XX (1945), 309–30.

ORREGO, Cristóbal, "La gramática de los derechos y el concepto de derecho humanos en John Finnis," *Persona y Derecho*, 59 (2008): 135–57.

OSBORNE, Thomas, "Francisco de Vitoria on the Nature and Source of Civil Authority," *The Review of Politics* 85 (2023): 1-22.

OSBORNE, Thomas, "Ockham as a Divine-Command Theorist," *Religious Studies*, 41/1 (Mar. 2005): 1-22.

PADUA, Marsilius of, *The Defender of the Peace* [*Defensor pacis*] (Cambridge: Cambridge University Press, 2005).

PADUA, Marsilius of, *Defensor Minor* and *The Translatione Imperii* (Cambridge: Cambridge University Press, 1993).

PALACIOS RUBIOS, Juan de López y, *Commentaria et Repetitio in rubricam et Cap. Per vestras, de donationibus inter virum et uxorem*, in *Opera varia* (Antwerp: Ioannem Keerbergium,1616), 1–468.

PELLETIER, Jenny, "Is There an Approach to the Transcendentals in Ockham: The Case of the Good," in *The Language of Thought in Late Medieval Philosophy*, eds. Pelletier & Roques (Springer 2017), 111-24.

PINCKAERS, Servais, *The Sources of Christian Ethics* (Washington: Catholic University of America Press, 1995).

PLATO, *Laws*, in *Platonis Opera*, volume V (Oxford: Oxford University Press, 1967).

PLATO, *Republic*, in *Platonis Opera*, volume IV (Oxford: Oxford University Press, 1972).

Popovic, Petar, "The Concept of 'Right' and the Focal Point of Juridicity in Debate between Villey, Tierney, Finnis and Hervada," *Persona y Derecho* 78/1 (2018). 65-103.

Rodríguez-Penelas, Horacio, "Francisco de Vitoria: la cuestión del dominio en la primera Relección *de indis*", in: Juan Cruz Cruz (Editor), *Ley y dominio en Francisco de Vitoria* (Pamplona: EUNSA, 2008), 165–73.

Rossiter, Elliot, "Hedonism, and Natural Law in Locke's Moral Philosophy," *Journal of the History of Philosophy*, 54/2 (2016): 203-226

Rovira Gaspar, María del C. *La influencia del nominalismo en el pensamiento de Francisco de Vitoria*, in: *Francisco de Vitoria en la Escuela de Salamanca y su proyección en Nueva España* (EUNSA, Pamplona, 2014), 61–70.

Rousseau, Jean-Jacques, *Le citoyen ou Discours sur l'economie politique* (Geneva: 1756).

Rousseau, Jean-Jacques, *The Social Contract and Discourses* (New York: Dent and Sons, 1761).

Schama, Simon, *Citizens, A Chronicle of the French Revolution* (New York: Alfred A. Knopf, 1989).

Schindler, David, *Freedom from Reality* (Notre Dame: University of Notre Dame Press, 2019).

Schindler, David, *The Politics of the Real* (Steubenville, Ohio: New Polity Press, 2022).

Schroeder, Joseph, "Francis of Vittoria," in *Catholic Encyclopedia* (New York: The Encyclopaedia Press, 1909).

Seagrave, Adam, "Locke on Natural Rights and Natural Law," in *The Foundation of Natural Morality* (Chicago: the University of Chicago Press, 2014), Chapter One, 27-51.

Shakespeare, William, *Troilus and Cressida*, in *Complete Plays in Nine Volumes* (London: William Pickering, 1825), Vol. 6, 259–348.

Sherer, Mark, "'Now let him enforce it.' Exploring the Myth of Andrew Jackson's Response to *Worcester vs. Georgia* (1932)," *The Chronicles of Oklahoma*, 74/1 (1896): 16-29.

SIMON, Yves, *Philosophy of Democratic Government* (Notre Dame: University of Notre Dame Press, 2017).

SOTO, Domingo. de, *De iustitia et iure* (Madrid: Instituto de Estudios Políticos, 1968).

SPINDLER, Anselm, "Law, Natural Law, and the Foundation of Morality in Francisco de Vitoria and Francisco Suárez," in *The Concept of Law (lex) in the Moral and Political Thought of the "School of Salamanca,"* eds. Kirstin Bunge, Marko J. Fuchs, Danaë Simmermacher and Anselm Spindler (Boston: Brill, 2016), 172-197.

STRAUSS, Leo, *Natural Right and History* (The University of Chicago Press, Chicago, 1953).

SUÁREZ, Francisco, *Defensio fidei*, Book III, *Sobre el poder y superioridad del Sumo Pontífice sobre los reyes temporales*, en: *Corpus hispanorum de pace* II (Consejo Superior de Investigaciones Científicas, Madrid, 1965).

TIERNEY, Brian, *The Idea of Natural Rights* (Grand Rapids: William B. Eerdmans Publishing Company, 2001).

TIERNEY, Brian, "Natural Law and Natural Rights Old Problems and Recent Approaches," *The Review of Politics*, Vol. 64, No. 3 (Summer, 2002): 389–406.

TIERNEY, Brian, "Author's Rejoinder," *The Review of Politics*, Vol. 64, No. 3 (Summer, 2002): 416–20.

TIERNEY, Brian, "Response to S. Adam Seagrave's 'How Old Are Modern Rights? On the Lockean Roots of Contemporary Human Rights Discourse,'" *Journal of the History of Ideas*, Volume 72, Number 3 (July 2011): 461–68.

TOYNBEE, Arnold, *A Study of History*, Abridgment by D. C. Somervell (New York: Oxford University Press, 1962).

UNITED STATES OF AMERICA, *Fourteenth Amendment*, https://www.archives.gov/milestone-documents/14th-amendment

VILLEY, Michel, *Seize Essais* (Paris: Dalloz, 1969).

VILLEY, Michel, *Estudios en torno a la noción de derecho subjetivo* (Valparaíso: Ediciones Universitarias de Valparaíso, 1976).

VILLEY, Michel, *Philosophie du droit* (Paris: Dalloz, 1978).

VINOGRADOFF, Paul, *Roman Law in Medieval Europe* (New York: Harper and Brothers, 1909).

VIRGINIA, State of, Declaration of Rights of 1776, https://www.archives.gov/founding-docs/virginia-declaration-of-rights

VITORIA, Francisco de, *Comentarios a la secunda secundae de santo Tomás* (Salamanca: Biblioteca de Teólogos Españoles, 1934), V. 3.

VITORIA, Francisco de, "Acerca de los indios recientemente descubiertos," in *El pensamiento político hispanoamericano. Vitoria* (Buenos Aires: Ediciones Depalma, 1967), 167–224.

VITORIA, Francisco de, "Cuestión sobre el Derecho de gentes," in *El pensamiento político hispanoamericano. Vitoria*, 293–310.

VITORIA, Francisco de, *Relectio de indiis*, in *Sobre el poder civil, sobre los indios, sobre el derecho de guerra*, Second edition (Madrid: Tecnos, 1998), 55–150.

VITORIA, Francisco de, *Fragmento sobre si es lícito guerrear a los pueblos que comen carnes humanas o que utilizan víctimas humanas en los sacrificios*. In: Francisco de Vitoria, *Relección sobre la templanza o del uso de las comidas and Fragmento sobre si es lícito guerrear a los pueblos que comen carnes humanas o que utilizan víctimas humanas en los sacrificios* (Bogotá: Universidad de Los Andes, 2007), 115–34.

VITORIA, Francisco de, *Relectio de potestate civili*, in *Relectio de potestate civili y Estudios sobre su filosofía política*, critical edition and other materials prepared by Jesús Cordero Pando (Madrid: CSIC, 2008), 1-67.

VITORIA, Francisco de, *De legibus* (Salamanca: Ediciones Universidad de Salamanca and Università degli studi di Genova, 2010).

VOEGELIN, Eric, *From Enlightenment to Revolution* (Durham: Duke University Press, 1977).

VOEGELIN, Eric, *The New Science of Politics* (Chicago: University of Chicago Press, 1952).

WARD, Thomas, "The Incoherence of Ockham's Ethics," in *Grounding in Medieval Philosophy*, eds. Normore & Schmid (Springer 2024), 225-37.

WEBER, Max, *The Meaning of 'Ethical Neutrality' in Sociology and Economics*, in: *Max Weber on the Methodology of the Social Sciences* (Glencoe, Illimois: The Free Press of Glencoe, 1949), 1–47.

WIDOW, Felipe, *Autonomía de la razón práctica y derecho subjetivo en la filosofía jurídica de John Finnis (Estudio crítico y confrontación con Tomás de Aquino)*. Doctoral dissertation submitted to the Faculty of Law of the Pontificia Universidad Católica de Chile, and approved on July 6, 2016.

WIDOW, Juan Antonio, "Non est potestas nisi a Deo," in *Sobre las relaciones y límites entre naturaleza y gracia* (Santiago: UST-Ril Editories, 2016), 645–57.

ZAGREBELSKY, Gustav, *El derecho dúctil* (Valladolid: Trotta, 1997).

ZORROZA, Idoya, "Francisco de Vitoria y Domingo de Soto: relación y comparación de sus respuestas a una problemática común," in: *Francisco de Vitoria en la Escuela de Salamanca y su proyección en Nueva España* (Pamplona: EUNSA, 2014), 113–29.

ZUCKERMAN, Charles, "The Relationship of Theories of Universals to Theories of Church Government: A Critique of Previous Views," *Journal of the History of Ideas* 35 (1973): 579–90.

ZUCKERT, Michael, *Launching Liberalism. On Lockean Political Philosophy* (Lawrence, Kansas: University Press of Kansas, 2002).

Index of names and things